D1613661

JINGLE BELLS

Solo (75)

Four Hands (1⁰⁰)

GRAND GALOP DE CONCERT.

BY FREDERIC E. WHITE.

BOSTON: WHITE, SMITH MUSIC PUBLISHING CO.

32 West Street corner Mason.

N. York. Bennett & Maguire.   Chicago. J. M. Himelman.   S. Francisco. M. Gray Music Co.   Portland Or. Wiley B. Allen.

Phil⁰ Nathan Darling Manager 1111 Chestnut St   New Orleans 24 Baronne St

Angels
We Have Heard

Angels We Have Heard: The Christmas Song Stories. Copyright 2002 by James Adam Richliano.
First Edition.

Published by:
   Star Of Bethlehem Books
   P.O. Box 116, Chatham, New York 12037.
   Email Address:
   StarofBethlehem7@aol.com

Please visit our Website at www.ChristmasSongStories.com for additional information and to order this book and other related products online.

First Printing September 2002

Cover and interior design by James Adam Richliano
Edited by Kenneth G. Dechman
Production coordinated by James Adam Richliano and Kenneth G. Dechman
Printed by Overseas Printing Corporation

ISBN: 0-9718810-0-6

LCCN 2002090798

Printed in Hong Kong

1 2 3 4 5 6 7 8 9 10

Angels We Have Heard

The Christmas Song Stories

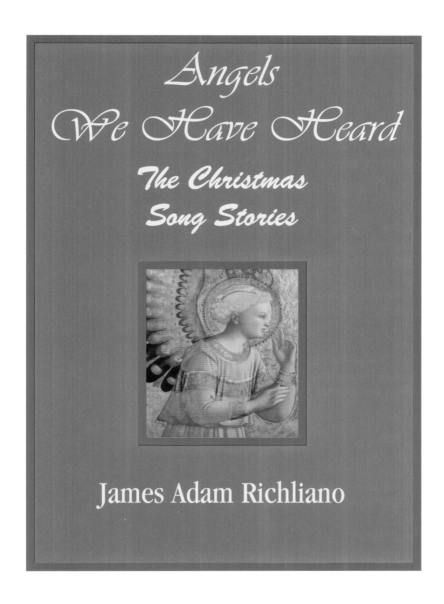

James Adam Richliano

Star Of Bethlehem Books

Contents

Foreword

Here is a new book about the origins of our favorite popular Christmas songs and hymns, and as you may have guessed by its thickness, this is by far the most detailed, comprehensive publication ever written on the subject.

To give you a bit of history as to how we met, James Richliano had been working on his dream book for years when we suddenly found each other in 1998. At that time, he was researching the *Rudolph* segment, and phoned Virginia Hertz, daughter of Robert L. May, the man who wrote the children's book upon which the Rudolph song is based. Virginia told him that I probably knew more about Rudolph than she did. Then I got the magic phone call at my home in Denver, Colorado.

I have been collecting historic information for thirty years on mostly pre-1950 Christmas songs for a television movie script I have written called *The American Festival Of Christmas*. James, being much younger than I, had been doing the same thing for many holiday songs, including ones that he remembered as a child. Talk about a match made in heaven! Well, that first phone call lasted nearly an hour-and-a-half, and we babbled in astonishment about the material that we could suddenly share for both of our projects.

Since 1975 I have been interviewing and recording the folks who wrote or sang our Christmas songs. The newest song that I covered was Johnny Marks' "Rockin' Around The Christmas Tree." I interviewed him a long time ago but never thought about trying to find Brenda Lee. James Richliano sure did, and her incredible story is in this book.

My interview with Johnny Marks was primarily to hear how he wrote the "Rudolph" song. Once that was done he wanted to talk about "Holly Jolly Christmas" and "Rockin.'" So I said, 'Go ahead, the camera is rolling.' Talk about a bonus!

It's exhilarating to know that between the two of us, we have actual accounts from both of them regarding the making of their yuletide classics, and that we have preserved for posterity a time of musical innocence that should never be forgotten.

Over the years, I have gleefully collected a ton of information on the magical world of Christmas music. James did this too, but he is a real writer. I am just an electrician who created a new line of holiday bubble lights and who, like James, somewhere along the way seriously fell in love with our Christmas music history and images. It is our fondest dream that you will fall in love as well with this wonderful part of our collective past.

And isn't it glorious when we can pass this enchantment on to the young ones in our lives, those who missed the golden era of American Christmas music? Isn't it also beautiful when their eyes light up on a snowy morning as they listen to a song like "Rudolph" for the first time? It's also nice to know that years from now, they may unexpectedly hear it again and suddenly be swept back to a few frozen-in-time moments of heavenly Christmas bliss. This book has tried to capture that bliss for you. Enjoy!

(l to r): Laura Kent, Spike Jones' drummer Joe Siricusa, Walter Kent (co-writer of "I'll Be Home For Christmas") and Thomas H. Carlisle

We wish you warmth and love at Christmas and always,

Thomas H. Carlisle
Christmas Historian
Denver, Colorado

Acknowledgments

This book is dedicated to my mother Christina Gizzi Richliano.

I would also like to honor my music teacher Elizabeth Venator, along with my sister Sherry Heflin, Kenneth Dechman, Thomas H. Carlisle, Justin Wilde, Anne Burt and all of the writers, singers, producers and musicians past and present, who helped create the timeless beauty of our Christmas songs.

In memory of Robert W. Noonan and all of our September 11th angels.

Thank you to you, the reader, and thank you to the following:
Art Austin, Gene Autry, Franny Bakos, Julie Bakos, Norman Bakos, Ken Barnes, Lisa Bartlett, Hal Belmont & Overseas Printing Corporation, Dr. Ranjan Bhayana, George Blane, Efrain Burgos, The Boston Public Library, The Buffalo New York Public Library, Owen Bradley, Fred Bronson, Alfred Burt, Diane Burt, Julia Cameron & *The Artist's Way,* Doreen Cardinale, Sharon Castricone, City Honors School (Buffalo, NY), Georgiann, Jim & Tony Cocuzzi, Dartmouth College, Ann & Joe Columbo, David Dechman, Don Dechman, Jim Dechman, Jonene Dechman, Kim Dechman, Danny DiBartolo, Joyce DiBartolo, Connie DiBuono, Tim DiPasqua, Ebay, Michael Ellis, Manya Fabiniak, Dr. Eli Farhi, Bob & Sandy Fellows, William & Pasco First, John Fricke, Philip Furia, Kim Galle, Audrey Gillespie, Adam & Nellie Gizzi, Marion Glastetter, God (my co-creator!), The Golden Glow of Christmas Past, Herbert Goldman, Rick Goldschmidt, Alex Gordon, Melva Grenier, Claudia Grenier, Debbie Grenier, Denise Grenier, Harvard's Houghton Library, Aaron Heflin, James Heflin, Ken Heflin, Mark Heflin, Nancy Heflin, Ryan Heflin, Robert Helms, Virginia Hertz, Lynne & Ron Hoogervorst, Dorothy Ives, Jeff Jardine, Maud Jennings, Barbara Madden Johnson, Anita Kerr, Jill Koons, Brenda Lee, Virginia Long, Babe Lorenzo, Michael Lupi, Gerry MacDonald, Antonette Marcinelli, Michael Marks, Hugh Martin, Anne Meacham, Michel Mercure, Jeanne Metzler, John Metzler, Johnna Metzler-Northrup, Tiffany Metzler, Erik Moore, Tom Noonan, Sam Northrup, Sumya Ojakli, Angela & Mark Overhoff, Frank Pooler, Amelia Richliano, Brenda Richliano, Gregory Richliano, Ralph Richliano, Richard Richliano, Michael Riff, Robert A. Schuller, Randi Sperber, Star Of Bethlehem Books, Lucille Stiglmeier, Paul Stiglmeier, Marty Szwed, Jason Szwed, Maryann & Jeff Torsell, Albert Wang, John Woolverton, Beverly Down, Anne Greco, Chris Holland, Reginald Knox, Patricia McCutchen, Tana Meadows, Carol Newlin, Nancy Simpson, Rev. Fred Shavor & His Capitol District Church. All of my friends, my entire family, and to all who create and seek beauty in the world!

Introduction

by songwriter Justin Wilde, co-author of "It Must Have Been The Mistletoe,"
recorded by Barbra Streisand and Barbara Mandrell

'Tis the season to be humming, singing, or just enjoying all those beautiful Christmas songs that add so immeasurably to our holiday traditions. This wonderful new book by James Richliano gives us the "behind the scenes" stories of how many of our perennial favorites came to be. James allows us to peek at the creative processes many of the songwriters went through, and the enormous efforts that were then required to launch your favorite holiday standards. From humorous anecdotes like which names Robert L. May first chose to call Rudolph, to the heartbreaking, yet inspirational story behind the Alfred Burt carols — it all makes for fascinating reading during "The Most Wonderful Time of the Year."

As the only publisher in the music industry who specializes strictly in holiday music, I'm often asked what makes a Christmas song become a standard? In my mind there's quite a difference between a "hit" song and a "standard" song. Hit songs come and go, but standards remain with us throughout the decades and possibly forever.

So what makes a Christmas song a potential standard? The first criterion is a great melody. By great, however, I do not mean intricate or elaborate. Melodic simplicity is the key. Try humming your favorite Christmas songs, and you'll notice how simple and easy they are to sing. I usually tell my writers that if I can't sing back the majority of their melody after hearing it only three to four times, it's not likely to become a standard. There are exceptions to this rule ("Sleigh Ride" comes to mind), but in general, the most memorable Christmas songs are the ones that can be sung by carolers, or the average man on the street. Add to that a joyous or emotionally moving lyric, and you've got the makings of a holiday "evergreen." But then comes the hard part.

Launching a new holiday standard has become extremely difficult, if not almost impossible in this day and age, for several reasons. I truly believe that if "White Christmas" was being released as a new Christmas song for the first time this year, it would probably not become the standard it is today, and the reasons have nothing to do with the quality of the song itself. If this sounds like sacrilege, read on.

The 1930's, 1940's and 1950's were the "Golden Age of Christmas Songs." During those decades, the record industry was a "singles" market. Artists released one song at a time, so it was very easy for them to release a new Christmas song every other year if they wished. When they did release one, if it was successful, the record label would continue to re-release and promote it each year thereafter for as long as it continued to sell. Thus, many Christmas singles were vigorously promoted for several years in a row. This no longer happens.

In today's market, everything is centered on the "album" concept. A few "superstar" artists will release two or three Christmas albums over the course of their careers, but most only do one or two at best. Artists no longer release yearly Christmas singles unless they are tied to the release of an entire Christmas album. And since most Christmas albums peak the first year they are released, there's no point for the label to continue promoting a CD that's no longer selling huge units like it did the first year it was recorded.

A second major factor is that for Christmas songs to become standards, they need to be recorded by several artists. Radio might play "White Christmas" every hour on the hour a few days before December 25th, but they won't play Bing's version every hour. They'll rotate by playing versions by different artists. So to get lots of radio exposure requires that multiple versions by different artists be available to radio.

Most of the major "pop" Christmas standards were released before the era of the "singer/songwriter" when artists like Bing Crosby, Nat King Cole, Brenda Lee, Judy Garland and others recorded songs written by other songwriters. These artists didn't care how many other versions of the song had been previously released. They put their own "vocal stamp" on their version. As a result, these songs from "The Golden Age" were often cut several hundred times over the course of those three decades.

Today, singer/songwriters usually only record songs they themselves have written. Call it vanity or greed, but if they do a Christmas album, although they will include some of the "old" standards, they rarely if ever record new Christmas songs that they, themselves, did not write. The result is that very few new holiday "standards" have surfaced since the 1970's. Luckily, we've been left with a treasury of wonderful holiday standards from years past, but only one or two new ones from each decade since the 1960's.

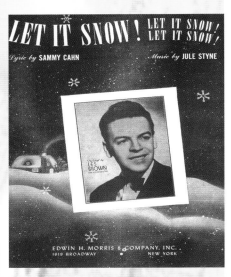

As you read through the coming stories of how these wonderful songs came to be, think back to that innocent, gentle, happy time when snowmen could dance and reindeer could fly — and you still believed in Santa.

Ho! Ho! Ho!

Justin Wilde
"Mr. Christmas"
January 29, 2002
Buena Park, California

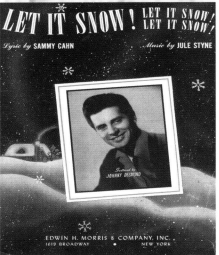

Over the years, "Let It Snow! Let It Snow! Let It Snow!" (written in 1945 by Sammy Cahn & Jule Styne) has become a holiday standard because it was recorded by many artists, including: (top right) Les Brown & His Orchestra, (bottom left to right) Frank Sinatra, Vaughn Monroe and Johnny Desmond.

The Golden Years
1930 – 1965

America's Brightest
Holiday Stars

I

"Santa Claus Is Comin' To Town" (Copyright 1998 by Thomas H. Carlisle and Harold Shuler)

SANTA CLAUS IS COMIN' TO TOWN — 1934

WRITERS —
  HAVEN GILLESPIE
  J. FRED COOTS

ARTIST —
  EDDIE CANTOR

Eddie Cantor (1933)

During the dimmest days of the Depression, tin-pan-alley songwriter Haven Gillespie left his childhood home of Covington, Kentucky, and took what would become a life-altering trip to New York City. He wasn't feeling well, his foot was sore, and rain water was leaking through his shoes. He was in no mood to fulfill the strange assignment his music publisher, Edgar Bittner of Leo Feist, Inc., unexpectedly thrust upon him and his partner, J. Fred Coots. One of the few comforts he relied on as he pondered the unusual request was a letter he carried with him from his wife, Corene, written on October 10th, 1933.

Haven Gillespie with grandchildren James & Carole Gillespie (1949, Covington, Kentucky)

On that drizzly autumn day in The Big Apple, Bittner wanted Gillespie, who had some earlier success with writing kid songs like "Tin Pan Parade" (1927), "The Sleepy Town Express" and "Bless Your Little Heart" (1930), to quickly concoct a children's Christmas song his company could turn into what was the hottest tune-selling format of the time — sheet music. With only days left before he was scheduled to return home, he was "pushed for time" and doubted Leo Feist could get a Christmas song out so fast. "Why do you want a song that's going to drop dead the day after Christmas?" protested Gillespie. "I told Mr. Bittner of the short time that remained before Christmas, but he remarked, 'we have offices in eighteen cities, and the radio, now won't you try?'"

Haven Gillespie

As difficult as the task at hand was, he had by 1933 acquired the necessary skills to meet such a daunting challenge.

James Haven Gillespie was born on February 6, 1888, in Covington, Kentucky, a small Ohio River town located near Cincinnati. Childhood life was harsh, and his most vivid memory of that time was a bleak portrait of "seeing whiskey bottles all over the house."[1]

This insecurity at home caused him to drop out of grammar school, and in 1902 he moved to Chicago where he became a printer's devil. For the next fifteen years he relocated several times working by night at a series of printing jobs, including a short stint at *The New York Times*, as he struggled by day to become a successful songwriter. "It was through printing that he gained a better understanding of words and the English language, and unknowingly fostered his talent for composing the lyrics which were to make him famous."[2]

In 1911 he published his first songs and received a big break that year when he was invited to write music for a vaudeville act appearing at a theater in downtown Cincinnati. The next twenty years were an extremely prolific period and he wrote and published close to 150 tunes, including two number one hits — Johnny Marvin's "Breezin' Along with the Breeze" (1926) and Rudy Vallee's "Honey" (1928). As other interpretations of his work, like Frank Coomb's "Harbor of Love" (1917), George Olsen's "Drifting and Dreaming" (1926) and Guy Lombardo's "Beautiful" (1927) became best sellers, he began writing songs for movies, Broadway revues and radio

1928

shows. In the tin-pan-alley tradition he learned to create these works rapidly, and "many of his masterpieces took only minutes to write. He often penned ideas for songs during a forty-five minute trolley ride to work."[3]

While working on a 1932 production called *Earl Carroll's Vanities*, Charles Tobias, a cousin of Eddie Cantor's wife, wrote songs with Gillespie for the show, and introduced him to Brooklyn-born J. Fred Coots.

Coots grew up in poverty, and as a child developed inflammatory rheumatism which paralyzed his hands for five years. In order to alleviate the condition, his mother prescribed piano lessons, and in 1917, at the age of twenty-three, he published his first work, "Mr. Ford You've Got The Right Idea." *Sally, Irene and Mary*, a Broadway show written for Eddie Dowling, followed, as well as subsequent sentimental hits such as "Love Letters In The Sand," "For All We Know" and "A Beautiful Lady In Blue."

Standing (l to r): Songwriter Abe Olman & Haven Gillespie
Seated at piano: J. Fred Coots

Gillespie and Coots formed a songwriting partnership in 1933. They went on to write many non-holiday gems including two 1938 hits — "There's Honey On The Moon Tonight" and "You Go To My Head." In addition, the pair collaborated on music for two 1930's Broadway revues — *Hollywood Holiday* and *Cotton Club Parade*, and later penned several children's songs together. The tune Mr. Bittner asked for became their biggest hit, however, and it was the only Christmas song they would ever work on jointly.

After agreeing to Mr. Bittner's request, Coots and Gillespie walked out of his Leo Feist office in October, 1933, and got on a subway train headed to the publisher's uptown office.

"We boarded the B.M.T. at Cooper Square," remembered Gillespie in a letter he wrote to Coots in 1971 describing the momentous event. "It was raining. I had a bad foot, but realizing the opportunity was a great one, I went to work."

Shown above is sheet music for songs performed by Eddie Cantor and Ethel Shutta from the 1920's through the early 1940's.

After thinking for a moment, Gillespie was swept back to his childhood and suddenly heard his mother's admonishing voice in his head. "If you don't wash behind your ears, Haven, Santa won't come to see you. You better be good." This day dream provided instant inspiration, and he began to scribble down some words on a letter he found in his pocket.

"You were chewing gum and reading the ad cards posted above the coach and moved down toward the rear," wrote Gillespie to Coots. "When we arrived at 49th Street and 7th Avenue, we left the coach. You asked me if I had anything. I said it's finished. In my records I see where it was written on the back of a letter from my dear departed wife Corene, dated October 10th, 1933."

According to Gillespie, he wrote the melody and lyrics for "Santa Claus Is Comin' To Town" in the fifteen minutes of time it took for their train to travel forty blocks. "We finally made it through the rain and the traffic, to the 50th Street office of Feist," he added, "I had five extra carbon copies

Corene Gillespie, nephew William First
& Haven Gillespie (early 1950's)

typed and gave you one. You read it over several times and asked me, 'How does it go?' I showed you."

Shortly after Gillespie demonstrated the melody and lyrics to his partner, Coots came up with an arrangement, and Leo Feist then set out to release the sheet music.

When comedian Eddie Cantor, one of the biggest radio stars of the time, was coaxed into singing it on his show, what happened to the song over the next two months went beyond the company and songwriters' most unrestrained expectations.

Weeks before "Santa Claus" rode the nation's radio airwaves, Gillespie said he asked popular singer/actress Ethel Shutta and her band-leader husband George Olsen to add the song to their "book." The two were friends of Cantor's, and Gillespie claimed he first offered it to them and then "had the tough task of asking them to stop doing it, as Eddie wanted to be the first on the air. Ethel graciously complied with my wish."

Ethel Shutta (1935)

Eddie Cantor (1934)

Eddie Cantor appeared on the original sheet music for "Santa Claus Is Comin' To Town" (1934, shown above)

While it's not known for certain where Shutta and Olsen initially performed "Santa Claus," according to *Who Wrote That Song* by Dick and Harriet Jacobs, they were the first to professionally introduce it. In 1933, Shutta was singing Friday nights on a radio show hosted by comedian Walter O'Keefe, and it's possible she sang it on that program.

It was Eddie Cantor's radio show, however, which became crucial to "Santa's" initial success, since it had a cutting edge in the 1930's similar to 1980's MTV in exposing music to a large audience. Just as Madonna was queen of television's music video, Cantor was king of radio's theater of the mind, and getting him to include Gillespie and Coots' Christmas song on his weekly program almost ensured that it would become a hit.

Although he is primarily forgotten today, Cantor was one of the biggest vaudeville and burlesque stars of the early 1900's to cross over to radio. His bulging eyes became his trademark, and he won the hearts of theater audiences when he stole the show in various *Ziegfeld Follies* and record-breaking productions such as *Whoopie* (1928), co-starring Ethel Shutta.

In 1931, he began hosting NBC's *The Chase & Sanborn Hour*, a variety show airing from 8 to 9 every Sunday night. His slapstick vaudeville sketches and crazy comic routines about his wife, Ida, led to the show becoming the most popular program of the early thirties, and one that ended up making ratings history. "It got beyond anything that anyone had ever dreamed of," said Cantor. "The rating climbed and climbed and stayed. During '32, '33, and '34 we had the biggest audience in America. It was wonderful."[4]

The ability for the show to reach such an enormous audience was revolutionary back then. When asked about radio's mass communication, Cantor admitted there was no power like it at the time.

"Say you played in a Ziegfeld show at the New Amsterdam Theater, which seats 1,600," he said. "In a week you play to

1962

Eddie Cantor on the cover of "Popular Songs" magazine (April 1937)

Eddie Cantor in a 1933 ad for Chase & Sanborn coffee

13,000. Play that Ziegfeld show for fifty weeks, you would play to 650,000. If you played it for ten years, you'd play to six and a half million. In twenty years it would be thirteen million. And if you played it for forty years, to packed houses, standing room only, you'd play to less people in forty years than you played to in one night on *The Chase & Sanborn Hour.*"[5]

Much like *The Tonight Show,* Cantor was known for introducing new talent on his program, and it became a marketplace for songwriters needing to promote new tunes. As much as he liked to sing fresh material however, he was at first opposed to "Santa Claus" because he felt it was too much of a children's song. In fact, when Leo Feist's promotional manager first started plugging it, like Cantor, someone sarcastically told him to "stop throwing corn all over Broadway."

Luckily there was one person who loved it — Cantor's wife Ida — and she finally convinced him to perform it on one of his upcoming shows. Since Gillespie had written songs in the past with three of Ida's cousins, Charles Tobias and his

Ida Cantor, Eddie and their five daughters in the 1930's

two brothers, it's possible his clout with her helped in pressuring Cantor to reconsider. Coots also may have influenced the comedian, since at the time he was writing special material for his *Chase And Sanborn Hour.*

There was a stipulation in his agreeing to sing this "children's" Christmas song, however, and he soon let Haven Gillespie know of his unusual demand. He wanted the songwriter to write a "Depression" version of "Santa Claus Is Comin' To Town." Gillespie agreed, and said at some time during the first week of November, 1933, he wrote a special "Depression" chorus for the song while drinking at a local bar in Covington, Kentucky. He then sent it to Leo Feist. What was once perceived as a lighthearted tune for tots was now something more topically adult, and this would be the version people first heard when they turned on *The Chase And Sanborn Hour* a few weeks later.

Although the exact air date for "Santa Claus" is unknown since records and transcripts of Eddie Cantor's "historically interesting Depression-era shows are lost and have yet to sur-

WINTER WONDERLAND

Words by
DICK SMITH

Music by
FELIX BERNARD

According to Christmas historian Thomas H. Carlisle, vocalist Joey Nash discovered "Winter Wonderland" at a neighbor's house in Brooklyn during the summer of 1934. In October, he sang it for the first time on the *Studebaker Champions Hour* radio show, accompanied by the Richard Himber Orchestra. Nash and Guy Lombardo were the first to record it, while follow-up 1940's renditions by the Andrews Sisters, Perry Como and Johnny Mercer further established its undying popularity. "Winter Wonderland" and "Santa Claus Is Comin' To Town" are the only two seasonal songs written in the 1930's which are still widely recorded today.

Published for

SONG
PIANO SOLO (SIMPLIFIED)
DANCE ORCHESTRA
QUICK-STEP BAND
CONCERT BAND
SYMPHONIC BAND
TWO PART (SA)
WOMEN'S VOICES (SSA)
MEN'S VOICES (TTBB)
MIXED VOICES (SATB)

Recorded By
JOHNNY MERCER
and THE PIED PIPERS
(CAPITOL)

SPECIAL EDITION

BVC
BREGMAN, VOCCO and CONN, Inc.
1619 BROADWAY   NEW YORK, N.Y

face,"[6] Gillespie states that it took place during the last week of November, 1933. It's quite possible it debuted on Cantor's November 26th show, since that evening his recurring topical "Night Court" segment focused on unemployment due to the Depression. Gillespie also recalled that as soon as Cantor sang the song it became an overnight sensation.

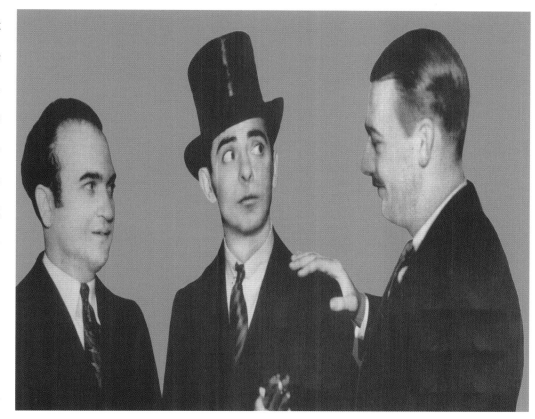

Eddie Cantor with "Chase & Sanborn Hour" cast members

With this immediate success, on December 5th, Mr. Bittner requested him to come back to New York City so he could show him something extremely surprising.

As soon as he arrived, his boss grabbed him and said, "I want you to see something that never happened in the music business before, and will never happen again."

"We went to the stock room," remembered Gillespie, "and Mr. Bittner asked the fellow in charge 'how many copies of "Santa Claus" is going out today?' The fellow answered, 'same as yesterday — 25,000.'"

The song's popularity continued to grow, and Cantor immediately became identified with it. He continued to sing it in subsequent years during the holiday season, and performed it on other radio shows he hosted after he left *The Chase & Sanborn Hour* at the end of 1934. Oddly enough, he wouldn't financially benefit from promoting "Santa Claus," since he never made a commercial recording of it.

It was only a matter of time before someone did release a single though, and on December 22, 1934, George Hall & His Orchestra, a New York based Big Band, debuted on the charts with "Santa Claus Is Comin' To Town," staying there for three weeks and peaking at number twelve. The featured vocalist on the Bluebird Records' track was Sonny Schuyler. Later known as Sunny Skylar, he became an important songwriter, and wrote the number one hits "Besame Mucho" and "You're Breaking My Heart."

JINGLE BELLS

Words and Music by J. S. PIERPONT
MODERN ADAPTATION BY
PATTY ANDREWS and VIC SCHOEN

As Recorded by BING CROSBY and THE ANDREWS SISTERS

Bing Crosby and the Andrews Sisters recorded "Santa Claus Is Comin' To Town" in 1943, and then released it as a single paired with "Jingle Bells," written by James Pierpont. Pierpont was the uncle of financier J.P. Morgan, and according to legend, he first played the tune on a piano at Simpson's Tavern in Medford, Massachusetts. It was initially published in 1857. Like "Winter Wonderland," it makes no reference to Christmas, and was actually conceived as a Thanksgiving song titled "The One Horse Open Sleigh."

Leeds Music CORP.
RKO BUILDING · RADIO CITY · NEW YORK

HOLLEY

Schuyler's recording of Gillespie and Coots' song was groundbreaking then, since it was highly unusual for anyone to record a secular Christmas tune other than "Jingle Bells," and very few ventured to do that. There was little public demand for it so few were being written prior to the 1940's. In fact, "Santa Claus Is Comin' To Town" and "Winter Wonderland" are the only two holiday songs written in the 1930's which are still widely popular today. Considering "Winter Wonderland" is really a song about the season in general with no reference made to Christmas at all, "Santa Claus" is the only true survivor from this period.

Popular singers didn't start regularly recording Christmas songs until Bing Crosby revolutionized the holiday music industry with the unprecedented retail success he achieved with "Silent Night" and "White Christmas." "Santa Claus Is Comin' To Town" finally benefited from that magic Crosby Christmas touch when he and the Andrews Sisters lent their voices to it on September 27, 1943, and released it as a single paired with "Jingle Bells."

Their duet sold a million copies and helped "Santa Claus" make the important leap from sheet music to records, allowing it to transcend rock music's usurpation of Tin Pan Alley. Over the years acts like The

1981

4 Seasons, the Jackson 5 and Bruce Springsteen continued to introduce the song to new generations of listeners.

By 1970 the golden radio days of stars like Eddie Cantor were long gone, yet *Santa Claus Is Comin' To Town* managed to become an enduring Rankin/Bass television special built around Gillespie and Coots evergreen. It starred Fred Astaire and Mickey Rooney's voices, and proved that a tiny remnant of Tin Pan Alley could somehow weave its way into the modern video age and survive beyond the new millennium.

Copyright 1970 Rankin/Bass Productions

The "Santa Claus Is Comin' To Town" animated TV special, produced by Rankin & Bass, first aired on ABC, December 14, 1970, from 7 to 8 PM. (Images: copyright 1970 Rankin/Bass Productions)

Immediately following "Santa Claus Is Comin' To Town," Haven Gillespie and J. Fred Coots released
"The Wedding Of Jack And Jill" (1935). Among the first to perform it was Ethel Shutta (pictured above).

1927

AN INTERVIEW WITH HAVEN GILLESPIE'S DAUGHTER-IN-LAW AUDREY GILLESPIE

Who owns the publishing rights for "Santa Claus Is Comin' To Town?"

My husband, who was Haven's son, died in 1990 and left the copyright to me. I'm the publisher of the words, and J. Fred Coots' daughters' copyright is owned by EMI Music. The song makes more money today than it ever has with all the different venues and different ways of performing it today. Sometimes I lose out on opportunities. Last year someone wanted to include it in a movie, but decided it was too much money and chose "Jingle Bells" instead, which is in the public domain.

What kind of person was your father-in-law?

He was a brilliant man with a very high IQ, who dropped out of school around the sixth grade. He came from a poor family, and his father was chased out of the house because, I think, he had trouble with the bottle. Haven worked at night printing so he could visit the publishers in the daytime and work on his music. He had a poetic mind. Writing words just came so easy for him — he had a vocabulary that wouldn't quit, and the printing business really helped him develop that.

Did he have a flair for writing children's songs?

Yes, it was an unusual thing. My father-in-law wasn't a person who showed affection for children and was matter of fact with them. Maybe it was his way of treating them as grown ups. But he was very successful with his kid songs. Most kids who learned to tap dance back then did it to songs like his "Tin Pan Parade" and "The Wedding Of Jack And Jill."

Did he write any other children's Christmas songs?

He wrote others like "Jiminy Christmas," but they didn't go over too well.

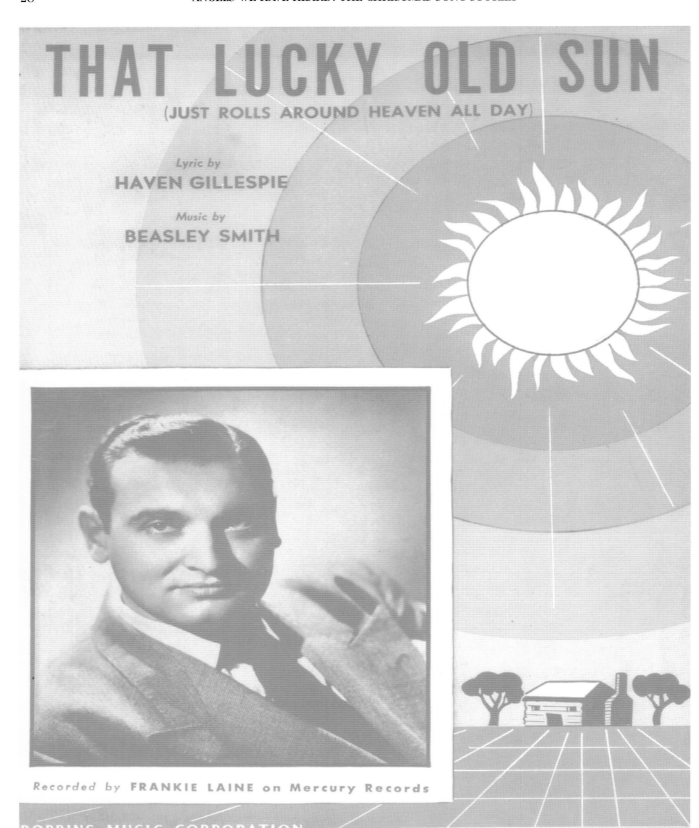

1949

Do you get a lot of requests for people to sing some of the other songs he wrote?

Oh quite a bit. "You Go To My Head" is requested often. "Right Or Wrong" and "That Lucky Old Sun" seem to be popular with country performers now.

How close were J. Fred Coots and Haven?

It was a very funny relationship. When J. Fred was interviewed on radio shows, he would say he wrote "Santa Claus," and didn't always mention my father-in-law. I don't think Haven liked that too well. I can't say they were in love with each other, but they must have worked well together. J. Fred was one of the best tune writers, and he was a wonderful Irish tenor performer who played the piano well. But he really was a true egotistical person, and I think that got under Haven's skin.

Was Haven a recovered alcoholic?

Yes. He once had a problem with alcohol, but a lot of the old songwriters had trouble with the bottle. In today's world they're more into drugs, but back then it was the booze.

How was Haven associated with Ida Cantor?

Haven knew the Tobias brothers, who were related to Ida, and that was his connection to her. Eddie Cantor performed "Santa Claus Is Comin' To Town" on his radio show, and when he did it became a hit.

What do you think of Bruce Springsteen's version of "Santa Claus Is Comin' To Town?"

He recorded the song in a way nobody had ever recorded it, and somebody said to me, 'I guess you don't care — you're smiling all the way to the bank.' His version was certainly unusual but I liked it. I'm sure my father-in-law would have liked it too — he was set in some of his ways, but whenever anybody records your song I think generally you're so pleased — it's such a joy and honor.

How about the Jackson 5's interpretation?

I love it. Michael made one mistake in the song, but that's ok since he was just a little boy at the time.

Did your father-in-law have a favorite Christmas song?

He thought the best Christmas song written wasn't his but Mel Torme's "The Christmas Song."

Haven Gillespie passed away on March 14, 1975. How would he like to be remembered?

He would often put his arm around me and tell me he loved me, and that if anybody ever did anything to make me unhappy he would take care of them. He never said an unkind word about me. I think he would like to be remembered as a good person and an excellent writer. He felt like he was actually Santa Claus, and he did a lot for people with that song.

c. 1955

AMERICAN SOCIETY OF COMPOSERS, AUTHORS AND PUBLISHERS
THIRTY ROCKEFELLER PLAZA
NEW YORK CITY

GENE BUCK
PRESIDENT

December 21, 1934.

Mr. Haven Gillespie,
511 Montgomery St.,
Covington, Kentucky.

Dear Mr. Gillespie:

The Writers' Classification Committee of this Society, after a great deal of deliberation in order to improve our present system of classification, decided to reward the outstanding songs of the past quarter in a concrete way. Pursuant to the unanimous resolution of the Committee, I am sending you enclosed our check in the sum of $2500.0, your song share of the composition entitled:

"SANTA CLAUS IS COMIN' TO TOWN".

In the absence of a program system, but with all the possible information we can obtain, the Classification Committee has decided to declare an extra bonus to the outstanding songs of each quarter. This is a new idea we are experimenting with with the view and hope that it will prove successful.

Classification is the most complex problem that confronts the Society. The Committee is conscious of the great changes that have taken place in our business and is doing everything possible to recognize initiative and activity.

We wish to congratulate you on your contribution.

With our genuine wish for continued success,

Faithfully yours,

AMERICAN SOCIETY OF COMPOSERS,
AUTHORS AND PUBLISHERS,

Gene Buck,
President.

GB:AH

August 18, 1971

Dear Fred:

     It was nice hearing from you, and, as you request, I am inclosing the New Orleans Clipping ~~xxxxxxxxxxxxx~~ so that you may have it included in your files.

     It may seem strange that I have all the data on the song, "Santa Claus Is Coming To Town", (it was written on the back of an envelope containg a letter from my dear, departed Wife, Corene. on October 15, 1933, while riding with you, returning from a visit to Mr. Bittner, at the Publisher's (Leo Feist) office, located at that time, on Cooper Square). Mr Bittner asked me to write a song for Christmas, as the children seemed to understand the vernacular I employed in a few other numbers. On returning to the 49th St. B. M. T. Station, we proceeded to the Feist Office, at 50th and Broadway, with the song finished, I had Marie Adams type the Lyric including five carbon copies, and, upon reading the lyric, I was asked "how does it go". Eddie Cantor introduced the Song on the Maxwell House Coffee program, on the evening of November 28, 19~~5~~3; 1933 I was in Kern Aylwards Bar three weeks previous to that date, and the 'special chorus was written there, and I phoned Johnny White and read that version to him, with instructions to get it to Eddie, as I had been informed by Johnny that Eddie was going to do it. I had Ethel Shutta, with Geo. Olson, doing the song (after some _rbdd selling_) and had the tough task of asking her to _stop_ doing it, as Eddie wanted to be first on the air...ethel graciously complied with my wish.

     Since those days, (from 1933, to the present) there has been much publicity on the song...and, I had often wondered who wrote the thing, but, at last, I have been duly informed by the clipping which I am returning to you...this had bothered me no end, and, thanks to you, now I know the full story. Thanks, again.

     As you know, Charley (Mousey) Warren has passed to his reward.

The above letter was written by Haven Gillespie to J. Fred Coots in 1971. In it, Gillespie mistakenly refers to Eddie Cantor's radio show as "The Maxwell House Coffee Program." In fact, "Santa Claus Is Comin' To Town" debuted on Cantor's "Chase & Sanborn Hour."

Coots—2

I should imaging his journey in his new world would have been eased had he received the <u>Luggage</u> which I had contributed to, and you were to present to him; somehow, he never got a glimpse of this gift.

Another matter which I have never been able to find the answer to: This concerns a 'Mack Davis' who was to spread the song I brought to you (Complete, words and music...ironically, Mousey, who accepted the song, along with "YOU GO TO MY HEAD" had you make changes in the melody as you demonstrated the song to him, and these changes put the melody right back to where I had it) and became an instant 'hit' and shared in the ASCAP PRIZE MONEY...which ASCAP asked <u>ME</u>, of all people, to forward Mack Davis' share of the Prize to him. I returned that check to ASCAP, with the information that I had never heard of him. I never did learn as to whether <u>Mack</u> received his nice check or not. The song, "There's Honey On The Moon".

My files are replete with these memos. and, in these salad days, I have much time to reflect back which affords me quite some amusement—amusement and amazement, as to what in the world some thing, or other does to a traveler, on his way through this short life.

I never give up hope, and am a firm believer in "turning the other cheek"....in this way, I may, or not see a better world; at least my prayers are bent in that direction.

As I quoted at the start of this letter, it was nice hearing from you...and with the best of wishes for you, Margie, and the children, I am

Due to corrections,   Yours,

<u>Please excuse appearance</u>
                                                      Haven
    P.O.Box 2140,
    Las Vegas, Nevada 89101

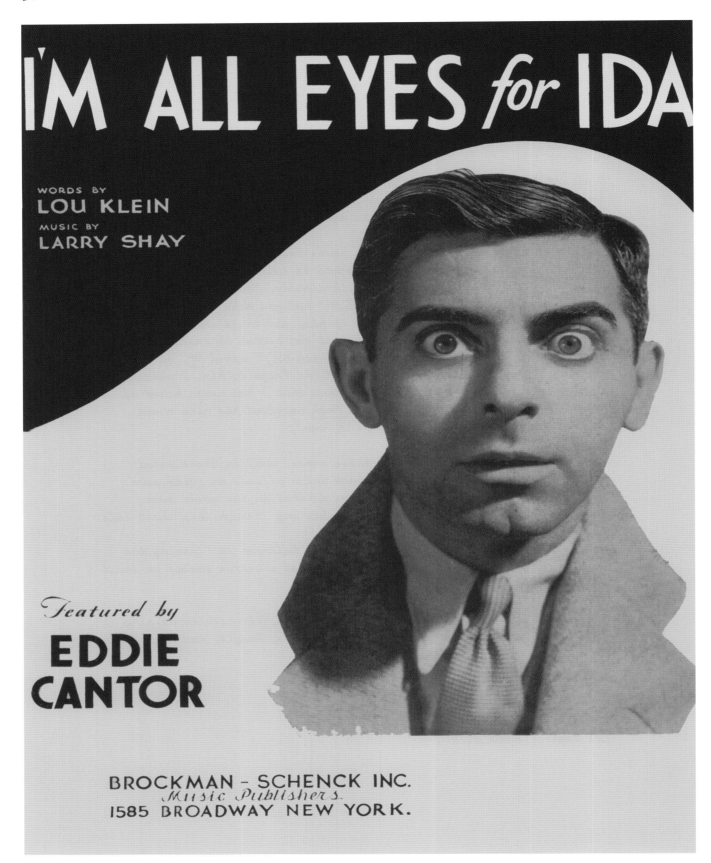

1931

HERBERT GOLDMAN, AUTHOR OF *BANJO EYES — EDDIE CANTOR AND THE BIRTH OF MODERN STARDOM*

Did you ever hear Cantor sing "Santa Claus Is Comin' To Town"?

Yes, I listened to transcripts of his shows privately held by the Cantor family. On his December 8, 1935, *Pebeco Show*, he started the song with its first verse, *I just came back from a lovely trip along the Milky Way.* He did the show from Los Angeles and was accompanied by the Lou Gress Orchestra. They opened up with an instrumental called "With A Song In My Heart," and then Cantor did a dialogue about Ethiopia. He then sang the song, "My Girl," followed by a segment called, *At The Movies.* At that point he sang "Santa Claus Is Comin' To Town" and ended the show with his closing theme, "I Love To Spend Each Sunday With You."

Do recordings of his 1933 and 1934 *Chase & Sanborn* shows exist?

I don't think any transcriptions of those shows have turned up.

Why would someone introduce a song on Cantor's show back then?

In my book, I make the point that in terms of the big star Cantor was, the length of time he was a star and the different media in which he was a star, Eddie Cantor is surely the most forgotten celebrity of the 20th century.

What's the reason for this?

Rock and roll altered our perspectives on performance quite a bit and made the old presentation of show business seem rather pretentious and corny. Cantor came up in an era, well before the 1920's, where the stage was it. It was about going out and performing in front of an audience, and it's the kind of performance art we really don't relate to today. It was a live art and had to be experienced live.

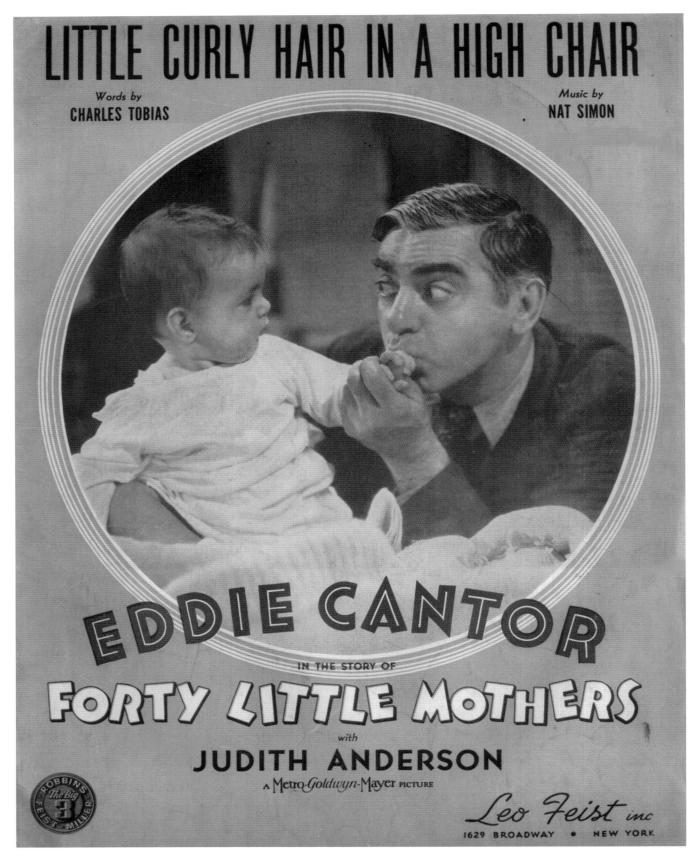

1940

The above Eddie Cantor ad appeared in "Life" magazine on June 23, 1952.

1932

BING CROSBY
FLORENCE GEORGE
RUDY VALLÉE
VICTOR YOUNG and His Orchestra
FRANCES LANGFORD

in an album of

VICTOR HERBERT
MELODIES VOL. 1

Three decades before "Santa Claus Is Comin' To Town" emerged, Victor Herbert (pictured at left) wrote "Toyland" with Glen MacDonough, for his operetta *Babes In Toyland*, which was produced first in Chicago and later at the Majestic Theatre in New York City on October 13, 1903. "Toyland" didn't start out as a Christmas song, yet it is now associated with the holiday, and has become one of the only yuletide gems written in the early 1900's that survives today.

DECCA
ALBUM
No. 38

DECCA RECORDS

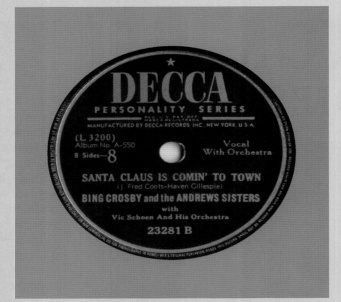

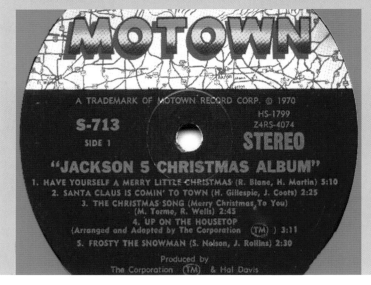

In 1981, Bruce Springsteen released his rockin' version of "Santa Claus Is Comin' To Town" (upper left). A decade earlier, the Jackson 5's R & B rendition of it became a number one hit on Billboard's Christmas Singles chart (lower left). Popular interpretations of Gillespie and Coots' masterpiece were also recorded in the 1940's by Bing Crosby with the Andrews Sisters (center) and Alvino Rey & his Orchestra with the King Sisters (upper right).

SANTA CLAUS IS COMIN' TO TOWN — SELECTED DISCOGRAPHY

SINGLES

ARTIST	FLIP SIDE	LABEL	YEAR
Eddy Arnold	White Christmas	RCA Victor	1950
Gene Autry	Up On The Housetop (Ho!Ho!Ho!)	Columbia	1954
Pat Boone	7-inch EP	Dot	1957
Jimmy Boyd	I Saw Mommy Kissing Santa Claus	Columbia	1953
Teresa Brewer	7-inch EP	RCA	1979
Carpenters	Merry Christmas Darling	A&M	1974
Perry Como	I'll Be Home For Christmas	RCA Victor	1949
Bing Crosby/Andrews Sisters	Jingle Bells	Decca	1943
The 4 Seasons	Christmas Tears	Vee Jay	1962
Benny Goodman	Jingle Bells	RCA Victor	1949
George Hall & his Orchestra	*vocal by Sonny Schuyler*	Bluebird	1934
Al Hirt	Nutty Jingle Bells	RCA Victor	1965
Jackson 5	Christmas Won't Be The Same This Year	Motown	1970
Sammy Kaye	Frosty The Snowman	Columbia	1951
Gladys Knight & The Pips	That Special Time Of Year	Columbia	1982
Chris Ledoux	'Twas The Night Before Christmas	Capitol	1996
Guy Lombardo	Jingle Bells	Decca	1952
The McGuire Sisters	Honorable Congratulations	Coral	1957
Johnny Mercer	Jingle Bells	Capitol	1950
Wayne Newton	Christmas Prayer	MGM	1968
The Osmond Boys	Kay Thompson's Jingle Bells	ARO	1987
Patti Page	Silent Night	Mercury	1951
Paul, Les & Mary Ford	Rudolph The Red-nosed Reindeer	Capitol	1955
Alvino Ray/King Sisters	Jingle Bells	Bluebird	1941
Soupy Sales	Santa Claus Is Surfin' To Town	Reprise	1963
Santa's Disco Band	Joy	Magic Disc	1977
Frank Sinatra	Have Yourself A Merry Little Christmas	Columbia	1950
Bruce Springsteen	Santa Claus Is Comin' To Town	Columbia	1981
The Three Suns	Adeste Fideles	RCA Victor	1949
Bobby Vinton	Santa Must Be Polish	Bobby Vinton	1987
Fred Waring & The Pennsylvanians	Rudolph The Red-nosed Reindeer	Decca	1954
Lawrence Welk	7-inch EP	Coral	1956

1926

"Merry Christmas Waltz" (1949) was co-written by Ida Cantor's cousin, Charles Tobias.
Tobias was responsible for introducing Haven Gillespie to J. Fred Coots.

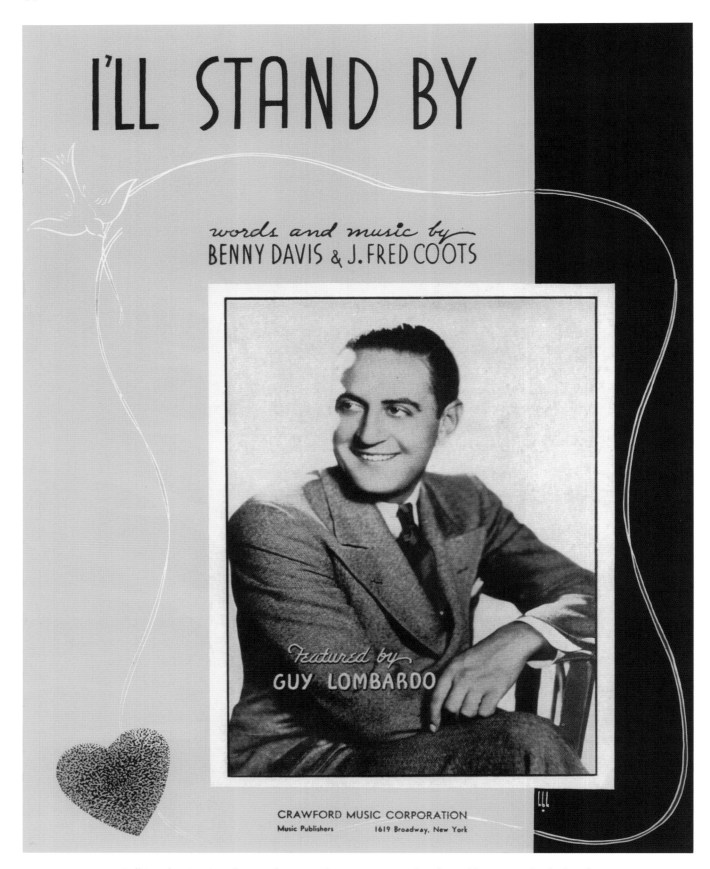

"I'll Stand By," written by J. Fred Coots with Benny Davis, and performed by Guy Lombardo (1936)

"Beautiful," written by Haven Gillespie with Larry Shay, and performed by Guy Lombardo (1927)

"White Christmas" sheet music (1943)

WHITE CHRISTMAS — 1942

**WRITER —
IRVING BERLIN**

**ARTIST —
BING CROSBY**

DECCA RECORDS

DL 78128   STEREO

Merry Christmas

DECCA RECORDS

Russian immigrant Irving Berlin's wistful dream of a "White Christmas," the most commercially successful seasonal song of all time, and a tune that is as much about a nostalgic snowy wish as it is about loss and longing for individual and universal peace, enormously influenced holiday music after its release in 1942. Berlin's tuneful finger was adroitly on the rhythmic pulse of the nation. He wrote his poetic Tin-Pan-Alley masterpiece around the same time that another timely popular treasure of his, "God Bless America," patriotically addressed an insecure country on the chilling brink of a second world war. After that war hit home, it seemed no song could better capture innocence lost than "White Christmas." No song stylist could better soothe the nation's frazzled nerves than America's most bubbly popular singer at the time — Bing Crosby — the human embodiment of Berlin's lost era, and a man considered by many to be the unassuming voice of Christmas long ago.

Irving Berlin Australian Song Folio (1940's)

Berlin was born in Russia on May 11, 1888, and emigrated to New York City five years later when conditions there became too politically dangerous for his persecuted Jewish family. His early musical life was greatly influenced by his religious father, a meat inspector and part-time Orthodox cantor, who encouraged his son to sing in their Lower East Side synagogue choir. "I used to sing in a choir with my father and made my first public appearance when I was ten years old," he once recalled. "For a boy whose father had been a cantor and grandfather a rabbi, singing was doin' what comes natur'lly."[1]

"I suppose it was singing with my father that gave me my musical background,' he later added. "It was in my blood."[2]

As a boy, the man who grew to become what many consider to be the greatest and most prolific Tin-Pan-Alley tune-smith of all time, faced the terrible gloom of poverty, fighting then to escape the dark forces which shaped his early life and threatened to consume him. One of his earliest memories involved a powerfully poetic Christmas image that stayed with him throughout his entire

Irving Berlin, approximately 1901

life. "I was a little Russian-born kid, living on the Lower East Side of New York City. I did not have a Christmas," he once remembered. "I bounded across the street to my friendly neighbors, and shared their goodies. Not only that, this was my first sight of a Christmas tree. They were very poor and later, as I grew used to their annual tree, I realized they had to buy one with broken branches and small height, but to me that first tree seemed to tower to Heaven."[3]

Irving Berlin may have tucked away this experience of the lonely outsider peering into a Christmas world he could never inhabit, subconsciously drawing from it when he wrote "White Christmas." Surely the untimely death of his father in 1901 left an indelible longing in his heart. He ran away from home and sang songs in New York City saloons for pennies he could send to help support his widowed mother. Early on, the young teenage panhandler learned people would often pay extra money to hear a heartfelt performance of sentimental tunes or bluesy popular songs known as "sob" ballads.

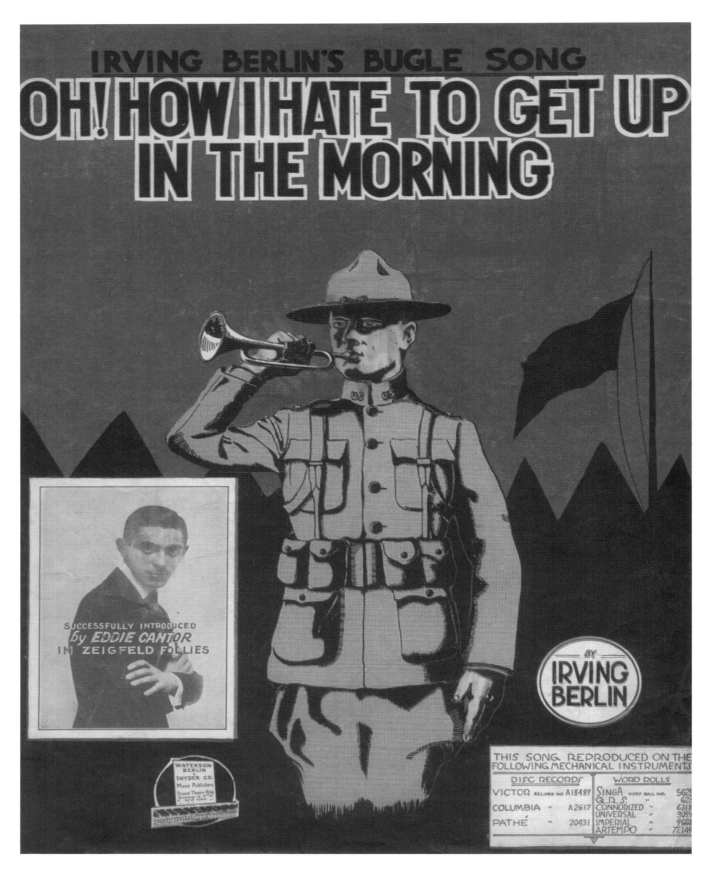

1918

do with the steady turn-of-the-century growth of Tin Pan Alley and the opportunities it presented to American immigrants. Tin Pan Alley was actually West 28th Street in New York City. It began in the 1880's as a place where many Jewish immigrants set up music publishing offices that produced sheet music for hungry consumers.

"In 1893, the year Irving Berlin came to America, Tin Pan Alley was galvanized by the sale of more than a million copies of sheet music for a single song, 'After the Ball.' Until then, no one imagined that songwriting could be such a profitable enterprise."[4]

By 1910, Berlin was working as a staff writer for one of those Tin-Pan-Alley publishing firms, and now had over fifty tunes under his songwriting belt. The following year completely redirected the young songwriter's life when his

The motley repertoire he gleaned on the gritty city streets of a bustling immigrant world soon helped Berlin support himself in his next job as a grave-yard-shift singing waiter in a smoky Chinatown tavern. It would be a sweet Tin-Pan-Alley love song called "Marie From Sunny Italy," and it serendipitously launched his incredible songwriting career in 1907 when his boss unexpectedly ordered him to pen its lyrics. Though Berlin had never learned to formally read or write music, he nevertheless saw this first song published just a few days before he turned nineteen.

The fluid nature with which this self-taught young man was able to move into the music publishing trade, had much to

Irving Berlin (1918)

Bing Crosby in "The Bells of St. Mary's" (1946)

"Alexander's Ragtime Band" opus became a worldwide smash. "That was the biggest hit anybody had ever seen up to that point and it became an international success," says Philip Furia, author of *Irving Berlin: A Life In Song.* "It was the song that singled out Berlin as a major songwriter."

Berlin once pointed out that this tune was really tapping into his somber Slavic roots, since played slowly it sounded very much like a mournful Russian-Jewish dirge. "And that certainly comes out in 'White Christmas,'" admits Furia, "which is also a very dark chromatic, almost mournful, melody."

At the same time Berlin was composing pop songs to sell as sheet music for the masses, he was also crafting and singing his own sophisticated show tunes for New York City's urbane theater crowd. In 1908, he wrote "She Was A Dear Little Girl," his first production number for a show called *The Boys And Betty.* "Alexander's Ragtime Band" appeared in *The Friars Frolic of 1911,* and over the next fifteen years he contributed songs for dozens of revue-oriented Broadway musicals ranging from *The Ziegfeld Follies* serial to 1918's *Yip Yip Yaphank,* a World War I satire in which he himself sang his comical military gem, "Oh How I Hate To Get Up In The Morning."

One of Irving Berlin's most well-known nuggets, "Blue Skies," appeared in an unsuccessful 1926 Richard Rodgers and Lorenze Hart musical called *Betsy.* Ironically, the song would reappear the following year in a groundbreaking movie when Al Jolson sang it for *The Jazz Singer.* That film would go down in popular history as Hollywood's first talking picture, and would create new opportunities for Berlin.

"Berlin's right there the minute the talkies come in, and he quickly began writing for Hollywood," says Furia. Among the additional films he helped score in the late 1920's were *Coquette* (Mary Pickford's talking debut), *The Cocoanuts,* starring The Marx Brothers, and *Puttin' On The Ritz,* whose title song evolved into yet another enduring Berlin classic.

In 1930, Irving Berlin began his historical movie collaboration with Christmas music king Bing Crosby, then a fresh-faced newcomer revolutionizing popular singing with his jazzy naturalistic vocal technique. Crosby's first spoken line, "Hello Gang," took place during his uncredited cameo in *Reaching For The Moon,* and he favorably stood out as he crooned its

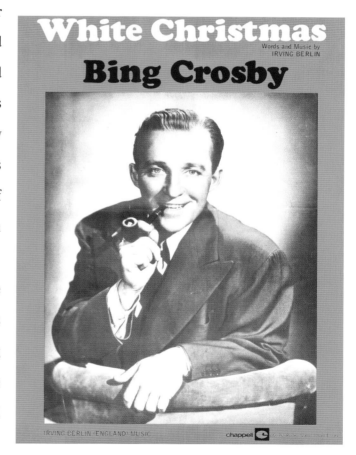

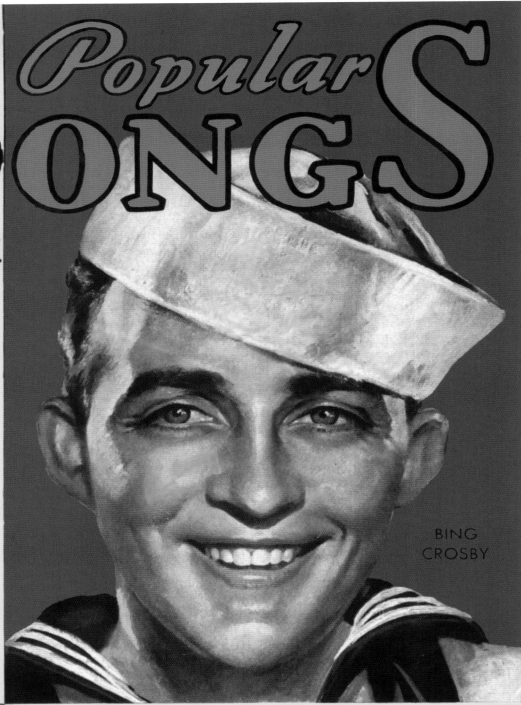

Bing Crosby on the cover of "Popular Songs" magazine (December 1934)

Bing Crosby (upper left) on the 1932 sheet music for "Please" from the movie, "The Big Broadcast"

Bing Crosby's first Christmas album (1949)

only song, "When The Folks High-Up Do that Mean Low Down," a tongue-in-cheek number written by Berlin himself.

"I think people should learn that Bing Crosby was the first really great popular singer," says Ken Barnes, author of *The Crosby Years,* and producer of his last albums. "He left behind a massive body of work, and was the first white singer to successfully incorporate Black jazz into popular music. He was also the first and probably the best of the naturalistic singers. Sinatra learned a lot from Crosby."

Born on May 2, 1901, in Tacoma, Washington, Bing Crosby began his professional recording career in 1926, and was greatly influenced by his friend, jazz innovator Louis Armstrong. In 1927, Bing's idol, Al Jolson, became the first actor to speak in a motion picture. The following year, Crosby formed a vocal trio known as the Rhythm Boys, and recorded "Sunshine," his first Irving Berlin tune.

As the Great Depression eclipsed the nation, Crosby was endearing himself to a downtrodden public voracious for his friendly voice. He began singing on his own long-lasting popular CBS radio show, and started releasing records as a solo artist first with Brunswick, and then Decca Records, racking up over ten number-one hits by 1935. He would end up recording close to 1000 songs in twenty years' time.

Matching his warm vocals to the cool silver screen, he also starred in his first movie musical, *The Big Broadcast,* when signed to Paramount Pictures in 1932. "I think the movies really helped his career," adds Barnes. "His face and voice went together so well for people."

The sunny casualness of that voice also went together well with Christmas music, and much of Bing Crosby's surviving legacy would be built around this incredible Yuletide marriage, when his seminal interpretation of the religious "Silent Night" quickly led to the overwhelming success of the secular "White Christmas."

Bing Crosby first professionally sang that holy carol with the Rhythm Boys in 1928, accompanied by The Paul Whiteman Orchestra. It turned out to be his first among dozens of popular holiday recordings, yet seven years would pass before a priest could persuade him to lend his solo voice to the hymn.

Crosby once expressed his initial reluctance to record "Silent Night:" "I thought it would be wrong for me to take

1936

income from the sale of such a record. The way I saw it, it would be like cashing in on the Church or the Bible."

He was finally compelled to do it in 1934 when a St. Columban missionary priest asked him for help with needy children in China. "He had just come from his mission with a film showing the work done there," said Crosby. "He planned to travel over the United States, showing the film in parish auditoriums to raise funds."[5]

Bing offered to cut "Silent Night"/"Adeste Fideles" for the missionary soundtrack. In what would become his first Christmas single ever, he recorded them once again when his brother suggested that any money made from the private sale of the record could be donated to the children. "The plan was to take the royalties from 'Silent Night,' and pour them into this fund. In that way I'd avoid cashing in on a religious song."[6] That fund would later go on to include additional charities.

The recording of Crosby's first solo Christmas song took place on February 21, 1935, with Bing backed by The Georgie Stoll Orchestra and The Crinoline Choir. Surprisingly, some music teachers and critics protested it, feeling Crosby's voice and style weren't appropriate for such spiritual songs.

After radio stations received a copy of it, however, people clamored for their own record of Bing crooning a holiday tune for the first time, and he was forced to go into the studio with a larger orchestra to commercially record the songs to meet this popular demand.

It would actually be his fourth session of "Silent Night"/ "Adeste Fideles." It would occur on November 12, 1935, with Crosby now accompanied by The Victor Young Orchestra and The Guardsmen Quartet. This recording became a million-selling seasonal single, and was a powerful hint of a new consumer market for Christmas music. As Decca continued to re-release it throughout the 1930's, and Bing began singing it live on radio, its popularity continued to grow, setting the stage for the arrival of his next phenomenal holiday coup — "White Christmas."

By 1938, both Crosby and Berlin had grown into two of the most powerful people in the entertainment industry. Berlin became part of the immortal Ginger Rogers/Fred Astaire triumvirate, writing scores for them to sing as they gracefully danced their way through surreal glamorous movies like *Top Hat* (1935), *Follow The Fleet* (1936), and *Carefree* (1938). Crosby extravaganzas such as *Pennies From Heaven* (1936),

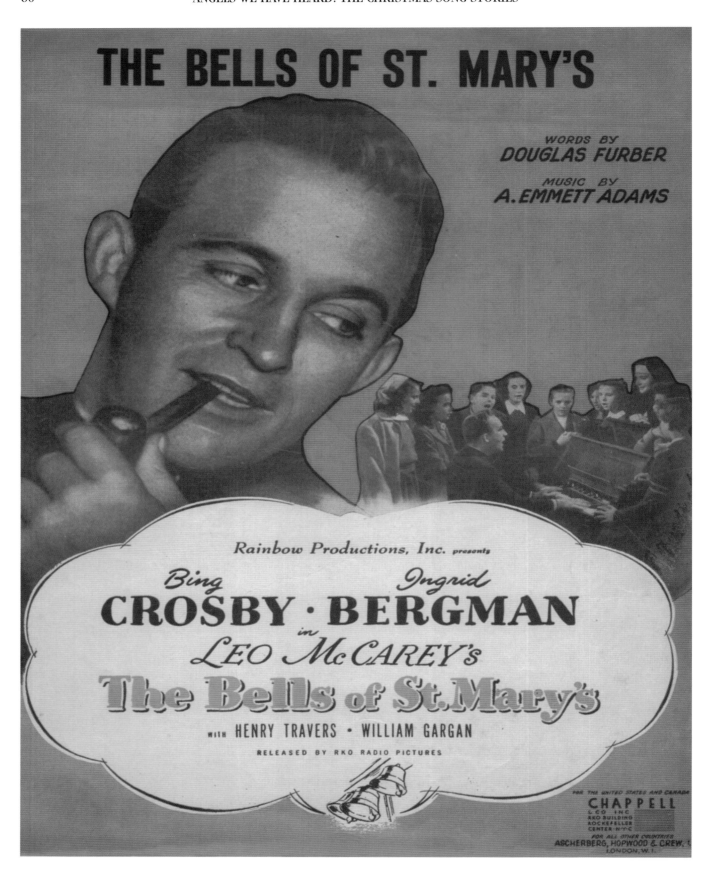

1942

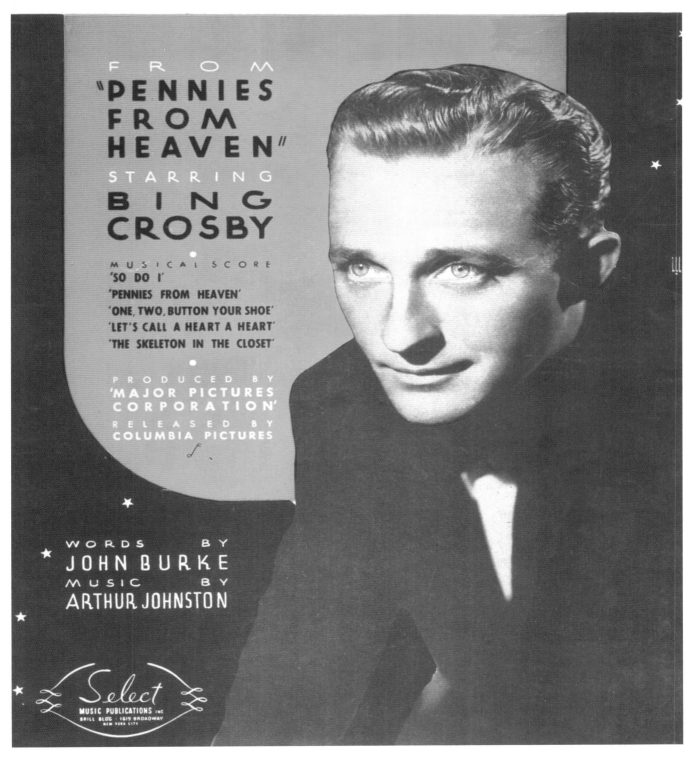

1936

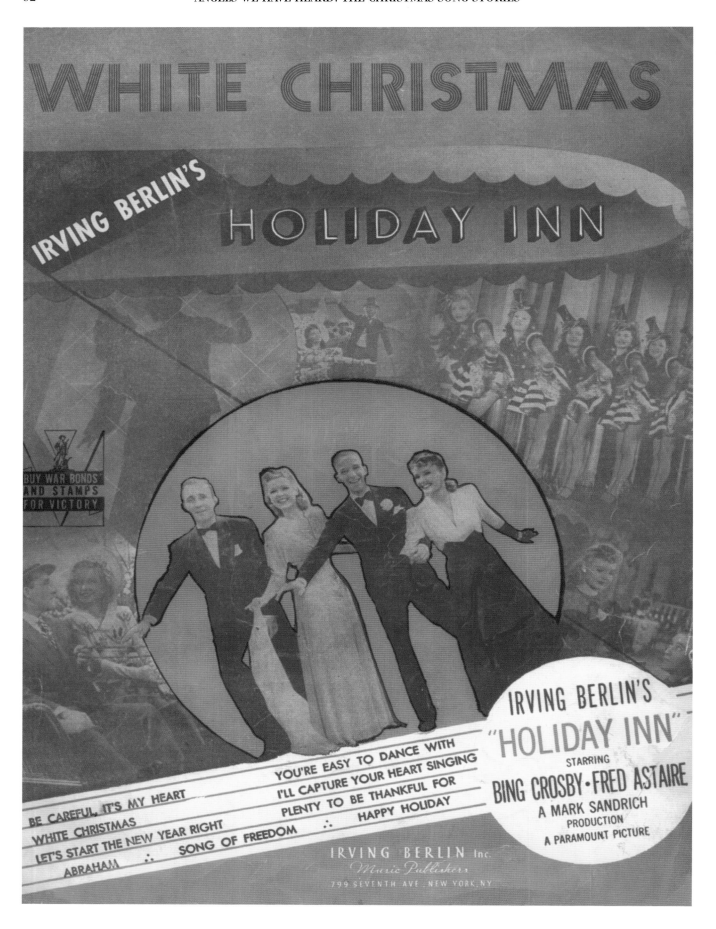

"Holiday Inn" debuted in New York City at the Paramount Theater, August, 1942 (shown above)

and *Waikiki Wedding* (1937), scored big at the box office, and with Academy Award voters as well, who nominated the former's title song while handing the statue to his "Sweet Leilani" from the latter.

The next Bing Crosby song to nab an Oscar was written by Irving Berlin. His "White Christmas" picked up the trophy on March 4, 1943, and would be the only Christmas song to ever accomplish this intoxicating feat.

Even though "White Christmas" wound up in a film, Berlin actually wrote it around 1938 for a Broadway play that never materialized. "I think he was planning to use it for a Broadway revue that never came off," admits Furia, who says Berlin wrote it for a show in which "each song" would be "tailored to a holiday." Berlin had written a 1933 production with Moss Hart called *As Thousands Cheer,* and each one of its tunes related to some part

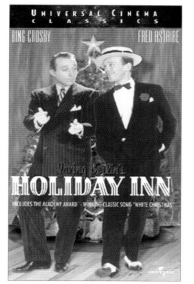

of the newspaper. "He wanted to do a follow up called *More Cheers* with Hart but never got around to doing it."

Instead, the songwriter secretly held on to "White Christmas" for quite some time, not revealing it to anyone in the business. "He would sit on some songs for a long time," says Furia. "'God Bless America' sat in his trunk for twenty years."

He hoped to insert the song into his new musical, but was unable to get anyone on Broadway to mount it. Finally, he decided to transfer the idea to a film about an entertainer who leaves the hustle and bustle of New York City show business life behind to run a quiet country inn in Connecticut, only open on holidays. He called the movie *Holiday Inn,* and it starred two familiar Berlin buddies — Bing Crosby, and a darker, less glamorous, Fred Astaire minus Ginger Rogers.

Furia stresses that the idea for *Holiday Inn* once again demonstrated Irving Berlin's unique ability to read the public's mind. "He picked up on the national mood — that it was time to recapture a kind of sentimentality. He had this wonderful line — 'there's nothing so corny as last year's sophistication,' and he really sensed that the Astaire/Rogers era was coming to an end and moving toward what it would become in the 40's when World War II hit — much more folksy and homey like the musical *Oklahoma.*

Caught between two worlds, when Berlin first sat down to write "White Christmas," he concocted an opening verse with a refined cocktail shaker mentality leftover from the glam days of the 1930's. Its story included everlasting sun, balmy palm trees and green grass growing in Beverly Hills. It was written for "sophisticates having martinis around a swimming pool." During the war "when he realized the verse was wrong, he pulled it very quickly," adds Furia, "and didn't want anybody singing it."

With the threat of war ominously lurking on the horizon, Berlin's intuition continued to push him away from urbane cocktail and slick city skyscraper tunes. He moved more toward home hymns like 1938's "God Bless America," and movie songs of white Christmas longing, tranquil rural living, and happy dreamy holidays, which to him had become much more important now for a somber nation yearning for domestic bliss. "Like 'God Bless America,' *Holiday Inn* would serve as a vehicle for endorsing the American way of life at a time when all hell was breaking loose in Europe."[7]

"In September, 1941, my father went to Hollywood to work on *Holiday Inn*, in production at last," said Berlin's daugh-

ter Mary Ellin Barrett. "All spring and summer he had been writing the songs, on keyboard and typewriter, a whole new batch to accompany the one written a year or more earlier called 'White Christmas,' a secret song he felt from the start so strongly about he'd made it part of the contract with Paramount."[8]

As time went on that secret song took on an enormous life of its own, unexpectedly upstaging *Holiday Inn* and spawning an unexplored consumer market for secular Christmas music, picking up where "Silent Night" left off. The story of its creation, cultural imprint and growth is legendary.

Irving Berlin wrote "White Christmas" at his New York City home in one long overnight session, unlike many of his ear-

lier tunes that took days, weeks and sometimes even years to craft. It was written using a piano that had a special lever for automatically changing keys, since he never formally learned to play, and only used the black keys of F sharp when composing.

He once described the inspirational process of its creation: "We working composers all too often, in the interests of expediency, sharpen our pencils, get out that square sheet of paper and become too slick. Those forced efforts are 'square' songs. But sometimes a song is a natural. We may start it to order for a specific scene or show, but our subconscious beings go to work and the song is just there. This is what I call a 'round' song."[9]

"It was morning when he finished the song. Instead of going to sleep, he went directly to his office, where his employees gaped at the sight of the boss appearing first thing on a Monday morning. He found his transcriber, and proclaimed, 'I want you to take down a song I wrote over the weekend. Not only is it the best song I ever wrote, it's the best song anybody ever wrote.' Irving sat down at the piano to play the song and, in his fashion, sing it."[10]

As Berlin readied "White Christmas" for Bing Crosby, he became more and more nervous about his *pièce de*

résistance. His musical orchestrator for *Holiday Inn*, Walter Scharf, was "impressed by the amount of energy and anxiety he expended during the final stages of preparation."

"It was as if he were going to have a baby when he was working on that song," he remembered. "I never saw a man so wrapped up in himself. It was all a tremendously traumatic experience for him."[11]

However, when Bing was finally introduced to it, the songwriter was given a bit of muted assurance. "Of course, he's not the one to throw his arms about and get excited," Berlin said later. "When he read the song he just took his pipe out of his mouth and said to me: 'You don't have to worry about this one, Irving.'"[12] Later Bing would say that the song was as much a part of him as his floppy ears.

It was now time for Crosby to go before the cameras and sing his soon to be trademark blockbuster. Berlin won the right from Paramount for final approval of every note in the film, and was so protective of "White Christmas" that he found a place to hide on the set, secretly watching while Crosby mouthed its words with co-star Marjorie Reynolds.

That scene in which movie goers were first introduced to the song on screen, serves to create a snowy fantasy world

for Crosby and Reynolds. They sing it as a duet while falling in love at the beginning of the story, alongside a blazing Yuletide fire. It reappears at the end of the film to reunite them, and fits in with other cheerful tunes like, "Let's Start The New Year Right," "Be Careful It's My Heart," "Easter Parade" (recycled from *As Thousands Cheer*), and a second enduring Christmas song, "Happy Holiday."

"Although 'White Christmas' became the bestselling song Irving Berlin — or anyone — ever wrote, Berlin had written most of his score for *Holiday Inn* with the realization that by tying each song to a holiday, it was unlikely any would achieve independent popularity. Not only did 'White Christmas' over-

turn that expectation, the all-purpose 'Happy Holiday' has also become an evergreen."[13]

Surprisingly, the song "White Christmas" and Berlin's entire *Holiday Inn* score failed to impress some critics from the start. When *Holiday Inn* opened in August, 1942, a journalist from *Daily Variety* said he "didn't think 'White Christmas' would make it" because it was "too schmaltzy."[14] In addition, one of Berlin's own lawyers said the song and its movie would "flop." Something those critics couldn't foresee, however, was the unexpected powerful influence World War II and Bing Crosby would initially have on its overall success.

Just as war was breaking out in America, Crosby publicly sang "White Christmas" for the first time during his *Kraft Music Hall* radio program on Christmas Day, 1941. Months after his *Holiday Inn* soundtrack take, he went into a Los Angeles studio to cut its first commercial single on May 29, 1942, accompanied by The John Scott Trotter Orchestra and The Ken Darby Singers. He recorded it twice that day. Either accidentally or to deal with the difficulty of singing the word "Christmases," he initially left out the word "your" in the song's last line, but replaced it on the second take. Decca released the latter version, while the former was locked away for over

fifty years until MCA decided to issue it on Crosby's 1998 *Voice of Christmas* disc.

Following its August, 1942, release on Halloween, "White Christmas" became the first Christmas song to reach number one, ringing in the New Year of 1943 and staying on top for eleven weeks straight.

American soldiers abroad longing for home quickly bonded with Bing Crosby's cozy interpretation of Berlin's pensive Christmas ballad, flooding Armed Forces Radio with requests and ultimately claiming "White Christmas" as their own personal anthem. "It became a peace song in wartime," said Berlin. "Nothing I'd ever intended. It was nostalgic for a lot of boys who weren't home for Christmas. It just shows that inspiration can pro-

duce anything."[15] Ironically, it was Berlin's later excised "palm trees" verse that really seemed to resonate with lonely soldiers stationed in the warm South Pacific, even though stateside audiences found it to be a disconcerting oxymoron.

Bing Crosby was able to use "White Christmas" as a bridge to personally connect with those homesick soldiers when he toured European army camps throughout the war years. In remembering his 1944 tour he said that "often in the midst of rainy muggy weather those kids still wanted 'Silent Night'

and 'White Christmas.' To be honest, I would rather not have sung them. I knew that those lads, away from home, were lonely enough without the additional nostalgia of Christmas memories. More than once I saw tears roll down their faces as they listened, their thoughts far away."[16] All of those tours were financed with charity money taken from Crosby's "Silent Night" recording.

At the end of 1944, Decca Records announced that "White Christmas" had sold two million copies, making it the biggest-selling single to date. In 1945 and 1947, it re-entered the charts, peaking again at number one.

By then the song's master had worn thin, and Crosby had to go back to re-record it on March 19, 1947. "When the first pressing had sold out seven times over and the die stamp had become worn from sheer overuse I got a call from Decca," remembered Ken Darby. "They wondered if I could gather together the same singers we had used on the original recording. I said they were all still in the business singing better than ever, and they set a date for a repeat performance in the old Decca studio on Melrose. We sang the same arrangement and John Scott Trotter conducted the same orchestration and used almost the same men."[17]

According to Decca, sales continued to skyrocket with five million records sold by the end of 1948. At the completion of the decade, with the birth of the long-playing album, Bing included "White Christmas" on his first holiday LP, *Merry Christmas*. He would ultimately record up to forty additional Christmas songs for subsequent Decca single and album releases through the late 1950's.

All of this incredible success spawned an entire 1954 movie named after the song, starring Bing Crosby, Rosemary Clooney, Danny Kaye and Vera Ellen. Like *Holiday Inn*, *White Christmas* employed a theme of rural paradise found at a blissful New England country inn. This time the romantic action took place in Vermont, and involved a retired army general yearning for the

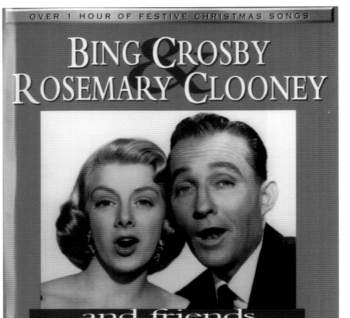

glory days of World War II. In its most festive scene, Crosby and his chirpy entourage cheerfully croon the title tune, cartoonishly dressed in bright red Technicolor Santa Claus suits.

According to Rosemary Clooney, Berlin was still very protective of his reappearing classic. "He looked quite worried when he listened to the first take of Bing prerecording it and began to pace up and down. Crosby, noticing it, shouted: 'Irving, why don't you go back to my dressing room and sit down and wait. We'll play the tape for you when it's finished. It'll be all right, because you know I did record it a long time ago — I really know the song!"[18]

After that soundtrack recording, Crosby went back into the studio once again to cut a new 1954 commercial single of "White Christmas," with Danny Kaye and Peggy Lee standing in for Clooney, whose Columbia record contract forbid her involvement in the competing Decca release. The film also included "Snow," a new seasonal Berlin evergreen, along with the hit "Count Your Blessings Instead Of Sheep."

The movie became one of Bing Crosby's biggest (as well as the top film of 1954), and fueled sales of his version of Irving Berlin's masterpiece, which continued to consecutively reenter the charts every year through 1962. On October 19, 1976, a year before his death, Crosby went back to record a thirty-eight-second version of "White Christmas," hoping to add it to a long medley of his hits for the album *Bing Crosby Live At The London Palladium*. He was unable to get permission from his record company to include it, however, and it has never been released.

Frank Sinatra's "White Christmas" (1946)

Eventually "White Christmas" was listed in *The Guinness Book of World Records* as the greatest selling song of all time with sales of 30 million units, a record it held until 1997 when Elton John's "Candle In The Wind" Princess Diana tribute pushed it to second place.

Those sales changed popular Christmas music forever, since before it came out only Crosby's rendering of the sacred "Silent Night" rang up substantial record store receipts. Not only did Berlin and Crosby's jewel lead to countless successful versions of it by artists like Sinatra (whose rendition upstaged Bing's on the charts in 1946), The Drifters and Andy Williams, but it would actually go on to create a brand new Christmas music industry, in which a popular face and voice could record and sell the sounds of the season.

Its unprecedented effect on the market place became important proof for record companies, songwriters and singers

of the 1940's onward, that writing, performing and releasing new holiday hits (while rejuvenating old ones like the 1943 million-selling Crosby/Andrews Sisters "Jingle Bells" duet) could reap great long-lasting financial rewards. Most of today's enduring secular American Christmas songs would be written post-1942, following the incredible success of "White Christmas."

The reason for that success is plain and simple — through his song Irving Berlin intuitively tapped into the dark side of Christmas — feelings of lost innocence so deeply personal that they became infinitely universal. "It's the loneliness of 'White Christmas that I think is so unusual," says Furia. "It's not like the group carol — the person singing it is off by himself and is almost shutout from the whole holiday world. The melancholy of it makes it unusual because Christmas is supposed to be such a time of ecstasy and joy. This song and

The Drifters' "White Christmas" (1962)

Irving Berlin

'Have Yourself A Merry Little Christmas' are, I think, two of the best Christmas songs ever written, and both of them have this kind of brooding darkness."

That "brooding darkness" was very much a part of Irving Berlin's personality, a simple sadness that repeatedly played itself out in the great body of work he left behind after his death on September 22, 1989. Since he never spoke on record about the wistful theme that runs throughout "White Christmas," it will always remain a secret as to which memories he called upon to express its masked sorrow. As he himself once said, the roots of its mournfulness could simply have come from his somber Russian-Jewish heritage.

But in addition to the early passing of his father, there were two other great losses in his life he may have conjured in writing his musical dream of things that once were, but can never again be attained.

In 1912, his first wife contracted typhoid fever on their honeymoon, dying barely five months after marrying him. In honor of her, Berlin paid a florist to place a white rose on her grave every other day for thirteen years, until he remarried.

"White Christmas" could also have been a way of honoring his first and only son, Irving Berlin, Jr. As a child, Berlin's daughter, Mary Ellin Barrett, stumbled upon an old newspaper clipping, and discovered a tragedy that broke her parents' hearts. It was an article announcing the death of her three week old brother.

Irving Berlin and his wife secretly went to the cemetery every Christmas Eve thereafter to put flowers on his grave. "Many years later, when Christmas was celebrated irregularly in my parents' house, if at all, my mother said, almost casually, 'Oh you know, I hated Christmas, we both hated Christmas. We only did it for you children,'" recalled Barrett. "The implication was that for them the happiness had drained out of Christmas on December 25, 1928, the day my brother died."[19]

IRVING BERLIN'S
REMEMBER

Irving Berlin, Inc.
MUSIC PUBLISHERS
1607 Broadway   New York

1925

White Christmas Facts

- Irving Berlin signed the Paramount contract to film *Holiday Inn* on May 14, 1940.

- Fred Astaire danced himself thin, losing fourteen pounds during its three-month shoot. He was offered the opportunity to reunite with Crosby for *White Christmas,* but reportedly turned it down because he was unhappy with its script.

- Although it looks like Bing is singing "White Christmas" as a duet with co-star Marjorie Reynolds, he's really singing it with Martha Meers, whose voice was later dubbed into *Holiday Inn.*

- On May 29, 1942, the historical day of the first "White Christmas" session, Bing also recorded two other songs from *Holiday Inn* —"Abraham" and "Song of Freedom."

- Two months before *Holiday Inn*'s release, its songs were plugged on Bing Crosby's *Kraft Music Hall* radio show. Crosby and Astaire acted out excerpts from the movie for Armed Forces Radio on November 4, 1942. The following

January, Dinah Shore starred with Bing in a complete radio version of it.

- Irving Berlin once bunked with Bing and Groucho Marx during a trip aboard the ocean liner *Queen Elizabeth.*

- Bing Crosby recorded over sixty Irving Berlin songs between 1928 and 1976, and re-teamed with Astaire in 1946 for the non-holiday Berlin movie, *Blue Skies* (Astaire would go on to star in Berlin's 1948 *Easter Parade* with Judy Garland). From 1943 through 1954, Crosby was one of the top-ten money-making stars at the box office, and number one for five of those years.

- In addition to "White Christmas" and "Sweet Leilani," two other Bing Crosby film tunes won Academy Awards for best song. After 1944's, "Swinging On A Star" (from *Going My Way),* and 1951's "In The Cool, Cool, Cool Of The Evening" (from *Here Comes The Groom)* picked up the coveted trophy, Bing became the singer with the most number of Oscar-winning film songs under his belt.

- Two other Irving Berlin/Bing Crosby musical collaborations were nominated as well — "You Keep Coming Back Like A Song" (from *Blue Skies),* and *White Christmas'* "Count Your Blessings Instead Of Sheep."

- Bing adamantly refused to dress in drag for a scene in *White Christmas* requiring him to impersonate Rosemary Clooney. Costumer Edith Head was eventually able to talk him into rolling up his pants and covering them with a shawl.

- Rosemary Clooney and Bing Crosby starred together in a CBS radio show which ran from 1960 to 1962.

- Kathryn Grant, Bing's second wife, met him on the set of *White Christmas* in 1954.

- If you include his movie soundtrack and single/ album versions, Bing recorded "White Christmas" seven times in thirty-five years. Additional recordings of him singing it live on radio, and taped television performances, helped to make "White Christmas" his signature song.

- In his 101 years, Irving Berlin wrote thousands of songs, often at the rate of one a day. 899 of them were registered for copyright. 282 became top-ten hits.

- When Berlin wrote "White Christmas," his second wife, Ellin Mackay, told him that his beginning lyric, which referred to "Beverly Hills, L.A.," was incorrect. His response was that was the way he wanted it.

- As *Holiday Inn* debuted, Irving Berlin was starring on Broadway in his World-War-II revue, *This*

Is The Army. Eleanor Roosevelt loved the show so much she saw it three times.

- Berlin wrote "Sittin' in the Sun Counting My Money" for *White Christmas*. It was cut from the movie and recorded by Louis Armstrong.

- In 1973, the International Society of Santa Claus gave their first Spirit of Christmas Award to Berlin's "White Christmas" and Johnny Marks' "Rudolph The Red-nosed Reindeer."

- A small group of people gathered in front of Irving Berlin's New York City home each Christmas Eve to serenade him with "White Christmas" when he was in his 90's. In 1983, he invited the carolers in to thank them, saying it was the nicest Christmas present anyone ever gave him.

Danny Kaye

Bing Crosby

Rosemary Clooney

Vera Ellen

1950

BING CROSBY'S SELECTED CHRISTMAS RECORDING HISTORY

SINGLES

LABEL	TITLE	YEAR
Columbia	Silent Night, Holy Night (*with The Rhythm Boys*)	1928
Columbia	Christmas Melodies (*with The Rhythm Boys*)	1928
Decca	Silent Night, Holy Night/Adeste Fideles (*charity version*)	1935
Decca	Silent Night, Holy Night/Adeste Fideles (*commercial version*)	1935
Decca	White Christmas/Let's Start The New Year Right/Happy Holiday	1942
Decca	Silent Night, Holy Night/Adeste Fideles	1942
Decca	God Rest Ye Merry, Gentlemen/Faith Of Our Fathers	1942
Decca	Jingle Bells/Santa Claus Is Comin' To Town (*with the Andrews Sisters*)	1943
Decca	I'll Be Home For Christmas/Faith Of Our Fathers	1943
Decca	The Bells Of St. Mary's	1945
Decca	Ave Maria	1945
Decca	White Christmas/Silent Night, Holy Night	1947
Decca	The Christmas Song/O Fir Tree Dark	1947
Decca	Happy Birthday/Auld Lang Syne	1947
Decca	Here Comes Santa Claus/The Twelve Days of Christmas (*with the Andrews Sisters*)	1949
Decca	You're All I Want For Christmas/The First Noel	1949
Decca	Deck The Halls/Away In A Manger/I Saw Three Ships/Good King Wenceslas/We Three Kings/Angels We Have Heard On High	1949
Decca	White Christmas/God Rest Ye Merry, Gentlemen	1950
Decca	Rudolph The Red-nosed Reindeer/The Teddy Bear's Picnic	1950
Decca	Mele Kalikimaka/Poppa Santa Claus (*with the Andrews Sisters*)	1950
Decca	Silver Bells (*with Carol Richards*)/That Christmas Feeling	1950
Decca	A Marshmallow World/Looks Like A Cold, Cold Winter	1950
Decca	A Crosby Christmas (*with Crosby's sons Gary, Phillip, Dennis and Lindsay*)	1950
Decca	Christmas In Killarney/It's Beginning To Look Like Christmas	1951
Decca	Sleigh Ride/Little Jack Frost Get Lost (*with Peggy Lee*)	1952
Decca	Sleigh Bell Serenade/Keep It A Secret	1952
Decca	White Christmas/Snow (*with Danny Kaye, Peggy Lee & Trudi Stevens*)	1954
Decca	Christmas Is A Comin'/Is Christmas Only A Tree	1955
Decca	The First Snowfall/The Next Time It Happens	1955
Decca	I Heard The Bells On Christmas Day/Christmas Is A Comin'	1956
Decca	Rudolph The Red-nosed Reindeer/I Heard The Bells On Christmas Day	1956
Kapp	How Lovely Is Christmas/My Own Individual Star	1957
Little Golden	Boy At A Window/How Lovely Is Christmas	1957
Columbia	The Secret Of Christmas/Just What I Wanted for Christmas	1959

SINGLES

LABEL	TITLE	YEAR
Warner Bros.	I Wish You a Merry Christmas/Winter Wonderland/The Littlest Angel	1962
Capitol	Do You Hear What I Hear?/Christmas Dinner Country Style	1963
Reprise	It's Christmas Time Again/Christmas Candles (*with Frank Sinatra*)	1964
Reprise	We Wish You The Merriest/Go Tell It On The Mountain (*with Frank Sinatra*)	1964
Reprise	The White World Of Christmas/The Secret Of Christmas	1965
Daybreak	A Time To Be Jolly/And The Bells Rang	1971
MCA	White Christmas/When The Blue Of The Night Meets The Gold Of The Day	1977
RCA	Peace On Earth/Little Drummer Boy (*with David Bowie*)	1982

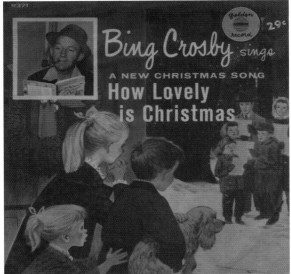

"Bing Crosby's Christmas Classics" (1999) was originally released on Warner Brothers in 1962 with the title, "I Wish You A Merry Christmas." The re-released set (shown left) contains four additional tracks.

ALBUMS

LABEL	TITLE	YEAR
Decca	Merry Christmas *(EP)*	1949
Decca	A Crosby Christmas *(EP)*	1950
Decca	White Christmas *(soundtrack)*	1954
Decca	A Christmas Sing With Bing Around The World	1957
Decca	That Christmas Feeling	1958
Decca	Holiday Inn *(soundtrack)*	1962
Decca	Two Favorite Stories by Bing Crosby	1962
Warner Bros.	I Wish You A Merry Christmas	1962
Capitol	Favorite Songs Of Christmas	1964
Reprise	12 Songs Of Christmas *(with Frank Sinatra)*	1964
Decca	Favorite Songs Of Christmas	1968
Daybreak	A Time To Be Jolly	1971
	A Christmas Star *(limited edition charity album)*	1972
Capitol	Bing Crosby's Christmas Classics	1977
Collectors Gold	Happy Holiday with Frank & Bing	1977
20th Century	A Holiday Toast	1977
Collectors Gold	Bing Crosby & Rosemary Clooney — White Christmas	1978
Fox American	Bing Crosby Sings Christmas	1978
Reader's Digest	Christmas With Bing	1980
Laserlight	Christmas Through The Years	1995
MCA	Sings Christmas Songs	1996
Mastertone	Bing Crosby & Rosemary Clooney and friends	1996
Capitol	Bing Crosby's Christmas Classics	1997
Polygram	Christmas Album	1997
Chicago Music	Christmas Classics	1997
Dejavu	Christmas Gift Collection	1997
Laserlight	Christmas Sing With Frank And Bing *(with Frank Sinatra)*	1997
Laserlight	It's Christmas Time *(Crosby/Sinatra/King Cole)*	1997
Laserlight	White Christmas	1997
MCA	White Christmas	1997
Laserlight	WW II Radio Christmas Shows	1997
KRB	Silver Bells Of Christmas *(with Rosemary Clooney)*	1998
MCA	The Voice Of Christmas — The Complete Decca Songbook	1998
Capitol	Christmas Classics	1999
Laserlight	Christmas With Liberace	1999
Laserlight	Christmas Collection	2000

MORE WITH PHILIP FURIA, AUTHOR OF
IRVING BERLIN: A LIFE IN SONG

What in Irving Berlin's younger life would eventually lead him to write a Christmas song?

Well, he talked about a time when he was young. He grew up in terrible poverty on New York City's Lower East Side. One of his best memories of childhood was of an Irish kid he played with, and of when this kid invited him over to his tenement. Berlin grew up in a place that didn't have any windows — this is really the Lower East Side at its most teeming. He remembered seeing this Christmas tree that absolutely astounded him. He realized years later that this Irish family was so poor that they had to take one of the trees with broken branches — one of the cheapest trees on the lot. But he said when he looked at that thing, it seemed to tower to heaven. It was just extraordinary, and it was a childhood memory of a tradition that was absolutely new to him.

Was his family very religious?

His father was a cantor and he was training Irving Berlin to also be a cantor. And his grandfather had been a rabbi. But his father died when he was eleven or twelve years old, and Berlin ran away from home shortly after that. He grew up in the Bowery, singing for pennies in the street. Yes, his family was very religious, but it didn't rub off on him.

Did he come from a musical family?

Yes, his father taught him how to sing, and he sang with the choir in church. His father couldn't get a job as a cantor in America as he had been in Russia. When he came here in 1893, there was just no work, and he basically worked as a meat inspector in a kosher meat factory to make ends meet. And all the kids had to work. On holidays he would help out with directing the choir, and that's where Irving began singing.

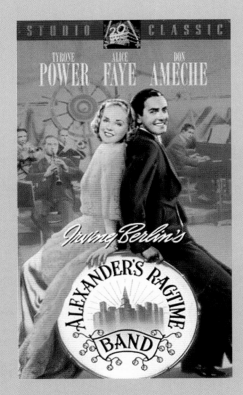

Shown clockwise above are the Irving Berlin movie musicals, "Alexander's Ragtime Band," "Easter Parade" and "Blue Skies." The sheet music for "I Used To Be Color Blind," from Berlin's "Carefree," is shown lower right.

Did Irving Berlin have a sense early on of his Russian heritage?

His sense of that heritage was that it was extremely melancholy and mournful. His first really incredible song — "Alexander's Ragtime Band" — really tapped into his Semitic and Slavic roots, because, he said, if you just listen to that melody played slowly, it's a mournful dirge-like song. This mournful feeling certainly comes out in "White Christmas."

Did his songwriting ability evolve over a long period of time?

No, it actually happened quite suddenly, because he began writing lyrics first when he was nineteen years old, and stayed on as a lyricist for a year or two. He then began composing his own melodies. Once he began doing both, he started having really big hit songs. By 1910, he was a major songwriter on Tin Pan Alley, particularly with ragtime songs. In 1911 when he wrote "Alexander's Ragtime Band," it became the biggest hit that anybody had ever seen up to that point. It was something like "After The Ball" from 1893, which was the first million-seller. "Alexander's" was an international success, and it was the kind of song where there were newspaper cartoons printed about it. It spawned editorials about the evils of ragtime, and was just this incredible achievement. George M. Cohan, who was probably the biggest thing at that point, singled Berlin out as a major songwriter. People were already saying then, if you look at *Variety* and newspapers of the time, that Berlin was already a cut above most of the other songwriters.

How did somebody without a formal musical education achieve this kind of success?

Well, he said that he thought that in some ways it was an advantage rather than a liability that he was stuck in one key — the key of F sharp, which is five black keys. But he said that if you let a child go to a piano and fool around, he'll instinctively get to the black keys. George M. Cohan played on the black keys. It was the standard way of a lot of untutored players to create songs. And Irving Berlin had a transposing piano that had a lever so that he could play in the one key he knew. It could be programmed so that every time you shifted the lever, you could hear how your songs sounded in another key. So all he needed was the key of F sharp.

1935

Did he reject a formal education?

Yes, he and Victor Herbert were working on a show in 1915, and he asked him if he should take lessons. Herbert said, 'well a little knowledge might be OK but don't ruin your gift.' Irving thought, though, that if he had not been stuck in one key, he would have been able to roam and do what other composers do. He pretty much felt he exhausted all of the possibilities of F sharp. In fact, George Gershwin wrote a piece called *Concerto in F*, and Berlin sent him a telegraph saying, 'Congratulations on your concerto in F, I'm still working on mine in F sharp.' But the notion of that utter concentration in one key, he thought, really gave him an advantage that he wouldn't have had if he could have done what other composers did.

What was happening to him that was leading him to "White Christmas" in the late 1930's?

He had done great things in Hollywood — several pictures for Astaire and Rogers — but they were breaking up. He was hoping to get back and do something on Broadway, which had suffered throughout The Depression. There were very few productions in the early 30's compared to what they were doing in the 20's. So many of the songwriters did what Berlin did — they went out to Hollywood where you could still get great work. I think he was sensing that a whole era, not just in musical culture, but in national culture, was shifting away from this kind of sleek Cole Porter elegant sophistication. Fred Astaire and Ginger Rogers break up their partnership in 1938. George Gershwin dies in 1938. Cole Porter has a crippling accident and doesn't write for several years. Berlin really had this incredible antenna about the national mood. With war coming on, there was a shift away from glitzy, glamorous art deco sets, and Astaire in top hat, white tie and tails. The country was moving toward what it would become in the 40's when World War II hits — much more folksy and homey. A musical like *Oklahoma* would have been unheard of in 1938, and I think he picked up on this national mood. It was time to recapture a kind of sentimentality. He really sensed that the whole Cole Porter/Rodgers and Hart/Astaire and Rogers era was coming to an end. In 1938, he was already thinking of doing a Broadway revue revolving around holiday songs.

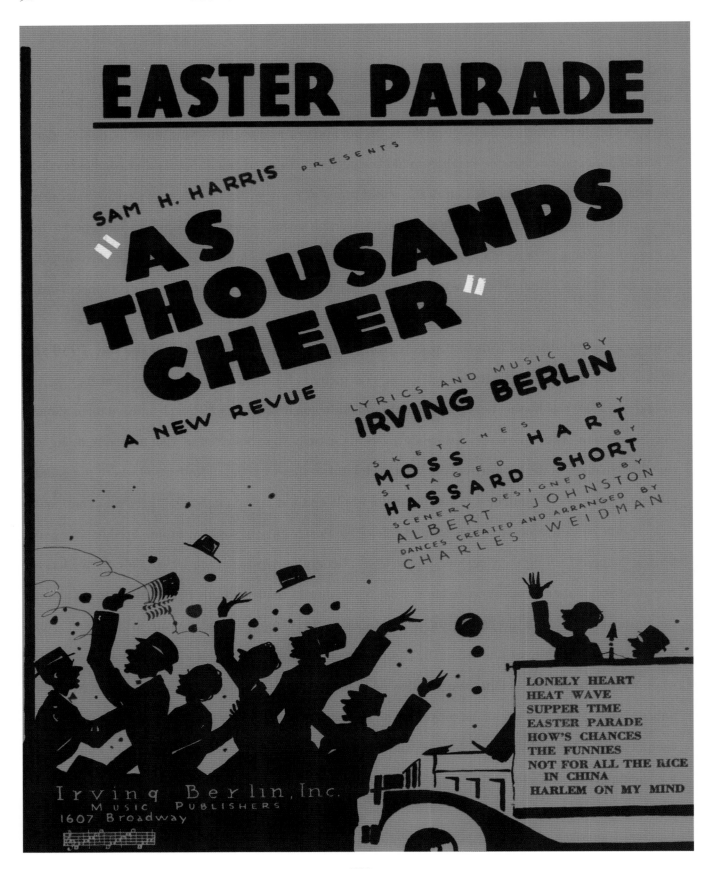

1933

At the time was he very much respected by Hollywood?

Oh yes, but he was a terribly insecure man. He would write a song and grab anybody that he found, and he'd sing it right in their face. He said if they blinked he lost all confidence in it. He really thought he had lost his talent in the early 30's, and he had a terrible time in Hollywood because they gutted one of his best films — *Reaching For The Moon*. He really resented that. But by 1938, after the movie of *Alexander's Ragtime Band*, he was considered the tops.

Do we know why Berlin withheld "White Christmas" from the public for so long?

I think he was planning to use "White Christmas" for a Broadway revue that never came off. The revue he had done before that in 1933 with Moss Hart was called *As Thousands Cheer,* and the gimmick for it was that every song related to some part of the newspaper. He wanted to do a follow-up to that based on a newspaper called *More Cheers,* but he and Hart never got around to doing that. He then wanted to do a Broadway revue where each song is tailored to a holiday, and I think he was probably hanging on to "White Christmas" to use as the Christmas song for that show. But he couldn't get anyone on Broadway to mount it, and the chance came up to do another picture. So he took the idea for the Broadway show and turned it into the movie *Holiday Inn.*

Is "White Christmas" a typical Tin-Pan-Alley song?

No, I don't think it is. I don't think it fits the same pattern, but it came out of the Tin-Pan-Alley tradition of songwriting. I'm sure it's probably a thirty-two bar song, and Berlin almost never strayed from that formula. He did wonderful things within it, but he was one of the few songwriters, who as far as I can tell, never aspired to do anything bigger — the way, say, Gershwin or Yip Harburg did. He was just perfectly content to do thirty-two bars. In fact, his daughter told me when I asked her about what he read, that he knew all these poets like Dorothy Parker and Robert Benchley. When I asked if he liked reading poetry, at first she said no, and that he just liked to read *True Crime* magazine. But then she remembered that actually there was one poet he did get to like — Alexander Pope. I thought it was goofy that he would pick such a classical poet, but then I realized that Pope wrote everything in two-line couplets. He even translated *The Iliad* into two lines of ten syllables each that rhyme. Students find it very boring to read anything long by Pope, because it's always these two-line units, but I thought Berlin probably saw that as akin to his staying within thirty-two bars, and the compression of working within the constrictions of a very small format. In an interview, Berlin said Pope managed to do everything in couplets, and would have made a good songwriter, because they have to do everything in fifty to seventy-five words. "White Christmas" is just that miracle of compression.

Did Berlin have a say as to who would record "White Christmas?"

He had a lot of say when he was with RKO in the 30's, but I don't think he would have had that much clout when they did *Holiday Inn.* I think that was probably set. It would be nice to think he wrote the song for Crosby, but if he wrote it in 1938, I don't think he was thinking of Crosby.

Do we know anything about the relationship between Crosby and Berlin?

They became very close. One of the most touching things occurred when they were doing the film of *White Christmas.* In the 1950's, Berlin was having another one of these terrible periods of depression and insecurity while putting together some new songs for the film. He was utterly terrified at having to demonstrate them for Bing Crosby. But Crosby, who could be a very kind man at times, just leaned over and said, 'Do you like them, Irving?' And Berlin could barely say yes. Then Crosby said, 'Then they're good enough for me — I don't need to hear them.' He was just sliding into the worst depression of his life during those years, and finally had to check into a mental institution by the end of the decade.

Was Crosby key to the success of "White Christmas?"

When people on the film were worried that nobody could sing the line 'may all your Christmases be white,' Berlin said Crosby could do it because he's one singer who can enunciate *that* clearly. Crosby makes it sound so effortless — that's a very tricky line to sing because of all the harsh consonants.

How typical of a Berlin song is "White Christmas" when you look at his whole output?

It's typical in that it has that kind of melancholy cast to it that runs through so much of his work. It really fits with his personality, which is surprisingly brooding and insecure.

MORE WITH BING CROSBY PRODUCER KEN BARNES

From a producer's standpoint, what was it like working with Bing Crosby?

Well, it was wonderful. I think he was just about the easiest man I ever worked with. He had a wonderful ear for music and you could play almost anything for him, however difficult, and he would sing it right back to you. He didn't read music, but he had a wonderful receptive ear. He had a very subtle ear for intervals and harmonies, and he was quite amazing to work with really.

What was the name of the first album you produced for him?

That's What Life Is All About — it's based on the single.

How many did you produce of his all together?

Six, and they were all released. The first five were on United Artists, and then we crossed over to Polydor because they gave us a much better deal. Bing never signed exclusively with anyone. I think if he had signed exclusively he would have had much better support from record companies, because if they know they're going to get the next album, they tend to spend more on publicity. But after spending all those years on Decca, he wanted to be loose. I think that's the weakness behind his thinking — if you look at his discography, he just went from label to label — anybody who wanted him to record, he would turn up.

Was he difficult to work with?

I was told in the beginning that he was a difficult man, cold and mean. I never saw any of that. Bing was exactly the way I expected him to be — easygoing. But he was nobody's fool. He was very intelligent, and I discovered that he spoke about four languages. He had many interests outside of music and didn't have to be singing all the time. He spent half an hour one time at dinner with me explaining how tequila was made. He owned a tequila factory. I mean I wasn't interested in tequila, but the way he explained it was fascinating. He was a constant surprise to me.

White Christmas

by

Irving Berlin

IRVING BERLIN
Music Corporation
29 WEST 46TH STREET, NEW YORK, NY 10036

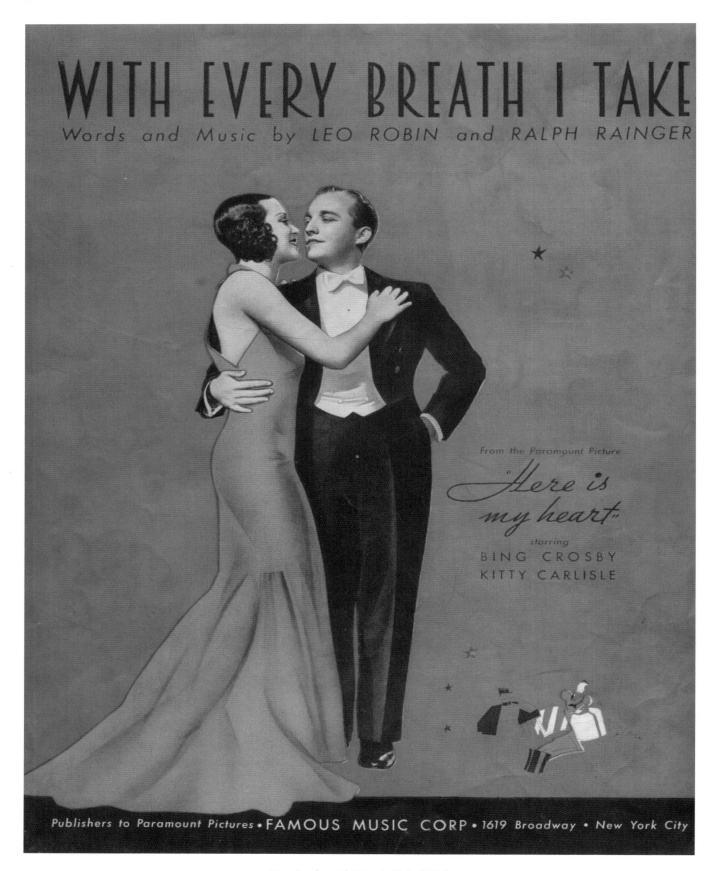

Bing Crosby with Kitty Carlisle (1934)

How did that intelligence manifest itself in his vocal performance?

He was just an instinctively good singer and blessed with a good ear. I think he had a better ear than Sinatra, who was the greater of the two as far as lyric interpretation was concerned, but in straight musical terms, Sinatra wouldn't learn a song as fast as Crosby would. Neither of them read music, but where Crosby's was the art that conceals art, which is the best kind of art, Frank would never conceal his art. He liked it all up front, and he let everybody know he was the greatest. I think Crosby was a little more intuitive, and a little more harmonious with things. If you listen to Crosby's latter-day performances, perhaps the upper notes weren't quite as strong as they used to be, but his intonation was absolutely spot on. If you listen to Sinatra from 1973 onwards, his intonation wasn't great, and all those live performances that were so wonderful, were marred for me by the sloppiness of it, which never happened with Crosby. It's difficult to say who is the greater of the two — they're both great in their own way.

Did Crosby influence Sinatra?

Oh yes — well, he came first. Frank idolized Bing, there's no question about that, but he did the sensible thing. When everybody else was copying Crosby, Frank created a style of his own, and that's how you become big. You don't become big by copying somebody else.

How much time did you spend with Crosby in the studio?

Nine hours in the studio on each album, and I worked with him on radio, and did a couple of TV shows with him. I went to dinner with him quite a lot, and I wouldn't say I became a close friend of his, but I certainly got to know him very well.

What was a typical session like with him?

It was wonderful. But he was difficult about one thing. Today we record apart from the orchestra, but that wasn't for Bing, he always wanted to be with the orchestra. One time he came over to London, and we did a little routine the day before just to run through the songs so he was fully familiar with them. The engineer came up and said, 'Pleasure to meet you, Mr. Crosby. This is where we're going to record tomor-

row,' and Bing said, 'Great.' The engineer said 'I'm going to put the brass over there, the strings over here, the reeds over there, and the rhythm here. You, Mr. Crosby, are going to go in that glass vocal booth.' Bing said, 'What do you mean? I'm not going to go in any booth, I might as well have stayed in California and sang to a track. Put me with the band — I'm an old band singer.' So the engineer said, 'Mr. Crosby, the brass can get awfully loud,' and Bing just shrugged and replied, 'Well, I'll get louder.' He could see the disappointment on the engineer's face, but said, 'Trust me, if it worked fifty years ago, it will work today.' Most engineers today have a certain way of working. In fact, sessions are sort of run by and for the engineer. In the end, though, he was amazed that Bing's voice did come through above the brass and everything else.

Did you have to direct him at all?

He took direction very well. If you had a suggestion, he would listen to it, but if you wanted another take, you had to have a damn good reason. One time I wasn't happy with his lyric reading on something, and after the session I said, 'Bing I'd like you to record this song again.' He said 'Jesus Christ, why?' And I said 'I just think you can give a little more in the lyric.' He said, 'Show me.' So I played the song to him and he replied, 'Well it's all in tune, the phrasings not square, you can hear every word.' I said, 'Sure,' and he said, 'Well that's it — I can't do it any better,' and he wouldn't do it.

Do you have a Bing Crosby story that stands out in your mind?

When we were recording the Astaire album, Bing was doing one of Fred Astaire's songs, and Fred was doing one of his, and a young assistant engineer got on the phone to his mother. She was a big Crosby fan, and he said, 'We've got Bing here and he's wonderful — listen to what he's doing.' We started playing back the tape for her while he's holding the phone up. Bing walked by and saw the kid holding the phone — and he looked at him — sometimes he got that severe school teacher look — and he said, 'What are you doing?' The kid got nervous and said, 'Oh Mr. Crosby, I was just letting my mother hear what you've recorded this morning if that's all right.' Bing said, 'It certainly isn't all right. Give me the phone, she'll never hear it that way.' He then said, 'Run the tape back and take my voice out.' Then he sang the whole song into the phone to this guy's mother.

How was Crosby groundbreaking during his time?

He started in the pre-microphone era. There weren't any mikes when he began, so when the microphone came along, he was the first one to realize its potential, and to sing in a relaxed and casual way, and phrase in a naturalistic way.

Why is he so closely associated with Christmas music?

I think first of all, when he was at his pinnacle in the 1940's, he did "White Christmas," which became the biggest seller of all time. And I think having the biggest hit of all time kind of identified him with Christmas. He became the voice of Christmas. There was no artist more Christmas than Crosby.

Was there something about his voice that lent itself to that genre?

I think so. I think it was the warm round sound — you could warm your hands on the sound of his voice.

Is there any way to explain the "White Christmas" phenomenon?

I think it just is that great song. Bing gave all credit to Irving Berlin, and thought he was lucky to get the first crack at it. It may not be Irving Berlin's best song, but it's a very simple straightforward tune. It isn't always the complex song that has to be the greatest.

Does Bing's version remain the most popular?

Absolutely.

What's your opinion of The Ken Darby Singers?

They were a marvelous group that worked with him on radio from time to time. Ken Darby was a great choral artist, and he did all the vocal arrangements for Twentieth Century Fox.

How about John Scott Trotter?

I understand he was a very nice man. His success with Bing had something to do with their personalities merging, because Bing was singing with the Dorsey Orchestra a lot on broadcasts in the 30's. When they split up, Bing knew he had to have a regular musical director who wouldn't run away and go off on the road. So he got John Scott Trotter from the Harold Kemp Band, and he just became the all-purpose arranger for Bing.

Why did Bing and the Andrews Sisters go together so well?

The amazing thing is when he recorded with the Andrews Sisters, what surprised me about those sessions is that the three girls were on one side of the mike, and Bing was on the other side. Nobody would dream of doing that today — it would be suicidal. But the blend that they got — the internal balance, the harmonics, and everything, was because it was just the four of them standing around the same mike.

Do you know anything about "I'll Be Home For Christmas?"

It was really the follow-up to "White Christmas." He did it in 1943, and it was a massive seller. It didn't do as well as "White Christmas," but I think he sold about 3 million of it or something in that year. It was just immense. Of course, it is a great Christmas standard because of Bing. He was the first to sing it, and who wouldn't want to get that song to Crosby after "White Christmas?"

Do you know how the writers got it to him?

I think what happened is that they may have submitted it to the head of his record company — Jack Kapp. I'm sure Jack Kapp found the song for him, because Bing said to me it wasn't any of his doing all of those things. He said Jack Kapp would have him record Irish songs, Hawaiian songs, patriotic songs, and everything that came along. Actually, he did a great modesty number. He always described himself as just a guy who could carry a tune. A regular guy — nobody special. It really was hilarious to hear him talk like that, because what he did in terms of world penetration was absolutely incredible.

Was he a very religious person?

Oh yes. He never missed church on Sunday. And no matter how hung over he was in his earlier days, he would drag himself to church on Sunday morning and would never miss mass as bleary eyed as he was.

Speaking of hangovers, one story has it that he would turn up drunk at a recording session, and they would have to hold him up to the mike, but he still sounded pretty good.

Was Bing a product of his time?

Yes, he was. To find singers who can perform as quickly and as good as he did would be a godsend. We spend weeks in the bloody studio with people who can't carry a tune more than four bars. You have to drop and punch them in all of the time — it's crazy.

What was the secret to Bing's success?

He had charisma. If he walked into a room, you certainly felt something. He had those great big blue eyes, and that smile that was such a winning smile. You just kind of liked the guy, and that came across on record. He had a very friendly voice, and he was the first and probably best of the naturalistic singers. Sinatra learned a lot from Crosby and took it a little further, but Bing went as far as he wanted to go. I think Bing was a better jazz singer. When you see the two of them together in *High Society,* and you look at how Bing does the last eight bars of "Now You Has Jazz," I don't think Sinatra could ever do that that way. Bing had a flexibility, and he sounded like a well-played bass. Frank was really more into lyrics than anything — he would do wonderful things with words. He tried his damnedest not to sing like Crosby. Of course, Dean Martin and Perry Como did sing like Bing, and there was room for those guys, because they were very charming in what they did, but none of them were as big as Crosby on record or movies. Bing was real, and his singing most closely approximated conversation, which is the best kind of singing there is.

Bing Crosby co-starred with Frank Sinatra in the 1956 movie "High Society" (upper left). He also starred in "Say One For Me" (lower right, 1959), which featured "The Secret Of Christmas," written by Sammy Cahn & James Van Heusen.

Judy Garland & Margaret O'Brien (1944)

HAVE YOURSELF A MERRY LITTLE CHRISTMAS — 1944

WRITERS — HUGH MARTIN
RALPH BLANE

ARTIST — JUDY GARLAND

DECCA RECORDS

There certainly was no place like home for seventeen-year-old Judy Garland, Hugh Martin and Ralph Blane during the summer of 1939, weeks before World War II portentously eclipsed Europe, and the now nostalgic time when two spectacular new events — *The Wizard Of Oz* and The World's Fair — simultaneously thrilled crowds in New York City.

That August, all three entertainers met for the first time in the Big Apple while singing together with Mickey Rooney for audiences at movie showings of *Oz*. Several years later, they would meet again to recreate another World's Fair for the film *Meet Me In St. Louis,* a groundbreaking Metro Goldwyn Mayer (MGM) musical, featuring Judy Garland tenderly crooning

Blane & Martin

Martin and Blane's "Have Yourself A Merry Little Christmas," as well as two other original songs the pair penned for the 1944 Vincente Minnelli-directed project.

"I met Judy Garland at The Capitol Theatre on Broadway, across from The Winter Garden Theatre, when the *The Wizard Of Oz* opened," recalls Hugh Martin, who was twenty-five years old at the time. "Ralph and I were in a quartet called The Martins, and we backed up Judy and Mickey for three weeks when the *Wizard* first opened on screen. We did five shows together, seven days a week. In those days, MGM would send their stars out to make personal appearances, and they would do a stage show after the movie.

1939 postcards depicting scenes from that year's World's Fair in New York City

But we didn't get to know Judy too well until we got to MGM in 1942 — and then of course, there she was — queen of the lot!"

It looked like royalty had arrived in New York City, August 17, 1939, the day of their debut at The Capitol Theatre. By then, Judy Garland had just completed the war-time musical *Babes In Arms,* her ninth film. This along with *Oz* was catapulting her into box-office bliss, establishing her as a legendary pop icon, and helping to make her one of the top-ten money-earning stars of the early 1940's.

It was an important turning point for the young performer, because up until now she had been playing only supporting roles. MGM's idea was to give *Oz* a huge send off in New York City — to really create a splash — especially since it had become such a huge investment for the studio, and was crafted from the start to be the ultimate Judy Garland star-making showcase.

Judy Garland with Tom Drake

The guileless on-screen Dorothy-next-door with the heart-breaking grown-up singing voice she continuously immortalized in film, powerfully endeared Garland to the public, and it's little wonder why ten thousand hysterical people flooded Grand Central Station when they heard she was coming to town.

As Martin and Blane prepared to open the show, fifteen thousand people lined up around the block, hoping to buy a ticket to see *Oz,* along with the real-life Judy and Mickey. After watching the mesmerizing movie, they anxiously remained in their seats while Georgie Stoll, MGM's musical director (who would later work on *Meet Me In St. Louis*), cued the orchestra to play a six-minute chorus of "We're Off To See The Wizard," sung by The Martins. Judy Garland then crooned "The Lamp Is Low" and "Comes Love," followed by three duets with Rooney, including two songs to promote their upcoming *Babes In Arms.*

That opening performance broke the house record at The Capitol — thirty-seven thousand spectators witnessed Martin, Blane, Garland and Rooney's tour-de-force performance, with many having been turned away throughout the day.

Those late 1930's were an exciting time of incredible destiny for Hugh Martin, born on August 11, 1914, in Birmingham, Alabama. At age five, Martin began studying classical piano at the Birmingham Conservatory, eventually graduating to that city's Southern College. He was soon inspired by George Gershwin to turn toward popular music.

From the M-G-M Picture "THE WIZARD OF OZ"

OVER THE RAINBOW

Lyric by E.Y. HARBURG • Music by HAROLD ARLEN

Belwin, Inc.
CPP
15800 N.W. 48th Avenue
Miami, FL 33014

A
bie3®
PUBLICATION

The 1939 film *Babes In Arms* was based on a play co-written by Richard Rodgers, who was instrumental in jump-starting Hugh Martin's professional music career. His 1959 musical, *The Sound Of Music*, which he co-wrote with Oscar Hammerstein II, spawned the tune, "My Favorite Things," a perennial holiday favorite. It was first sung on Broadway by Mary Martin, and immortalized on film in 1965 by Julie Andrews.

Strike Up The Band (1940)

Richard Rodgers responded to a letter he wrote the famous songwriter, and soon invited him to vocally arrange a tune for his 1938 show *The Boys From Syracuse*. Around this same period, Martin would also develop an important creative friendship with his soon-to-be fellow songwriting partner — Ralph Blane — a union which lasted for over fifty years.

"Ralph and I met in the chorus of a 1937 Broadway musical called *Hooray For What*," he says. "We sang together in the show at the Winter Garden Theatre for about nine months. During that run, he asked me if I would coach him — he had been singing only classical music and wanted me to help him become more pop, like Bing Crosby. So I worked with him for several months, and auditioned him for NBC radio, which loved him and put him on the air."

Born Ralph Blane Hunsecker on July 26, 1914, in Broken Arrow, Oklahoma, the multi-talented tenor dropped out of high school in Tulsa, later resuming his studies at Northwestern University. According to his only child, George Blane, he moved to New York City when he was sixteen years old. "He started when he was so young," says Blane. "I've got pictures of him dancing with Judy and Mickey at The Capitol when they were all just kids. He was a character and had great sport with everything."

Ralph Blane was featured in the Broadway production, *New Faces Of 1936*, and over the next five years, The Great White Way and radio would figure prominently in his and Martin's early collaborations. As The Martins, they sang on a popular radio program called *The Fred Allen Show*, and appeared together not only in *Hooray For What* (the crew of which coincidentally included a pre-Hollywood Vincente Minnelli), but also in Irving Berlin's 1940 musical *Louisiana Purchase*.

As a vocal arranger, Martin was repeatedly hired for his unique talent of bringing a jazz-oriented contemporary-pop

Ralph Blane

1941

flair to his work. Those innovative arrangements were featured in many important productions including Richard Rodgers' 1939 *Too Many Girls,* Cole Porter's 1939 *DuBarry Was A Lady,* and Vernon Duke's 1940 *Cabin In The Sky.*

A 1941 show entitled *Best Foot Forward,* choreographed by Gene Kelly, led to a very unexpected career change for Martin and Blane. "We were never songwriters, but in 1941 we got this lucky break to write the music for *Best Foot Forward,*" remembers Martin.

"One day a popular actor at the time by the name of Van Johnson, who was originally hired as Judy's love interest in *Meet Me In St. Louis,* and who lived in the same building as Ralph, was walking down the hall, ran into him and said, 'Hey did you know George Abbott is looking for a new team of songwriters for a show he's gonna do?' Ralph said, 'So what? We're not songwriters, we've never written a song in our lives!' Van replied, 'Well, I bet you could be, why don't you get Hugh to help you?' And that's how the team of Martin and Blane was born. Ralph called me up and asked me if I'd help him do an audition for Abbott. We did it together and much to our astonishment got the job!"

That job led to the team's first musical score. *Best Foot Forward,* produced by Abbott and an unbilled Richard Rodgers, opened on Broadway at the Ethel Barrymore Theatre in October 1941, two months before war broke out in America. It starred June Allyson and Abbott discovery Nancy Walker, and included "Buckle Down, Winsocki," Martin and Blane's first hit song. In 1963, Liza Minnelli made her New

"In The Good Old Summertime" (1949)

York debut in the play's off-Broadway revival, and the success of the original production quickly led to the songwriters' musical reunion with her mother, Judy Garland.

"When *Best Foot* came out it was a great big hit and resulted in MGM Hollywood hiring us to work on the Technicolor 1942 movie version of it starring June Allyson and Lucille Ball," says Martin. "All of this brought us back to Judy, and we began getting to know her more since we now started working with her as vocal arrangers on her movies."

Since their *Oz* meeting at The Capitol, Judy's career continued to reach unparalleled new heights — in three years'

The original album for "Meet Me In St. Louis" was a three-record set released in 1944, which contained
Martin & Blane's "Have Yourself A Merry Little Christmas."

time she had won a special Academy Award, starred in eight movies, entertained war troops, recorded dozens of songs for her Decca Record label, repeatedly appeared on popular radio shows — and would soon be celebrating her twenty-first birthday.

1943 saw Martin and Blane musically involved in all of Garland's filmic output that year — *Presenting Lily Mars,* Gershwin's *Girl Crazy,* co-starring Mickey Rooney, and the war revue, *Thousands Cheer,* in which she made a brief appearance belting out the duo's boogie-woogie nugget, "The Joint Is Really Jumpin' At Carnegie Hall."

Their next project brought them back to The World's Fair, and its innocent story included a wistful Christmas song that powerfully touched the heart of its war-torn audience.

Meet Me In St. Louis represented MGM's desire to place Judy Garland in a movie similar to *Oz* in scope and theme. It would be the first integrated big-budget Technicolor musical (in which the songs actually advanced the plot) she would star in since then, and would once again focus on a sentiment that had high-charged significance for World-War-II movie goers — "there's no place like home."

After easing into more adult roles, it would also return her to playing a juvenile on screen. Judy Garland's dissatisfaction with this reversal, along with her disapproval of an inferior initial script, almost stopped the cameras from ever rolling.

The story, which centered around a year in the domestic life of the all-American St. Louis Smith family, was plucked from the pages of a well-known New York magazine. "MGM producer Arthur Freed conceived the idea of filming author Sally Benson's autobiographical serialized story, then called *5135 Kensington Avenue,* which ran from 1941 to 1942 in *The New Yorker,*" says Martin. "He invited me into his office to hear a pupil of mine sing a vocal arrangement I had done for 'Skip To My Lou,' listened to it, and hired me and Ralph to write the music for *Meet Me* the next day."

Work on the film began in November 1943. New writers were hired to hone the script, and director Vincente Minnelli eventually

Sally Benson

Judy Garland with Margaret O'Brien & Tom Drake (1944)

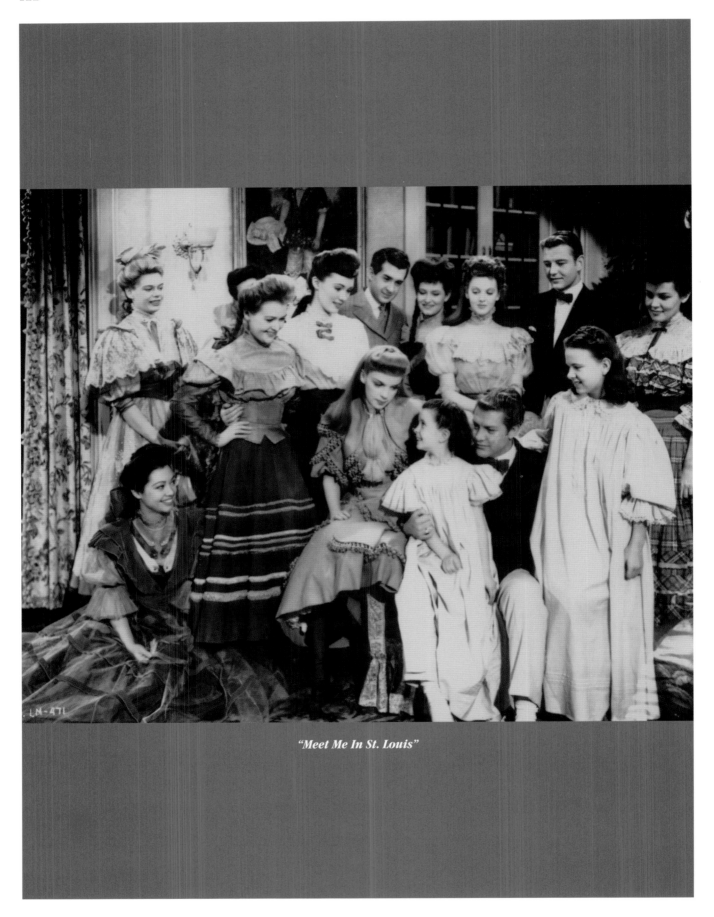

"Meet Me In St. Louis"

convinced Garland the role of seventeen-year-old Esther Smith would be beneficial to her career. It was decided that the dramatic center of the story would revolve around a minor incident in Benson's version — the fact that the family might be forced to move from its beloved St. Louis to New York City, thus missing the 1904 World's Fair held at home that year.

In December, as cameras started rolling, Garland began recording Martin and Blane's music for the film's soundtrack. They had written three exclusive new solo tunes for her — "The Boy Next Door," "The Trolley Song" and "Have Yourself A Merry Little Christmas" — while reworking several old turn-of-the-century songs like "Skip To My Lou" and "Meet Me In St. Louis, Louis," which she sang with other cast members. Originally on this list was Rodgers and Hammerstein's "Boys And Girls Like You And Me," later cut because it was thought to slow the movie down.

At MGM's recording studio in Culver City, California, on December 4, 1943, Judy Garland became the first artist to record "Have Yourself A Merry Little Christmas," a song which would in time transcend its movie and continue to reintroduce itself on a yearly basis for decades to come. She sang it six times with MGM printing takes three and six. "The Boy Next Door" was also recorded on that same day.

At the end of filming, she would re-record both tunes on April 20th, 1944, for a commercial single released that November (Decca had already released "The Trolley Song," which sold half a million copies before the movie even opened). During that session, an alternate take of "Have Yourself" was recorded as well, but stayed in a vault for fifty years before its final release in 1994 on a CD entitled *The Best Of The Decca Years, Vol. 2* (audiences would also have to wait over fifty years to purchase the original soundtrack recording, released by Rhino Records in 1995). The first take contains a minor lyrical oversight, with Garland singing "faithful friends who are near to us will be dear to us once more." In the second alternate take she corrects herself, singing "faithful friends who are dear to us will be near to us once more." Decca re-released the single in 1945 with a new B-side, "You'll Never Walk Alone," mistakenly using Garland's incorrect version.

"Have Yourself A Merry Little Christmas," was the film's most poignant song, and the minor-key ballad established a

MARGARET O'BRIEN - Metro Goldwyn Mayer

critical turning point for the Smith family. After returning from a romantic Christmas ball, Esther sings it to broken-hearted Margaret O'Brien's seven-year-old character Tootie, as a way of expressing their shared sadness. They believe it's their last St. Louis Christmas, that they're leaving home for good, and that they will never see The World's Fair. The scene is the epitome of "Meet Me's" "no place like home" theme,

and the song whisks Tootie outside, where she dramatically destroys her family of snow people. Upon witnessing this, Mr. Smith humbly decides to keep his family in St. Louis.

In real life, Hugh Martin remembers how the emotional power of Garland's recording seemed to touch everyone in the studio the day she recorded it: "We had a tough old engineer who was at the controls while Judy was singing 'Have Yourself A Merry Little Christmas.' He became unable to see the controls because his eyes were so full of tears, which were flowing out onto the knobs. It really moved everyone very much."

But the journey to that recording session would be fraught with danger — on two separate occasions the song was completely abandoned. The first occurred in 1943 at the time of its conception, when Martin and Blane were first reading the movie script. "I saw there was a Christmas scene," recalls Martin, "and I began to cast about for an appropriate melody. I got about as far as the sixteenth bar and my inspiration just gave out. I thought, I'm not going to finish this because it's not going anywhere. A couple of days later Ralph Blane said 'whatever became of that little magical melody you were playing over and over two days ago — you've got to finish it because it's one of the prettiest things you've ever written."

With Blane's encouragement, Martin went back to the piano to work on the song, "evolving its bridge, release and ending."

"I played it for Ralph and he loved it," he says. Soon however, he would give up on it a second time due to a troublesome problem Judy Garland had with some of its lyrics: "Reading the script, it seemed that what was required was kind of a plaintive song, but everybody hated the first lyric I wrote. It went like this: 'Have yourself a merry little Christmas, it may be your last, next year we may all be living in the past.' The next eight bars went 'Have yourself a merry little Christmas, pop that champagne cork, next year we may all be living in New York.'"

"So the rest of it went on more or less like the song you are familiar with, but instead of 'Faithful

The dynamic songwriting duo of Sammy Cahn and Jule Styne wrote "Let It Snow! Let It Snow! Let It Snow!" in 1945. The following year it became a number one hit for Vaughn Monroe, who was the first to record it. Frank Sinatra's version was released in 1950 as the B-side of "Remember Me In Your Dreams." Within a twenty-five year period, Sinatra recorded over two dozen Cahn and Styne tunes, and in 1954 he asked them to write a Christmas song just for him. Without hesitation, they gave Old Blue Eyes "The Christmas Waltz," which was released first as a single, and later included on Sinatra's 1957 *A Jolly Christmas* LP.

EDWIN H. MORRIS & COMPANY, INC.
1619 BROADWAY • NEW YORK

friends who are dear to us will be near to us once more,' it was 'faithful friends who are dear to us will be near to us no more.' When Judy heard it she adored the melody but said that if she sang that lyric to little Margaret O'Brien, the audience would think she was a monster."

At first Martin was irritated and refused to change the lyric, offering instead to come up with a brand new song. "I was stubborn and stuck to my guns for about a week. Then one day Tom Drake, who was playing Judy's love interest, invited me to have coffee with him, and convinced me that my stubbornness was keeping a very important song from being realized. After thinking about it, I went back to the drawing board, sharpened my pencils and wrote the lyric you hear in the film."

Years later, Martin would change the lyrics once again to accommodate Frank Sinatra, who desired a more positive interpretation: "I got a call from Frank. He said he'd love to do my song but was bothered by the line, 'Until then we'll have to muddle through somehow,' which is in the movie. You don't say no to Sinatra if you have any brains at all. So again I went back to the drawing board and came up with 'Hang a shining star upon the highest bough,' as an alternate lyric for him. I was really relieved when I thought of it, because I wanted to end with the word, 'now,' and other than 'cow' there aren't many appropriate rhymes for 'ow.'" This updated version was first included on Sinatra's 1957 *A Jolly Christmas* set (later repackaged as *The Sinatra Christmas Album*).

Martin also admits he eventually re-wrote the song's first verse, written for but never used in the movie: "I didn't like the first verse so I wrote a second one, this time to please myself." Those words, published with the song's original sheet music began: "When the steeple bells sound their A, they don't play it in tune," and were replaced with the more familiar verse, which starts out: "Christmas future is far away, Christmas past is past." Neither Garland nor Sinatra recorded it, but it can be found on later interpretations of the song by singers like Barbra Streisand and the Carpenters.

"And there's still another lyric," admits Martin. "In 1995, a friend of mine named John Fricke interviewed me for A&E's Judy Garland *Biography*, and sent me a letter a few weeks after we met saying that his mother had browbeaten him to sing in church. So he took my Christmas song, wrote a sacred version of it, sang it in church, and everyone loved it."

Afterwards, the two worked together polishing it, keeping the melody intact while completely overhauling the lyrics. The

Judy Garland with Frank Sinatra

sheet music for their religious collaboration became the fourth major change the song has experienced over the past fifty years, and can be purchased in stores across the country.

At the same time the tune was undergoing a sacred transformation, Garland's daughter, Lorna Luft, went into a London studio to record a vocal of it she could merge with her mother's, technically and emotionally similar to Nat King & Natalie Cole's 1991 "Unforgettable" duet.

Although she died in 1969, "Have Yourself A Merry Little Christmas" now bridged lost decades of time, resurrected a mother's voice, and in song and spirit reunited Judy Garland with her youngest daughter. The 1995 single of that magical pairing includes two other Lorna Luft songs ("Me And My Shadow"/"The Nearness Of You"), and was released in England by Carlton Home Entertainment, Ltd. It has yet to be domestically distributed.

The overwhelming success of *Meet Me In St. Louis* allowed Garland the opportunity to reunite with Martin and Blane many times after the war, and dramatically changed the lives of all involved. On the set, Garland fell in love with Vincente Minnelli, later marrying him. After the film's debut in St. Louis on November 22, 1944, it broke box office records, becoming her greatest hit to date (and MGM's biggest money maker since *Gone With The Wind*). Margaret O'Brien won a special Academy Award for her role as Tootie, while Martin and Blane picked up a nomination for "The Trolley Song." (In 1947, they would nab a second nomination for "Pass That Peace Pipe," from the film *Good News.*)

All three of the film's original songs quickly turned into Judy Garland classics, and up to the mid-1950's she re-teamed with Martin and Blane on separate occasions. After the duo parted, she worked with Blane on two subsequent films (*The Harvey Girls* & *In The Good Old Summertime*), and with Martin on *A Star Is Born*. In 1951, the two reconvened in

"Meet Me In St. Louis" original Broadway cast CD (1989)

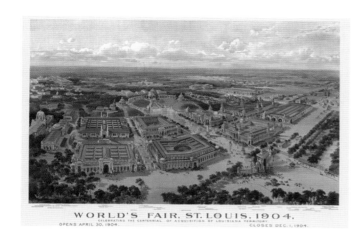

World's Fair, St. Louis (1904)

New York City for her record-breaking nineteen-week concert engagement at The Palace. Martin accompanied her on piano as she sang what had become a well-loved repertoire, including songs from *Meet Me,* and her standard, "Over The Rainbow."

Judy Garland's yearning for home and The World's Fair followed Martin and Blane for the rest of their lives. In 1960, the songwriters met again in St. Louis to produce a summerstock stage version of the movie at that city's Municipal Opera House. A second theatrical version of *Meet Me In St. Louis* opened at The Gershwin Theatre on Broadway in 1989. "Have Yourself A Merry Little Christmas" was featured in both shows, along with the movie's other music, paired with new songs exclusively written for the stage.

Ralph Blane died on November 13, 1995, and according to his son, before passing away he had visions of Judy Garland, whose life tragically ended at the age of forty-seven.

"God gave her this innate musicianship, and a tremendous sensitivity to a point that I think it was a burden to her," says Martin. "It was hard to be Judy Garland because she was just so aware of everything and everybody. But I adored her, we were soul mates and were meant to be good friends. I still have dreams about her."

One of Judy Garland's dreams came true the time it all began with Martin and Blane back at The Capitol Theatre in 1939. Due to the hysteria of the crowds, she became a virtual prisoner in the theater, and was disappointed that she wouldn't get out to see The World's Fair in Queens, New York. But on August 27th, Mayor Fiorello La Guardia provided a police escort, finally making it possible for her to attend with Mickey Rooney. It seemed to be a moment of pure freedom for her, and she later described the event in an interview: "We raced from one exhibit to the next," she said. "We saw everything. We rode everything. I still remember it as the most wonderful night of my life."

"The Clock" (1945)

1947

MORE WITH HUGH MARTIN

Hugh Martin

Did you have any idea "Have Yourself A Merry Little Christmas" would become such an enduring classic?

Heavens, no. I didn't even have commercial values in mind when I wrote it. I was thinking strictly of the movie. I was totally surprised, although I will say this — just before I left MGM to go into the army, we had a meeting with Arthur Freed and the publishers of the songs from *Meet Me In St. Louis.* The question that was asked was, 'Which of the songs do you think has the best possibility of success on the airwaves and in recordings?' Everyone voted for a different song, and I was the only one who said, 'Well, I think the Christmas song might have a chance.' So I had the last laugh on that one.

Did the song's lyrics have anything to do with World War II?

No. If it did it was just a coincidence. I wasn't thinking about World War II at all — I was thinking of 1903 in St. Louis. I do think it was fortuitous that the bridge — 'Faithful friends who are dear to us will be near to us once more' — was easy to relate to soldiers being away. The war was raging in Europe at this time.

Meet Me In St. Louis **was based on Sally Benson's childhood life in St. Louis. Did you read her** *New Yorker* **stories before writing the songs for the film?**

Oh yes. I read them before Arthur Freed ever thought of doing them and loved them. And I adored Sally — what a darling woman she was — she came out to MGM as an advisor on the film and I loved her. I also met her family — all of the stories' prototypes — and had dinner with them at the Astor Hotel the night the movie opened in New York City. It was very exciting.

CHRISTMAS 1999

Kind hearts and gentle people,

Old age announces itself in different ways to different people. My style seems to be falling down. As 1999 commenced, I was recovering from a 1998 fall. I took a six months breather, then did a spectacular nose dive off an over-excited escalator. Ill effects: minimal. There was surgery for a broken elbow and my piano technique is somewhat diminished, but I feel better at 85 than I did at 25, so what is there to say except Praise the Lord!

I chipped away at my memoirs throughout the year and finally finished them, but polishing takes almost more time than writing. I already had one fine editor, Reg Fulton; now I have two: Terry Driscoll came aboard as my archivist but since Reg is 500 miles away, I drafted Terry as Editor # Two to augment Reg's work. Terry has that precious editor's instinct for zeroing in on the long-winded and boring and shouting "off with its head!" Thank you, Reg and Terry!

This was the year I reluctantly gave up on my musical, MAGGIE AND JIGGS. Mickey Rooney commissioned me to write it for him and the late Martha Raye in 1983 and I've been working on it off and on ever since. Bob Hilliard, who wrote the hilarious script, perceived it as a tough-talking no holds barred romp in the vernacular of today's sitcoms. Like Bob, I wanted a rough and tumble romp but clean enough that audiences could include children. We tried to resolve our differences but they were deep-seated and passionate.

I'm in my tenth year as "pianista" for the Hispanic branch of the Solana Beach Presbyterian Church. I do not exaggerate when I state that Pastor Galdino Don Juan and his wife, Francisca, comprise the greatest husband-and-wife ministerial team I've ever encountered. They work around the clock and miracles happen every day.

Almost at year's end, I had an even greater joy: Joni Eareckson Tada celebrated the twentieth anniversary of her marvelous ministry, JONI AND FRIENDS. Joni is a true Renaissance lady: an outstanding Christian who has written twenty devotional books: in addition she preaches, conducts a radio ministry, paints (brush between teeth since she is quadriplegic) and sings, all of these endeavors being accomplished with excellence! JAF sends thousands of reconditioned wheel chairs to disabled persons around the world, many of whom (in Africa, especially) are crippled children crawling in the dirt. Joni (pronounced "Johnny") designed the concert in Thousand Oaks, California on 30 November around my Christmas song. She sang it, using the special lyrics John Fricke and I wrote for it — lyrics suitable for worship services in Christian churches. I accompanied her — not without a sense of awe at the degree of inspiration this Hollywood-beautiful lady brings to millions of disabled people.

I'm often asked how I happen to be living with the Harrisons. Twenty years ago, a hit-and-run truck driver knocked me down in a pedestrian crosswalk and broke my shoulder and leg. (Accidents are a way of life with me). Because Elaine is by nature a giving person, as much as anyone I've ever known, after my surgery she invited me to convalesce in her home. Like Sheridan Whiteside in THE MAN WHO CAME TO DINNER, somehow I never got around to leaving.

The house is gloriously situated on a bluff overlooking the blue Pacific. I flatter myself that a bit of that ocean is finding its way into my music. Unless I push my gracious hosts too far with my eccentricities, I'm not liable to seek greener pastures. I may be old but I'm not crazy.

With loving thoughts,

Hugh

A Christmas letter from Hugh Martin (1999)

What did you think when you saw your song matched with what was on screen?

It was exactly right. Minnelli was a marvelous director and I was so lucky to have him.

How did you and Ralph Blane end up singing together in the 1937 Broadway show *Hooray For What?*

The leading lady of that musical was Kay Thompson — an absolutely dynamic, marvelous, sensational woman — whoever worked with her thanked God they were allowed to learn from her. She taught me almost everything I know about music, and selected Ralph for the chorus of the show. When he auditioned at her apartment, I happened to be there, and she invited me to play the piano while Ralph sang. Then she took me into the show as a singer as well. I owe her, Richard Rodgers, George Abbott and my mother. Those are the four people who taught me everything.

Did you coach him for his own NBC radio show?

Yes. It was on once or twice a week and was called *Young Man Of Melody*. It was just fifteen minutes of Ralph singing, and it was a lovely program.

What was it about Ralph Blane that allowed you to work with him for so long?

Ralph was a wonderful man and a great artist. First of all, he sang better than any pop singer I've ever heard, including Sinatra. Secondly, he sparked me and gave me wonderful ideas. Some of the best songs were really suggested by Ralph in a subtle sort of way. Thirdly, Ralph was a life enhancer, a very happy person, and very pleasant to be around. I write better when I'm happy, so being with Ralph was when I wrote my best, because he kept me in such a wonderful mood. Also, if I had an idea for a song, I had this great voice to try it out on. I'd say, 'Ralph sing this,' and he would sing it. And then I'd say, 'I can do better than that,' and go back to the drawing board. I think we complemented each other in a rather unique way.

"Girl Crazy"

But you didn't always write together — he did things on his own and vice versa?

That's right. But I never had nearly as much success without Ralph as I did with him. There was something synergistic about the two of us, and I almost regret that I broke up the team, because I wanted to write alone. After the army, I struck out on my own, and had some successes with a Broadway show called *High Spirits* and a show called *Love From Judy,* which ran for two years in London. But it was nothing like the Martin and Blane stuff. Our best songs might never have been written if Ralph hadn't been there. He had a wonderful effect on me.

Was Ralph with you on the days the soundtrack was recorded?

Yes. In fact they actually used Ralph's voice for the "Skip To My Lou" recording. We used Ralph's voice a lot with the groups and choruses. I had used his voice earlier to dub for Chuck Walters in the film, *Girl Crazy,* for the scene when he's dancing with Judy Garland and they're singing "Embraceable You." That was actually Ralph's beautiful voice!

Who arranged your songs for *Meet Me?*

Conrad Salinger arranged them, and Georgie Stoll conducted the orchestra.

How well did you know Judy Garland?

I got to know her intimately when we worked together at The Palace in 1951. We ended up sharing the same dressing room, because she wanted me to be close to her. She said to Sid Luft, 'Can't we put Huey in my dressing room?' He gave us kind of a funny look and she said, 'Well, I'm gonna put a sheet between us!' We were there for nineteen weeks and we talked a lot.

Did you vocally coach her for *Meet Me?*

No, her mentor Roger Edens did all that and set the keys. Incidentally, I thought the key for "Have Yourself A Merry Little Christmas" had gone too high, but that's just me — I'm real particular about keys and would have liked it a half tone lower.

Hugh Martin & Michael Feinstein

Were you there the day she recorded her soundtrack version of "Have Yourself?"

You bet, and I cried and was moved beyond words. I loved the song, and for me there's no other singer but Judy — she's just queen of song as far as I'm concerned. And to have her doing it I thought I'd died and gone to heaven.

Did you enjoy working with her?

She was a sweet wonderful gal, but she could also go the other way if she had been on drugs. I had a terrible fight with her on *A Star Is Born,* and left the picture because she wasn't nice to me. But that was only because she was on drugs. If I had known that she really loved me, and that it was the drugs

speaking and not Judy, I would have stayed on the picture. But almost all of the vocal arrangements for the film were done by me, even though I was never given credit for them.

Why do you think your Christmas song has lasted for over fifty years?

I think it was a gift from God. I think he just gave me this beautiful song. It's just a very sweet gift from my creator. I don't know why it touches people — it touches me too. But there's a lovely lyric from the Richard Rodgers' musical *South Pacific* — 'Who can explain it, who can tell you why, fools give you reasons, wise men never try.'

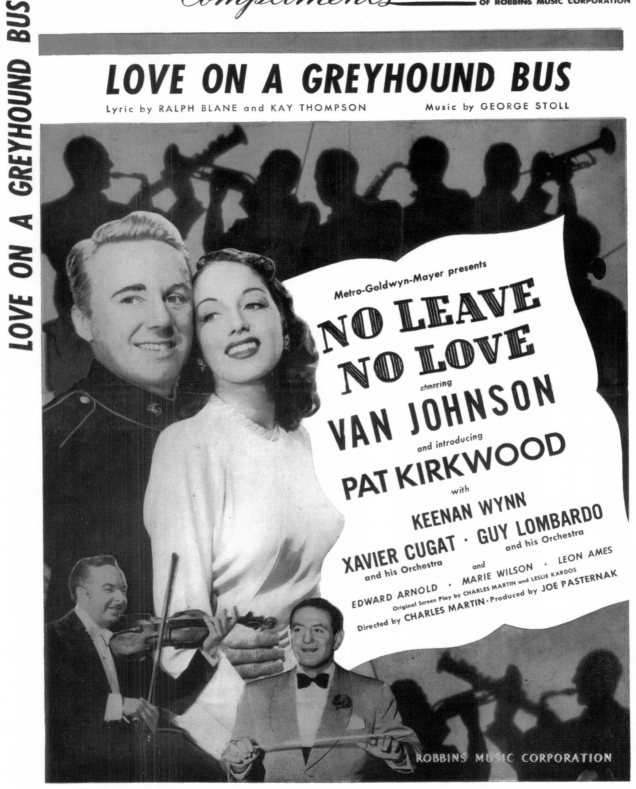

"Love On A Greyhound Bus," written by Ralph Blane, Kay Thompson & Georgie Stoll (1945)

GEORGE BLANE REMEMBERS HIS FATHER AND "HAVE YOURSELF A MERRY LITTLE CHRISTMAS"

Blane & Martin

Did your father and Hugh Martin ever make their own record together?

There's an album called ***Martin & Blane Sing Martin and Blane***, and they do all of their hits accompanied by **The Ralph Burns Orchestra**. It was recorded in 1956 — dad sings half the songs and Hugh sings half of them. Dad sings "Have Yourself A Merry Little Christmas." A CD of it was released in 1994 by **DRG Records**.

Note: In 1995, Nonesuch Records released "Michael Feinstein Sings The Hugh Martin Songbook," with Hugh Martin accompanying him on piano. It includes Feinstein singing "Have Yourself A Merry Little Christmas."

Did he ever song write with other people or for his own Broadway show?

Yes, his most famous songs were written with Hugh, but there were some wonderful songs written with Harry Warren and Harold Arlen. He solely wrote the music and lyrics for a show called *Three Wishes For Jamie*, that opened on Broadway in the early 50's. Bonnie Raitt's father John Raitt starred in it, and he sent flowers to my dad's funeral.

Hugh Martin thought of your father as a great singer — did he ever perform their Christmas song for a live audience?

Yes, he sang it at Disney World during the holidays for over twenty years.

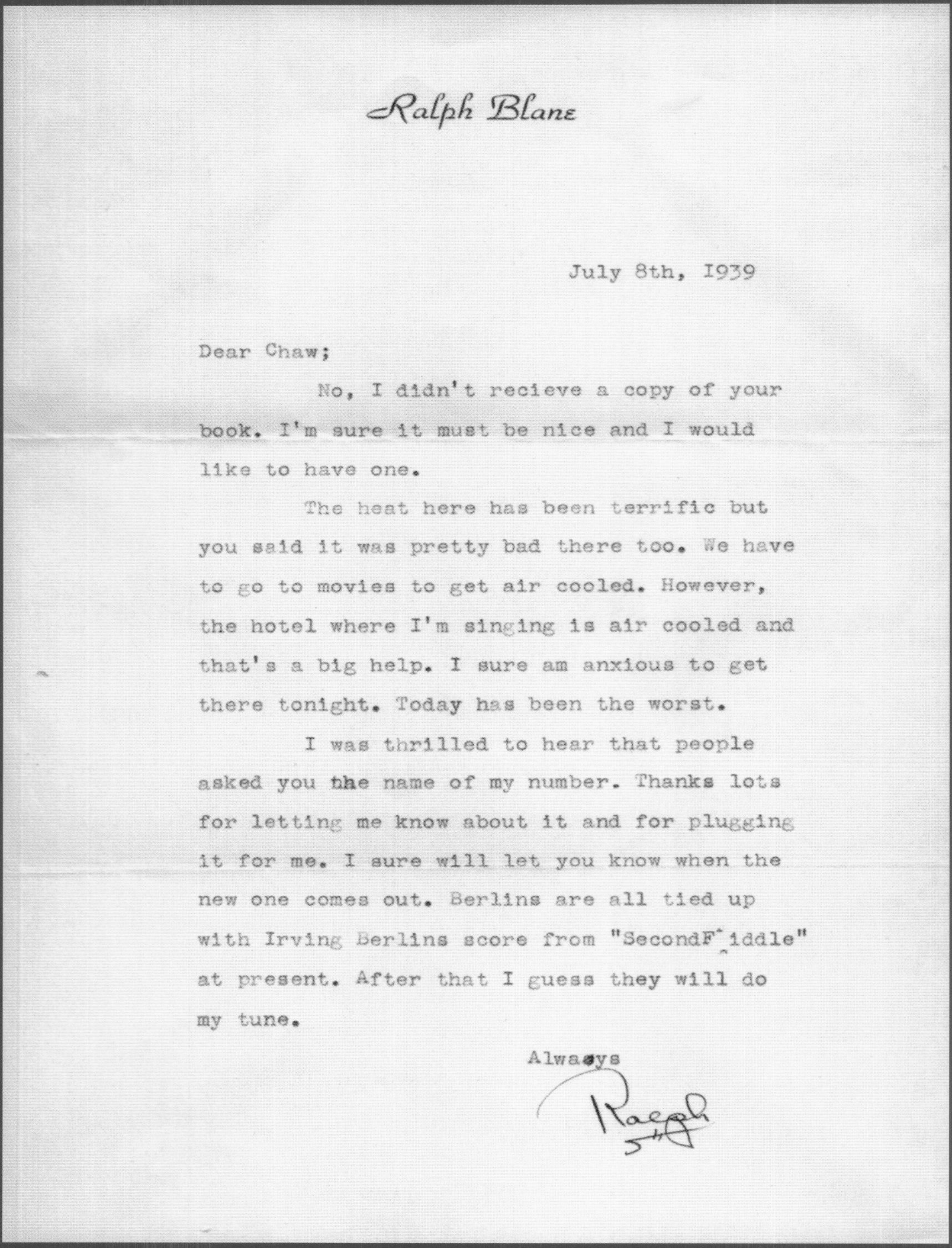

Ralph Blane

July 8th, 1939

Dear Chaw;

    No, I didn't recieve a copy of your book. I'm sure it must be nice and I would like to have one.

    The heat here has been terrific but you said it was pretty bad there too. We have to go to movies to get air cooled. However, the hotel where I'm singing is air cooled and that's a big help. I sure am anxious to get there tonight. Today has been the worst.

    I was thrilled to hear that people asked you the name of my number. Thanks lots for letting me know about it and for plugging it for me. I sure will let you know when the new one comes out. Berlins are all tied up with Irving Berlins score from "SecondF*iddle" at present. After that I guess they will do my tune.

                  Always

                  Ralph

A letter written by Ralph Blane on July 8, 1939

Was he at the Broadway opening of *Meet Me In St. Louis* in 1989?

He was there with Hugh on opening night at The Gershwin Theatre. It got mixed reviews, but I thought the girl who played Judy Garland's part — Donna Kane — was excellent. And there were some added songs, one called "Banjos," that was fabulous. My dad was in heaven. Margaret O'Brien was at the after-party.

Are you protective of your father's song?

Yes. At one point Willie Nelson wanted to record it and change the lyrics to "Have yourself A Willie Nelson Christmas, let your hair down long, grab an old guitar and play a country Christmas song." But I said, 'I ain't fallin' for that. The original lyrics will be lost before we know it if you allow this.'

How has the song grown over the years?

When I was growing up, the song probably paid, in its first ten years, five or six thousand dollars in royalties. And then it made a little more and a little more, until the country people started picking it up in the 1970's. Then it snowballed and went from making 10,000 dollars to 250,000 dollars a year. In fact the song won two ASCAP awards in 1990. One for being among their most performed standards from 1979 through 1989. The other award was for the most performed standard song from a feature film for that ten-year period. One of the earlier films it was in was *The Godfather*, and it ended up making a lot of money because the movie made a lot of money. In 1997, according to a *Newsweek* article I have, the song was its publisher's number one earner that year, grossing 2.9 million dollars.

Can you talk about the experience you had with your father's song shortly before he died?

When Dad was getting bad at the later part of his life — he had Parkinson's Disease — I walked into the hospital one night. He was laying there not able to recognize me, and the nurses asked him to sing his famous Christmas song. He started singing "You Are My Sunshine," and I walked out of the room with tears in my eyes. Then I went to see a movie — the updated version of *Miracle On 34th Street* — and as I sat there, Kenny G's saxophone take of "Have Yourself A Merry Little Christmas" was playing on screen. It made me cry, and I said, 'Gee, look at my dad, he wrote this song.'

Have Yourself A Merry Little Christmas

(Have Yourself a Blessed Little Christmas)
Words and Music by HUGH MARTIN and RALPH BLANE
Sacred Lyrics by HUGH MARTIN and JOHN FRICKE

The sacred version of "Have Yourself A Merry Little Christmas" (1996)

JOHN FRICKE, AUTHOR OF *JUDY GARLAND — WORLD'S GREAT-EST ENTERTAINER* & *THE WIZARD OF OZ: THE OFFICIAL 50TH ANNIVERSARY PICTORIAL HISTORY*, DISCUSSES HOW HE ENDED UP CO-WRITING THE 1998 SACRED VERSION OF "HAVE YOUR-SELF A MERRY LITTLE CHRISTMAS" WITH HUGH MARTIN

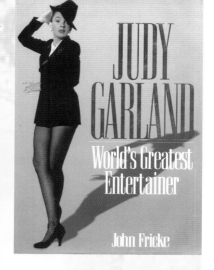

It all started when my folks changed churches in 1979, and I began singing every Christmas Eve for this new Lutheran church they had joined in Brookfield, Wisconsin, a suburb of Milwaukee. In 1996, I wanted something new to sing, and realized I had written so much special material for my own club acts, why not write a sacred lyric for "Have Yourself A Merry Little Christmas," which is such a beloved song and such a great show tune. So I wrote new lyrics for it, and kept the melody intact.

In Spring, 1996, I was in Los Angeles working as the co-producer/writer of the A&E Judy Garland *Biogra-phy*. Part of my duty was to track down the people we wanted to interview associated with Judy, and natu-rally I thought of Hugh Martin. He admired my work, and we became friends over the next two months, corresponding by letter, talking on the phone, and getting to know each other in person at the taping.

Hugh is so faith-fully religious, and we got to be such good friends that I thought he might like to see what I had done with his song. That summer, I sent him my lyrics, and not only did he not take of-fense, but liked the idea so much that he said he couldn't believe he had never thought of it himself. He kept part of what I had done, reworked some of it to suit himself, and added some of his own new words.

He then sent it off to his publisher and asked if they would be interested in it. They accepted it, and the first official sheet music of it came out in the fall of 1998, with "Have Your-self A Blessed Little Christmas" underneath the original title of the song. I sang it for the first time in church, Christmas Eve, 1996.

1. HAVE YOURSELF A MERRY LITTLE CHRISTMAS (RADIO EDIT) (3.26)

(Martin-Blane) EMI United Partnership Ltd. WITH JUDY GARLAND

2. ME AND MY SHADOW (4.38)

(Dreyer-Jolson-Rose) Francis Day & Hunter Ltd./Memory Lane Music Ltd.

THE NEARNESS OF YOU

(Washington-Carmichael) Warner Chappell Music Ltd.

3. HAVE YOURSELF A MERRY LITTLE CHRISTMAS (EXTENDED EDIT) (4.02)

(Martin-Blane) EMI United Partnership Ltd. WITH JUDY GARLAND

T.P.L.12'08"   Produced by Gordon Lorenz

Christmas is the most special time of year for me. It was my mother's favourite time also and no matter where we were in the world my mom always made Christmas magical and wonderful. She especially loved all the traditions that Christmas brought, so much so that I now celebrate the same traditions with my family.

I'm so very proud that "Have Yourself A Merry Little Christmas" is part of my mother's musical legacy having been expressly written for her to introduce in the 1944 MGM musical "Meet Me In St. Louis".

Since then countless recordings and performances have made this one of the most beloved songs for this time of year. This project has been a complete joy for me and I hope it brings as much happiness into your home over the Christmas season as I had recording it.

Merry Christmas   30360 00172

                                                        CARLTON SOUNDS

In 1995, Carlton Home Entertainment, Ltd., released a Judy Garland/Lorna Luft duet version of "Have Yourself A Merry Little Christmas." In the liner notes for that project, Garland's daughter describes how special Christmas was to her mother.

"Screen Songs" magazine (September 1947)   **"Song Parade" magazine (May 1944)**

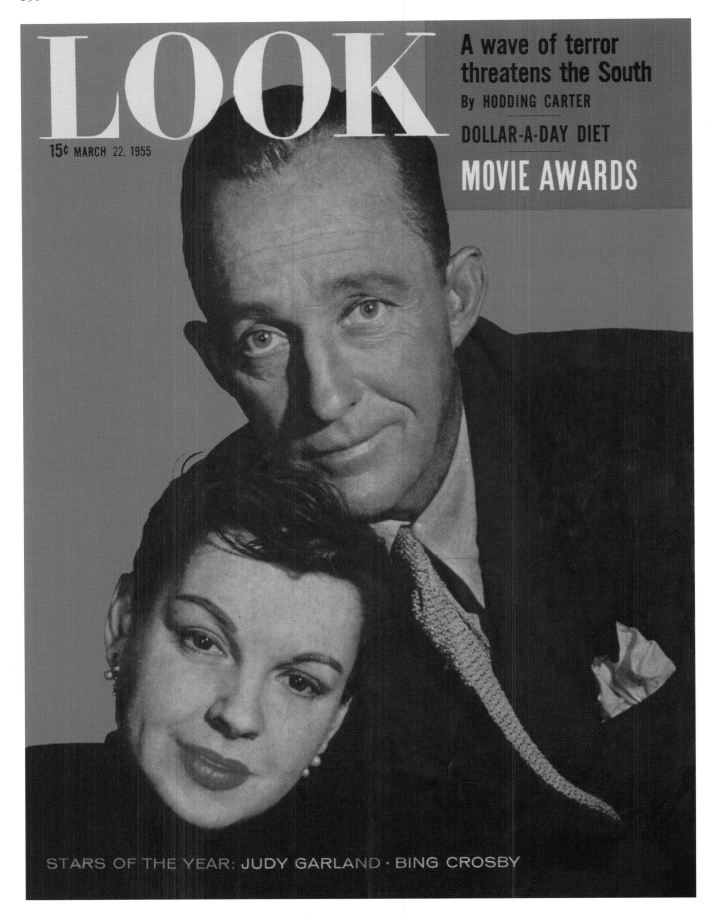

Judy Garland's Christmas Legacy

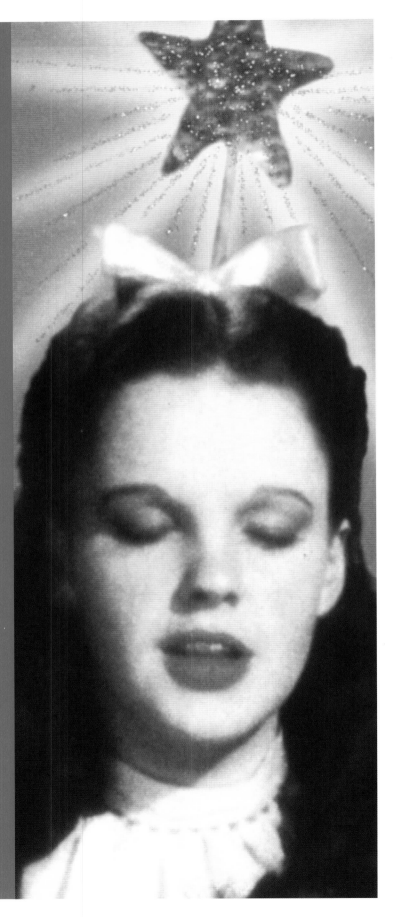

- "Jingle Bells" was Judy Garland's formal debut as a performer. She sang it when she was two years old, on December 26, 1924, at The New Grand Theatre in her home town of Grand Rapids, Minnesota.

- Judy Garland never recorded a Christmas album, but the songs from her December 22, 1963, CBS Christmas television show are now commercially available on CD and home video. Some of the holiday tunes she sang then were "Have Yourself A Merry Little Christmas," "The Christmas Song" (a duet with its co-writer Mel Torme), and "Caroling, Caroling." On that show she also sang a number of Christmas songs with her daughters Liza and Lorna.

- The movie *Meet Me In St. Louis* contains a second Christmas song — "The First Noel" — which is playing in the background after Mr. Smith announces the family won't have to move.

- On December 2, 1946, CBS presented an hour-long Lux Theatre *Meet Me In St. Louis* radio show, written by Sally Benson and starring Judy Garland, Margaret O'Brien and Tom Drake. Garland sang her hit songs from the movie including "Have Yourself A Merry Little Christmas." On Christmas Day a year earlier, she sang it for *The Armed Forces Radio Service* program, starring Bob Hope and Bing Crosby.

- Judy sang a duet of "Rudolph The Red-nosed Reindeer" with Bing Crosby for his December 6, 1950, radio show.

- A second Garland Christmas film song, "Merry Christmas," appears in her 1949 movie *In The Good Old Summertime*. Ralph Blane contributed music for that project (see pg. 151).

- In 1937, Judy sang "Silent Night" with the St. Luke's Episcopal Church Choristers of Long Beach, California, for an MGM radio Christmas trailer. Two years later she recorded a pair of sacred tunes for Decca — "The Birthday Of A King" & "The Star Of The East." (See page 149)

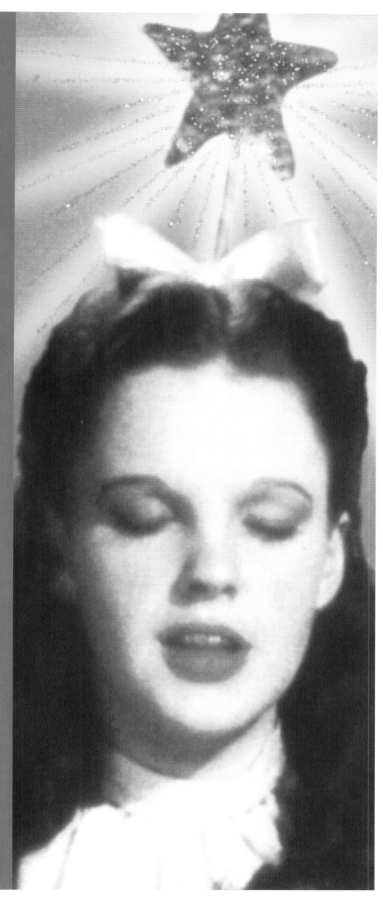

HERE COMES SANTA CLAUS — 1947

WRITERS — GENE AUTRY
OAKLEY HALDEMAN

ARTIST — GENE AUTRY

PRODUCER — CARL COTNER

COLUMBIA RECORDS

Following World War II, a nation recently held in the dark, foreign twilight of universal conflict, yearned for domestic fantasies, metamorphosis and renewal. No one could better represent this awkward transition than Gene Autry, America's most beloved singing cowboy, whose rags to riches life embodied the halcyon era of Hollywood's early days. Military turmoil had dramatically altered the country's palate, and it could no longer easily embrace the kind of pre-war, western escapist fantasies that made Autry, star of over ninety movies, a multi-millionaire before the age of forty. Once again, there simply was 'no place like home.'

To deal with these sudden changes in tastes, Autry became a successful businessman, a popular television entertainer, and a man who shrewdly aligned himself with holiday song. Aided by a host of cheery childhood characters like Frosty The Snowman, Rudolph The Red-nosed Reindeer, Peter Cottontail, and of course, Santa Claus, it wasn't long before he was 'back in the saddle again.'

"After the war, the music industry began a massive hunt to find a new Christmas number that would appeal to kids," said Autry, in his 1978 autobiography. "'Jingle Bells' was wearing thin. In the summer of 1947, well ahead of the holiday season, we recorded 'Here Comes Santa Claus (Down Santa Claus Lane).' That winter it swept the country as the first new Christmas song in years."[1]

Gene Autry

That charming holiday jingle, written by Autry and Oakley Haldeman, definitely helped put him back on top again, pivoting him for the second phase of his life as a multi-faceted entertainer. This new role of Christmas cowboy quickly led to the western-film star lassoing 1949's "Rudolph The Red-nosed Reindeer," a song that would go on to become the second largest-selling seasonal hit in American history.

Texas-born Orvin Gene Autry came into the world on September 29, 1907. At the age of five his Baptist-minister grandfather, in need of a soprano, encouraged him to sing in the church choir. Sadly, his mother, a church organist who sang nightly psalms, hymns and folk ballads to her young son, died in 1930 due to a lack of money for proper medical care. Her passing came before Autry's star had risen, and after his father drifted off, he was left to support his abandoned siblings.

But the man who helped create a brand new musical movie genre had an early talent humorist Will Rogers noticed late at night when passing through the pastoral Chelsea, Oklahoma, Frisco Railroad Station Autry worked at as a teenager. In the 1927 summer quiet of the room, he overheard the young man passionately singing while strumming his guitar. Impressed, Rogers advised him to go to New York and get a job on the radio.

Not long after that fateful encounter, the Jimmie Rodgers-influenced singer was signed to the Big Apple's American Record Corporation label headed by legendary producer Art Satherley, a pioneering record executive who discovered many important singers in the 1930's and 40's. Satherley convinced Autry to stick with his rural roots when he was yearning to imitate smooth pop crooners of the time like Rudy Vallee.

Soon billed as "Oklahoma's Yodelin' Cowboy," in the early 30's Gene Autry became the hottest performer on Chicago's nationally heard WLS radio station, appearing regularly on *Barn Dance* and his self-hosted *Conqueror Record Time*, two highly popular concurrent shows that gained him a legion of loyal fans, and made him the first American country music celebrity. His recording career took off simultaneously, and in 1931, the depression-era mountain song, "That Silver Haired Daddy Of Mine," a tune he co-wrote with his wife Ina's uncle, turned into his first million-selling single.

1950

Shown above and on the opposite page are two Autry souvenir programs from the 1950's.

Gene Autry

1951

During that same period, Autry helped architect a new category of international filmic entertainment when he was cast as a singing cowboy in the 1934 film *In Old Santa Fe*. He was recast dozens of subsequent times in movies that saw him drop into song at the drop of a hat, while heroically galloping across the western ranges of his youth. This cinematic success exposed him to a much broader audience, and in an effort to reach out to his growing middle-class fan base, he sought the softer less twangy musical sound heard on "Here Comes Santa Claus," his first Christmas hit.

In October 1997, shortly after his 90th birthday, Gene Autry reflected on where he found the notion for his jolly post-war opus. "I got the idea for 'Here Comes Santa Claus' when I

heard the kids shouting that during the Christmas Parade in Los Angeles in 1946, when I was Grand Marshal and Santa Claus was on his float behind me," he recalled. "It seemed like a good idea for a song."

"This was an event that combined the spirit of the season with all the trimmings the fantasy factory can muster. It had been a tradition for cowboy stars to appear."[2]

"The parade route jangled right down Hollywood Boulevard, leading to what the promoters called Santa Claus Lane. The curbs and sidewalks were lined with kids, thick as chinch bugs, craning their necks, some perched on the shoulders of their dads. Santa was in the big sleigh a few rows back and as I rode past each block I could hear the kids, already looking behind me, shouting to each other, 'Here he comes, here comes Santa Claus.'"[3]

Hurrying to turn this holiday vision into a song, Autry brought "a few scribbled notes" about the parade experi-

Gene Autry with actor Smiley Burnette

Oakley Haldeman (1948)

ence to tunesmith Oakley Haldeman, manager of his music publishing company set up after the war.

Haldeman was born into a musical family in Alhambra, California, on July 17, 1909. He frequently appeared onscreen as a background orchestra trumpet player in movies of the 1930's until an unfortunate lip injury ended his instrumental career. According to his daughter, Virginia Long, after working as a promoter for Warner Brothers, her father established a songwriting partnership with Autry and began writing for him and other artists like Doris Day, Dale Evans and Nat King Cole. Those years resulted in a number of 1940's gems like "Brush Those Tears From Your Eyes," and "I Wish I Had Never Met Sunshine," as well as several other Christmas songs the pair penned including "He's A Chubby Little Fellow" and "Santa, Santa, Santa."

Long claims it was her mother Dixie Haldeman who came up with the song's moniker on the eve of one of her childhood birthdays: "At night, around eight o'clock, we were having a hamburger dinner outside and it was the day before my birthday, so I was really excited. I was sitting at the table with my parents, and I remember my dad telling my mother that Autry wanted him to write a song for the Santa Claus Parade because he was going to be the grand marshal. My dad had writer's block, couldn't come up with anything that he liked, and was saying something like 'Santa Claus comes but once a year full of good cheer.' My mother said, 'Oh, Oakley, that is such a cliché, why don't you just say here comes Santa Claus right down Santa Claus lane?'"

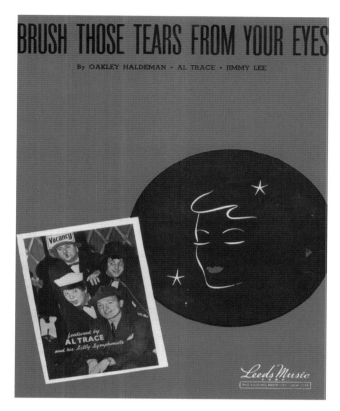

"Brush Those Tears From Your Eyes" co-written by
Oakley Haldeman (1948)

After their death, Virginia Long was bequeathed her parents' share of the song's royalties. She now admits her mother was never given credit for creating the "Here Comes Santa Claus" title, yet has warm thoughts of her father's Christmas legacy. "Luckily he was able to catch a star, and write a song that is such a part of our memories," she says. "It's like a nursery rhyme you want to pass on to your children."

That everlasting 'nursery rhyme' full of childhood wonder was first recorded on August 28, 1947, at a CBS studio in Los Angeles. According to Alex Gordon, VP of Autry's film company, the song was produced by Carl Cotner. Cotner was the Christmas cowboy's now-and-then movie stand-in, as well as his musical director, and he honed his talent playing the vio-

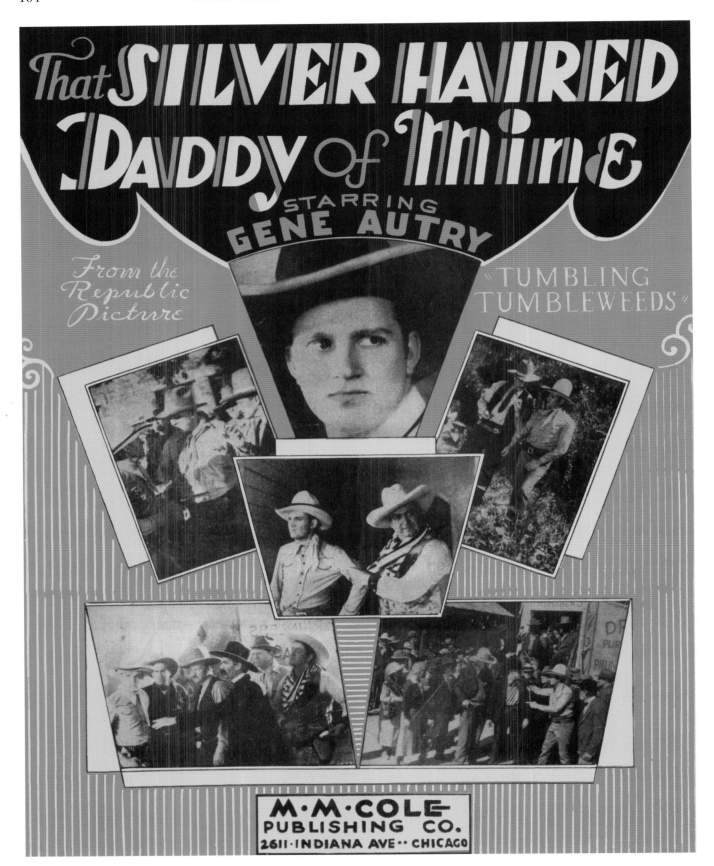

1932

Oakley Haldeman (1928) & Dixie Haldeman (1939)

He's A Chubby Little Fellow

By GENE AUTRY, A.S.C.A.P.
and OAKLEY HALDEMAN, A.S.C.A.P.

Featured by Gene Autry

Recorded by GENE AUTRY on Columbia Record No. 20616

WESTERN MUSIC PUBLISHING CO
6520 Selma Avenue, Hollywood 28, Calif. ● 146 West 54th St., New York 19, N. Y.

*"He's A Chubby Little Fellow," written by Oakley Haldeman &
Gene Autry (1949)*

1950

lin in an early 30's pop/jazz western outfit called The Georgia Wildcats. His eclectic knowledge of popular music helped in the evolution of Autry's pleasing style, and the phenomenal success he experienced with his songs after the war is largely due to Cotner smoothing out his vocal delivery and replacing some of his rougher country elements with softer tin-pan-alley pop sounds. This ultimately helped America's ever-growing urban middle class accept the fact that their cinematic cowboy was now in their living room singing happy-go-lucky Christmas songs.

Gordon revealed more about the process of creating "Here Comes Santa Claus:" "Gene turned a sketch he had of the song over to Oakley Haldeman and Art Satherley, who had become head of Artist and Repertoire at Columbia Records. They completed the lead sheet, hastening a copy over to singer/guitarist Johnny Bond's home to make an acetate disc of the finished product. A cocktail was mixed for Art, who sipped

near the microphone while Bond sang 'Here Comes Santa Claus' for the first time. When the group heard the ice cubes jingling so merrily on the playback, they were inspired to use a 'jingle bell' sound on Gene's record!"[4]

Over the years different versions of that record would be sung by dozens of acts like the Jackson 5, the Carpenters and The Chipmunks. It went on to become one of many hits from a batch of 300 songs Autry cut between 1929 and 1964, and his own recording of it debuted on Billboard's pop singles chart December 27, 1947. His song sold over a million copies, and cracked the top ten then, and once again in 1948. The following year Autry says it became an even "bigger hit with new versions released by Bing Crosby with the Andrews Sisters, and Doris Day among others."

It was resurrected once again in 1949 when Autry sang it onscreen in *The Cowboys and The Indians*, which also included his version of "Silent Night." "I thought it might fit

(l to r): Carl Cotner, Gene Autry & Christmas historian Thomas H. Carlisle (1983)

BLUE CHRISTMAS

Words and Music by
BILLY HAYES and JAY JOHNSON

Sung by Elvis Presley in "Elvis' Christmas Album"

Elvis Presley recorded "Blue Christmas" in Hollywood, California, on September 5, 1957, one day before his session for "Here Comes Santa Claus." Both would make it onto Elvis' first Christmas album. Written in 1948, the song first gained popularity in 1949 when Russ Morgan recorded it for Decca Records. Dueling versions of it by Hugo Winterhalter and Ernest Tubb debuted the following year.

CHOICE MUSIC, INC.
9109 Sunset Boulevard
Hollywood, California

into the movie, whereas 'Rudolph' might not have," he says. "Also we had the publishing rights on it but not on the other, which was being used in a cartoon."

"I tried to stick with my policy of including one or more popular songs in each picture. The plot of *The Cowboys and The Indians* had me, as an Arizona ranger, helping the Navajos defend their land against the palefaces. But we still managed to work into it that year's Christmas favorite, 'Here Comes Santa Claus.'"[5]

While the song has gone through a variety of interpretations, the celebrity most closely associated with it other than Gene Autry is Elvis Presley, who included it on *Elvis' Christmas Album*, his first holiday set, released in 1957. "Elvis knew Gene from his very early days in the business and was a great admirer of his," says Gordon. "He was greatly influenced by Gene and sang some of his songs on his early recordings." Presley recorded "Here Comes Santa Claus" on

September 6, 1957, at Radio Recorders studio in Hollywood, California, with a group of other songs including the non-holiday ballads, "My Wish Came True" and "Don't." His versions of "White Christmas" and "Silent Night" were also cut on that same autumn day.

Although both have passed away, over the years Presley and Autry's versions have remained highly popular, and it's an incredible testament to the staying power of Haldeman and his western partner's whimsical opus. Of course this mirrors the country star himself, who found success with "Here Comes Santa Claus," despite the fact that he returned from the war to find his movie studio had tried to replace him with his rival Roy Rogers. He also discovered that the type of films he was making were on the verge of obsolescence.

RADIO RECORDERS
7000 SANTA MONICA BLVD., HOLLYWOOD 38, CALIF.

SPOT OR MASTER NO.	R. R. MASTER NO.	TITLE
H2PB-5525-3		BLUE CHRISTMAS
H2PB-5524-28		MY WISH CAME TRUE
H2PB-5527-2		HERE COMES SANTA CLAUS
H2PB-5528-9		SILENT NIGHT
H2PB-5526-9		WHITE CHRISTMAS
H2PB-5529-7		DON'T
H2PB-5530-4		LITTLE TOWN OF BETHLEHEM
H2PB-5531-9		SANTA BRING MY BABY BACK TO ME
H2PB-5532-7		CHRISTMAS BLUES
H2PB-5533-15		I'LL BE HOME FOR CHRISTMAS

Elvis' 1957 session sheet for his first Christmas album

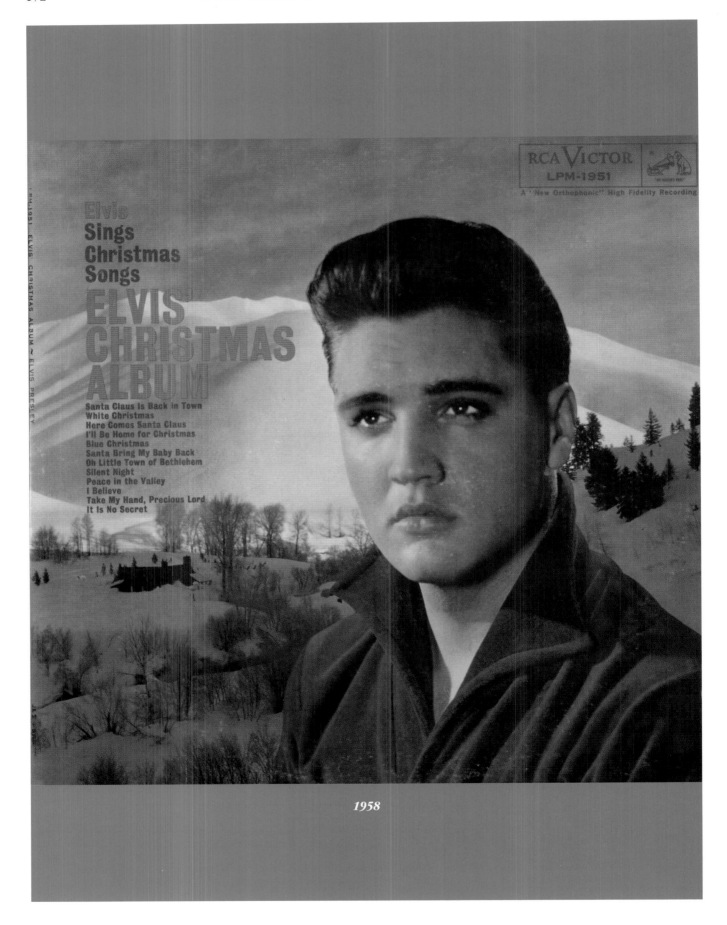

1958

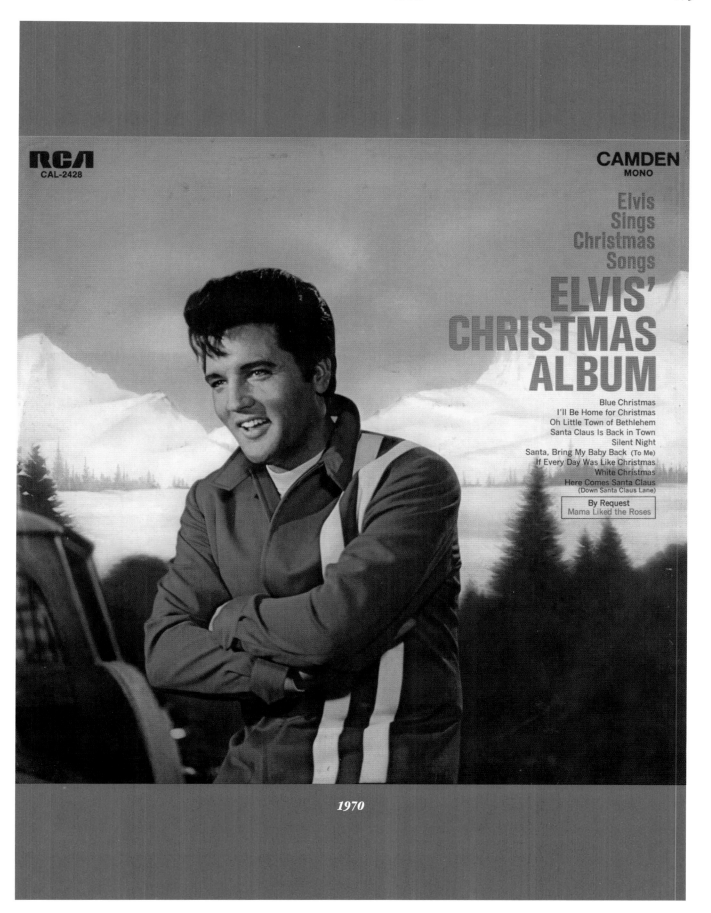

1970

1952

We find comfort in the reliability of Christmas, and that Santa Claus will come back down the lane once again in December of every year to greet them. The public grew to rely on Gene Autry coming back in the same way they could rely on the return of holiday spirit, which may best explain his incredible rebound, and his Christmas cowboy transformation. "People like him," wrote a *Life* reporter in 1948. "He is a natural actor in the sense that he always acts naturally. He makes no pretense at trying to be or wanting to be anybody other than himself."[6]

"You hear all the time about performers, who were simply transformed when they hit that stage and felt the glow of the lights and the warmth of the crowd," said Autry who passed away on October 2, 1998. "I never experienced that. So many singers would not only sing down the audience's throats, but they had to have a runway so they could get closer. They just overpowered you. I could never do that. I just laid back and let the audience come to me. It was like listening to the boy next door sing. I never tried to be more or less than Gene Autry."[7]

FROSTY THE SNOW MAN

Words and Music by STEVE NELSON and JACK ROLLINS

Two children's songs closely associated with Gene Autry were "Frosty The Snowman" and "Peter Cottontail." Both were written in 1950 by Steve Nelson and Jack Rollins. In 1951, Autry, Nat King Cole and Guy Lombardo all released their own versions of "Frosty," which is now closely associated with the voice of Jimmy Durante. Like "Rudolph The Red-nosed Reindeer," both "Frosty The Snowman" and "Peter Cottontail" would go on to inspire successful Rankin & Bass television specials.

HILL AND RANGE SONGS, INC.

*Oakley Haldeman (seated on arm of chair) with
his mother, father, and brother (1912)*

Oakley Haldeman (second from left, 1928)

MORE WITH VIRGINIA LONG, DAUGHTER OF OAKLEY HALDEMAN

What kind of musical background did your father have?

My father was a total music buff. He played in the school marching band, and the trumpet was his instrument. He was completely passionate about it and would drive for hours between LA and San Diego just to have a private lesson with a mentor. Later on he played in bands, the circus, traveling orchestras, and taught Henry Fonda and Jimmy Stewart how to play the trumpet for movies they were in. He did a lot of stuff for radio too, and was in backup bands for a lot of movies from the 1930's.

Do you remember any of your father's songs other than "Here Comes Santa Claus?"

I remember when I was a teenager that I found all kinds of 78 records, which I had never heard of, that my father had written. One was called "Red Letters," and it sounded a little like "On Top Of Old Smokey."

Other than his famous Christmas song, do you have a favorite song that your father wrote?

One of my favorites was "When Easter Sunday Comes On Monday I'll Be Coming Home To You." And my dad wrote another Christmas song that I really liked called "He's A Rootin' Tootin' Santa Claus," but it just didn't go anywhere. There was a song he wrote before his heart attack at age fifty-one that I really loved, which made me shake, called "There Are Two Sides To Every Heartache."

Aside from Gene Autry, did any other famous people record your father's songs?

There was a song he wrote called "I Wish I Had Never Met Sunshine," which was recorded by Jimmy Davis, who later became governor of Louisiana. Doris Day and Dale Evans also recorded some of my dad's music.

What was one of your father's most popular non-seasonal tunes?

I still get royalties from "Brush Those Tears From Your Eyes" — that was a huge hit for him.

What kind of a relationship did your father have with Gene Autry?

I don't think that my father liked Autry very much, and I think it was purely a business relationship, not a

Oakley Haldeman (1911)

social one. I remember my father being very upset once because Gene's brother was in jail on a drug charge, and he wouldn't put up his bond money. But my parents both adored Ina Autry. From what I could gather, Gene Autry was a real straight arrow, and I think my father respected the hell out of him for being a top business man. My parents did go to Gene's Christmas party at his house once a year, and every Christmas we got incredible gifts from the Autry's.

What kind of songwriting collaboration did they have?

My father always wrote both the lyrics and the music. Quite frankly, I don't recall Autry ever writing a song. He just put his name on all of the music. But that was part of their partnership, and it didn't bother my father. That's just how business was done in those days. I remember my mother telling me years ago before she died, that she listened to Autry on television tell the story of how "Here Comes Santa Claus" was written, and it made her so damn mad because it wasn't the truth at all. I said, 'Mother, why don't you tell somebody?' and she said, 'Are you kidding? I don't want to jeopardize my royalties.'

Was there ever a lawsuit regarding who wrote "Here Comes Santa Claus?"

My mother told me that after the song had been out for a couple of years, there had been a lawsuit because it mimicked a tune that was copywritten. Autry was afraid of getting caught up in that mess and pulled his name off the song for a few years until the lawsuit was over. He ended up winning, and put his name back on it.

Your father passed away in December 1987. What kind of memories do you have of him?

Alcohol was his downfall, but I remember that he had a great sense of humor and that he was a very handsome man, who was very charming and a very good people person. We had a tiny piano in our house, and even though he never really had piano lessons, he would just sit down and start playing the piano. And he was always piddling around with song ideas. But when he retired at the age of forty-three, that was the end of it. He went fishing, and he and my mother lived off the royalties for "Here Comes Santa Claus" until they died.

GENE AUTRY'S SELECTED CHRISTMAS RECORDING HISTORY

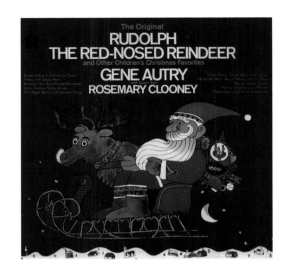

SINGLES

LABEL	TITLE (FLIP SIDE)	YEAR
Columbia	Here Comes Santa Claus/An Old-Fashioned Tree	1947
Columbia	Rudolph The Red-nosed Reindeer/If It Doesn't Snow On Christmas	1949
Columbia	Frosty The Snowman/When Santa Claus Gets Your Letter	1950
Columbia	Frosty The Snowman/An Old-Fashioned Tree	1951
Columbia	Here Comes Santa Claus/He's A Chubby Little Fellow	1951
Columbia	Poppy The Puppy/He'll Be Coming Down The Chimney	1951
Columbia	Rudolph The Red-nosed Reindeer/Here Comes Santa Claus	1951
Columbia	Santa, Santa, Santa/If It Doesn't Snow On Christmas	1951
Columbia	Thirty-Two Feet And Eight Little Tails/(Hedrock, Coco and Joe) The Three Little Dwarfs	1951
Columbia	When Santa Claus Gets Your Letter/He's A Chubby Little Fellow	1951
Columbia	The Night Before Christmas Song/Look Out The Window (*with Rosemary Clooney*)	1952
Columbia	I Wish My Mom Would Marry Santa Claus/Sleigh Bells	1953
Columbia	Merry Texas Christmas, You All!/The Night Before Christmas (In Texas, That Is)	1953
Columbia	Where Did My Snowman Go/Freddie The Little Fir Tree	1953
Columbia	Santa Claus Is Comin' To Town/Up On The Housetop	1954
Columbia	Round, Round the Christmas Tree/Merry Christmas Tree	1955
Columbia	Everyone's A Child At Christmas/You Can See Old Santa Claus	1956
Challenge	Rudolph The Red-nosed Reindeer/Here Comes Santa Claus	1957
Republic	Nine Little Reindeer/Buon Natale (Means Merry Christmas)	1959
Republic	Santa's Comin' In A Whirlybird/Jingle Bells	1959
Republic	Rudolph The Red-nosed Reindeer/Here Comes Santa Claus	1969

ALBUMS

Columbia	Merry Christmas With Gene Autry	1950
Grand Prix	Gene Autry Sings: The Original Rudolph The Red-nosed Reindeer and Other Children's Christmas Favorites	1959
Harmony	The Original Rudolph The Red-nosed Reindeer and Other Children's Christmas Favorites	1964
Mistletoe	Gene Autry Christmastime	1974
Republic	Christmas With Gene Autry	1976
Chicago Music	Christmas Classics	1997
Sony	A Gene Autry Christmas	1997
Madacy	Rudolph The Red-nosed Reindeer	1997
Laserlight	The Christmas Cowboy	1998
Sony	Christmas Favorites	1998
Legacy Int'l	Gene Autry: His Christmas Album	1999
Varese Vintage	Here Comes Santa Claus	1999

Gene Autry's first Christmas album (1950)

Robert L. May (1939)

RUDOLPH THE RED-NOSED REINDEER — 1949

WRITER: JOHNNY MARKS
BASED ON THE STORY BY ROBERT L. MAY

PRODUCER: CARL COTNER

ARTIST: GENE AUTRY

COLUMBIA RECORDS

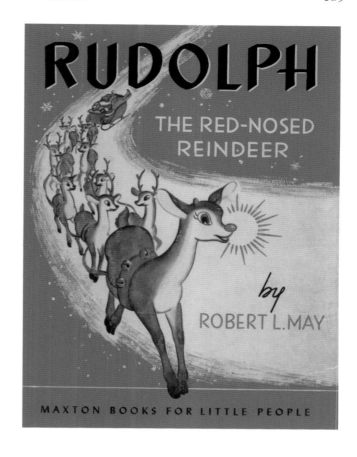

RUDOLPH THE RED-NOSED REINDEER by ROBERT L. MAY

MAXTON BOOKS FOR LITTLE PEOPLE

R udolph The Red-nosed Reindeer" is the story of an ugly duckling who turns a painful handicap into a magnificent personal achievement, and grows up to become an immortal holiday hero. Likewise, it's the story of Robert L. May, a humble Montgomery Ward copywriter, who created the 1939 tale as a free gift for his store's customers. At the time it was written, May had just lost his wife to cancer, and wrote Rudolph while coming to terms with her death. It was also a way for him to finally deal with the childhood inadequacy he experienced as a result of being the smallest boy in his class. "It seemed I'd always been a loser," May told an interviewer in 1975. "Frail, poorly coordinated, I was a scrawny kid, not accepted by my peers and I was never asked to join the school teams."[1]

Rudolph was never intended to be a commercial product, and Robert May always looked upon his character's eventual flight into the world's imagination as a miraculous gift. Little did he know that those privately held feelings of awkwardness projected onto his endearing creation would almost automatically strike an unceasing global demand. Over decades of time, May's ugly duckling metamorphosed into one of the most successful popular icons of the twentieth century.

The beginning of that century marked the birth of the author, born in 1905 in New Rochelle, New York. Much of his unhappy childhood could be attributed to the fact that he skipped a grade in school — his small size made him a conspicuous target for bullies, instilling in him an underdog sense of not belonging. This insecurity haunted him throughout the years he spent as a student at

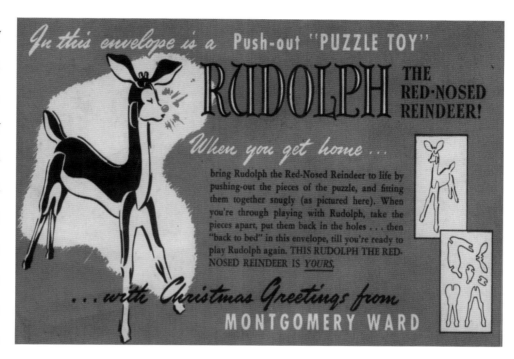

Montgomery Ward's 1947 customer giveaway

Dartmouth College, from which he graduated Phi Beta Kappa in 1926.

In 1935, May fatefully began working as a writer in the advertisement department of Montgomery Ward's Chicago-based office, a company that began as a catalog house in 1872. It opened its first department store the year he left Dartmouth. Thirteen years later, 600 stores were in operation across the country, breaking sales records annually. With the end of the depression, the chain looked forward to even greater expansion. One of the best ways to keep growing was by keeping its patrons happy. With this in mind, Robert May's boss, H.E. MacDonald, began planning a new customer giveaway project for the 1939 holiday season.

At Christmas time in past years, Montgomery Ward Santas handed out free presents to children visiting their toy depart-

ments, gifts that varied depending on the retail establishment's location. For the 1939 season, the company wished to nationally unify its giveaway, and to do so, MacDonald asked May to write an animal story appealing to youngsters that would uniformly be distributed as a pamphlet in all of its stores.

MacDonald knew his employee had a talent for writing comic sketches — a year earlier he asked him to concoct something entertaining for the company's Christmas party. Remembering the success he achieved at Dartmouth with parodies he wrote on special occasions, May came up with a similar witty idea for Ward's holiday bash.

"In January 1939, MacDonald summoned May to his office and said, 'That parody you wrote for the Christmas party wasn't bad. It gave me the idea that maybe you could write

Clement C. Moore's poem, "Twas The Night Before Christmas," helped inspire Robert L. May to write "Rudolph The Red-nosed Reindeer." Here Clement C. Moore is shown on Christmas Eve, 1882, in New York City reading that famous poem to his family. (Copyright 1996 by Thomas H. Carlisle and Harold Shuler)

some kind of Christmas story that we could use as a giveaway promotion in all our stores next Christmas. For instance, an animal story for kids. Have you read *Ferdinand the Bull?* Read it and then let's see you come back with some bright idea.'"[2]

"First I decided that, nuts, for Christmas there was only one animal," May told *Newsweek* in 1964. "No matter what, it had to be a reindeer. But I needed a reindeer who was different from the rest — an ugly-duckling type, one that children could identify themselves with vicariously."[3]

May himself needed to vicariously identify with Rudolph. As he spent days working on the story, struggling to parody it after Clement C. Moore's poem *Twas The Night Before Christmas* (thinking of naming it "The Day Before Christmas"), he was heavily in debt. He was also on the brink of becoming a single parent, as his wife lay dying in their small apartment on Chicago's north side.

His unique tale was actually serving a dual purpose — as it fulfilled a company obligation, it also attempted to answer a devastating question his four-year-old daughter Barbara asked regarding her dying mother: "Why isn't my mommy like everyone else's mommy?"[4] Her father's answer became part of Rudolph's metaphor, and he would read the story to his daughter nightly after her mother died.

He worked on through a deep state of depression, making many changes to the fearless reindeer before coming up with a final version. One change involved the reindeer's name — among other monikers, he thought of calling his furry friend

Robert L. May worked at the Chicago Montgomery Ward building, depicted above in this 1907 postcard

Rollo or Reginald, finally settling on Rudolph. The greatest alteration however was made to Rudolph's face. At first the hero had huge glowing cat eyes, but the writer was inspired to replace them with an even stranger dramatic feature — a shiny red nose.

"Separate analyses of Santa's needs and a reindeer's anatomy eventually pinpointed the idea of the shining red nose that would be a foggy-night asset to Santa," said May, "but something less than a social asset to the youthful deer."[5]

According to Christmas historian, Thomas H. Carlisle, who interviewed May in 1975, the idea for Rudolph's red nose came at a pivotal moment when the author was gazing out his

Front

This original 1939 Rudolph booklet was given away as a free gift to 2.3 million Montgomery Ward customers.

Back

window. "He was sitting in his little apartment looking out towards Lake Michigan, and the fog was coming off the water making a big glow around the street lights. That gave him the idea to create a deer with a red nose that would light up the fog so that Santa could see."

"A red-nosed reindeer? For chrissakes, Bob, can't you do better than that?" was his boss' response when he first brought the idea to him, admits Carlisle. Apparently he was concerned that customers would associate the florid nasal organ with alcoholism. But intuitively knowing the power of his imaginary character, May asked his friend, Denver Gillen, a Montgomery Ward's art department employee, to create an actual drawing of him. Since the pair decided to make him as lifelike as possible, they spent hours at Chicago's Lincoln Park Zoo sketching deer resting and at play, eventually creating a Rudolph that MacDonald finally approved.

It was now time to deliver the finished fable to Montgomery Ward. "I'll never forget that day," said May. "I was so nervous I couldn't eat lunch." This event was made more nerve-wracking due to MacDonald's summoning the whole copy staff for a special meeting to hear May read Rudolph. "I knew kids liked it," he added. "My daughter and her friends laughed and enjoyed it as if someone else had written it. But to get up and read it to a room full of hard-boiled copywriters!"

Although several employees criticized Rudolph, some wanting May to dramatically alter or abandon it altogether, MacDonald gave his story and Gillen's crayon illustrations, a green light for production. "From then on it was smooth

1950

sailing," said May," and I heaved a sigh of relief, thinking I had waved good-bye to Rudolph."[6]

In reality, he was just saying hello to the exponential growth of a serendipitous cottage industry.

That growth started when 2.3 million lucky 1939 Montgomery Ward Christmas shoppers were given a free twenty-nine-page Rudolph booklet of May's original story including a scene (omitted in subsequent printings) of the reindeer almost crashing into an airplane while guiding Santa's sleigh. This giveaway campaign was halted during World War II, due to a paper shortage, and fear that Rudolph's name was too German sounding. Ward's resurrected it in 1946, and distributed 3.6 million more copies to its customers.

What took place over the next three years fueled a worldwide Rudolph phenomenon that lasts to this day.

Front

Back

In 1947, RCA Victor released Rudolph's story on record (above). It was narrated by Paul Wing, and set to the music of George Kleinsinger.

In an act of corporate generosity unheard of today, May's company granted him the copyright to Rudolph in 1947, allowing him to receive royalties for any subsequent products bearing the character's image. And there would be an abundance of them, soon making May, who was given a mere 300 dollar company bonus for his booklet, a wealthy man.

That same year saw the first commercial printing of Rudolph as a hardcover children's book when Maxton & Co., a small Chicago publisher, took a chance and issued an edition with Gillen's illustrations. It sold 100,000 copies within two years' time, and became the company's first best-seller. In addition, RCA Victor released an album of the story narrated by Paul Wing, and set to the music of George Kleinsinger. Simultaneously, Ward's, an exclusive seller of many Rudolph products, received orders up to three times the amount manufacturers could handle for stuffed toys and slippers.

The list of items ranging from Rudolph rings to Rudolph underwear grew tremendously in 1948, the year the world

Johnny Marks (1947)

saw the screen debut of the red-nosed star in a Technicolor nine-minute cartoon sponsored by Ward's and directed by Max Fleischer. It was shown in over 900 cities and towns across the country. Ironically Rudolph, now a Parker Brothers game and a Ringling Brothers Barnum & Bailey Circus pony with an electric nose, overshadowed a second children's book May wrote then entitled *Winking Willie.*

To feed the reindeer frenzy even further, a song about Rudolph was in the planning stages. Its writer turned out to be New York tunesmith Johnny Marks — the man married to Robert May's sister.

"In 1946, they started thinking about making a Rudolph song," says Thomas H. Carlisle, "particularly after 1948 when they made the cartoon and it didn't have a good song in it." May told Carlisle several songwriters had been courting him, but in the end he chose Marks due to their family connection. "Marks threatened to shake up the family if May didn't let him write Rudolph. He was very arrogant, and was going to cause a family fight if Bob gave that song to somebody else."

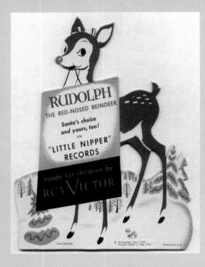

RCA Victor Rudolph record store display

When you're at Wards ... be sure to see all these

NEW DELUXE EDITION OF FAMOUS RUDOLPH STORY

- *Handsomely Bound.*
- *42 Illustrations.*

The touching tale of the funny-faced deer who made good with Santa. 32 pgs.; 4 colors.

PAUL WING HAS RECORDED RUDOLPH FOR RCA-VICTOR!

- *Hit of the Year!*
- *Unbreakable!*

Paul Wing at his best! Kleisinger-composed music! Album of 10-inch records; 4 sides.

GAY RUDOLPH SLIPPERS JINGLE ALL THE WAY!

- *The Bells Jingle!*
- *The Eyes "Roll."*

"Bells on their toes!" Soft, warm shearling, in red-and-white. Sizes 6 to 12. Gift boxed.

BOX OF 3 RUDOLPH PUZZLES FOR CHILDREN

- *3 Action-Scenes!*
- *Easy; Big Pieces!*

Exciting pictures; verses with each. Cut in big pieces, perfect for young children's play.

BIG RUDOLPH CUDDLE-TOY AMAZINGLY LOW PRICED!

- *15 inches Tall.*
- *His Eyes "Roll."*

Soft, life-like, lovable! A size and quality usually sold at far higher price than Wards.

RUDOLPH SWEAT-SHIRTS FOR YOUNG CHILDREN

- *Blue and Maize.*
- *Sizes 2 to 6.*

Long-sleeved cotton sweat-shirts, bearing red-nosed Rudolph's picture and "signature."

Grand New RUDOLPH TOYS and GIFTS!

Rudolph the Red-Nosed Reindeer Gifts

[A] LAMP. Perky figurine of Rudolph, molded of sculptor's plaster. Highly glazed finish, hand-tinted, accented by famous red nose. Translucent White paper parchment shade, 10-in. diam. Bulb not included. Ht. 15½ in.
66 T 57 L—Ship. wt. 3 lbs........3.29

[B] RUDOLPH VIEW-MASTER OUTFIT. Full color, 3-dimension, real-as-life pictures of Rudolph, with printed story. Plus Alice in Wonderland; Night Before Christmas. 3 reels, 7 scenes each. With View-Master Stereoscope. *Postpaid.*
67 TN 3405—Complete Outfit......3.00
67 TN 3406—3 Reels only........1.00

[C] INFLATED PLASTIC RUDOLPH. Tots will love riding this frisky reindeer. Tough Vinyl plastic with heat-sealed seams; weighted bottom; "squawker" in head. Easily inflated. About 21 in. high. Ship. wt. 1 lb. 8 oz.
48 T 3538....1.39

[D] NEW RUDOLPH SCHOOL BAG. Artificial leather, double stitched. Zipper pencil pocket; book, lunch compartments. New hard bottom—bag expands to abt. 4 in. 14x9½ in. Wt. 1 lb. 6 oz.
53 T 1525—Shoulder Strap.2.19
53 T 1526—Plastic Handle..2.19

[E] PLASTIC MUSICAL MILK MUG. As child sips, Swiss movement plays "Rudolph the Red-Nosed Reindeer". Cup releases for washing. Abt. 7 in. high.
53 T 5508—Wt. 12 oz......5.95

[F] RUDOLPH PULL TOY. Bells tinkle merrily as Rudy gallops along with Santa. Of wood with enameled wood beads on strong cords; harmless colors. 8¾x5½x7½ in. high. Pull cord.
48 T 1250—Ship. wt. 1 lb...1.79

[G] [H] PENCIL, PEN. Watch tiny Rudolph float in falling snow through transparent center. Maroon plastic, gold-color metal caps, clip, trim. Gift box.
(G) 53 T 2345—AUTOMATIC PENCIL. Propels-repels lead. Concealed eraser, extra leads. Abt. 5¼ in. long. Wt. 4 oz..98¢
(H) 53 T 2347—BALL POINT PEN. With cap, clip (not shown). Abt. 5¼ in. long. Wt. 4 oz..98¢
53 T 2349—PEN AND PENCIL. Ship. wt. 7 oz........Set 1.89

For similar items, other toys see Index and General Catalog.

[J] RUDOLPH WATCH. Red nose glows in dark. Easy-to-see red hands, numerals. 30-hour movement. Chromed case, stainless steel back, unbreakable crystal. Vinylite strap. 10% Federal Excise Tax included. Shown actual size.
45 T 99—Ship. wt. 4 oz......4.49

[K] CHILD'S 3-PC. DISH SET. Rudy's cheery face and red nose on 6½-in. Cereal Dish, 7⅜-in. Plate, 6½-oz. Mug. First quality lustrous white semi-porcelain.
86 W 9504L—Wt. 2 lbs. 4 oz.1.49

[L] KIDDY PROJECTOR. Easy for a child to use; nothing to get out of order, no threading or rewinding. Plastic, abt. 4¾ in. high. Cardboard box becomes theater screen. With 20-picture Rudolph color film disc. Extra films below. 7-watt lamp; 6-ft. cord. For 110-120 volt AC, DC. UL listed.
48 T 2006—Ship. wt. 2 lbs....2.59

EXTRA FILMS FOR (L). 4 film discs per set (1 in color); 20 pictures on each. Ship. wt. set, 2 oz.
48 T 2040—Noah's Ark (color); Old Woman in Shoe; 3 Bears; Nursery Rhyme Medley..Set 89¢
48 T 2041—Pinocchio (color); 3 Little Kittens; Old Mother Hubbard; Old McDonald had a Farm................Set 89¢
48 T 2042—Sinbad the Sailor (color); Hare and Tortoise; Puss in Boots; Koko.........Set 89¢

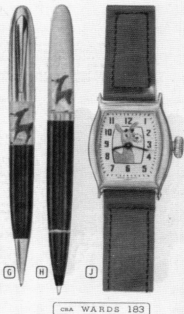

CBA WARDS 183

Rudolph products advertised in Montgomery Ward's 1953 Christmas catalog (above)

Shown above: Johnny Marks, age six (upper left), Marks' wife and Robert L. May's sister, Margaret Marks (upper right), and Marks playing the piano for World War II servicemen in France (1945, lower left)

In 1949, "Song Hits" magazine named Johnny Marks its Songwriter of the Year for "Rudolph The Red-nosed Reindeer."
Shown above is Marks accepting that award on NBC radio.

Marks was born in Mount Vernon, New York, on November 10, 1909. He started songwriting at the age of thirteen, and worked as a radio producer as well as a nightclub pianist. He received a Bachelor's degree in English from Colgate University in 1931, studied music in Paris, served as a captain in the Second World War, and with the success of Rudolph, formed his own music publishing company in 1949. New York City was home for most of his life, and he died on September 3, 1985.

Although he is best known for writing Christmas hits including "I Heard The Bells On Christmas Day," "Rockin' Around The Christmas Tree" and "A Holly Jolly Christmas," he professionally started songwriting in 1935, penning non-seasonal pop songs for performers like Kate Smith, the Ink Spots, Bing Crosby and Glenn Miller. "Address Unknown," "Who Calls" and "She'll Always Remember" were among some of those well-known chestnuts within a catalogue of 900 published and unpublished tunes, which encompassed a host of many other lesser-heard Christmas songs. May's brother-in-law was also a prolific television composer. He wrote General Electric commercial jingles for three years, along with music for five children's TV specials like 1964's *Rudolph The Red-Nosed Reindeer, The Tiny Tree* and *The Ballad Of Smokey The Bear.*

While Marks told *Time* in 1960 that Rudolph's lyrics came to him as he casually walked down the street one spring day in April, and that he created the music on his piano only

Johnny Marks

hours after this inspiration, May told Carlisle he fed his brother-in-law lyrics during phone conversations taking place in the late 1940's. "I would say that eighty percent of the lyrics came from Bob May and that Marks just put them all together," says Carlisle. According to *Newsweek*, May received five percent of the song's royalties, yet was never given writer's credit for the song's lyrics.

"Bob May always gave Johnny credit for writing the song even though he gave him most of the lyrics, but Johnny would do a whole interview for a newspaper and would never mention Bob," continues Carlisle. "May was the nicest guy and would always talk about Rudolph as if he were his child. Marks was more like a song factory. In a way he stole Rudolph from Bob and never looked back. After he divorced May's sister things kept getting worse and worse over the years."

Despite this family feud, Rudolph's song proved to be unstoppable. The first recording of it, however, almost never happened.

Its demo tape was sent around to many singers, but the tune was perceived as a novelty children's record and was turned down by virtually everyone in the business. The man who eventually ended up lending his voice to Rudolph's first vinyl pressing initially disliked it as well. "Johnny Marks sent me the song after Bing Crosby and many others rejected it," says Gene Autry. "I did not think it was right for me but my wife Ina persuaded me to do it."

"In 1949, I was in the market for another Christmas song as a follow-up to 'Here Comes Santa Claus,'" continues Autry, "and I sifted through dozens of lead sheets and demo records that came through the mail, most of them unsolicited. It was decided that we would cut two records, meaning four sides. We quickly agreed on three of the songs: 'He's A Chubby Little Fellow,' 'Santa, Santa, Santa,' and one I especially liked, 'If It Doesn't Snow On Christmas.' But we had no prospects for the fourth side."

"Meanwhile, Johnny Marks had mailed me a home recording of a number called 'Rudolph The Red-nosed Reindeer.' I played it at home that night for my wife. It not only struck me as silly but I took the position that there were already too many reindeer flying around. 'Hell,' I said to Ina, 'how many kids can get past Dancer and Prancer right now?' But to my surprise, Ina loved it. There was a line in the song about the other reindeer not letting Rudolph join in any reindeer games,

Gene & Ina Autry

and she was touched by it. 'Oh Gene,' she said, 'it reminds me of the story of the Ugly Duckling. I think you ought to give it a try. The kids will love it.'"[7]

Autry recorded "Rudolph The Red-nosed Reindeer" at the tail end of a session on June 27, 1949, with a background female vocal group called The Pinafores, who previously sang with him on his successful radio shows. It was done at a Los Angeles studio with Carl Cotner directing the session, writing Rudolph's arrangement and conducting the band, which included legendary guitarist, Johnny Bond. Luckily, Ina's words remained in the back of Autry's mind that day — at the last minute he overcame his resistance and quickly recorded the "children's" song.

1949

BEULAH ★ IONE ★ EUNICE

*Clockwise from upper right: Johnny Bond, The Pinafores, Carl Cotner, who all contributed
to the first recording of "Rudolph The Red-nosed Reindeer."*

1952

"We finished the first three numbers and Carl Cotner said, 'Gene we have less than ten minutes left. What do you want to do?'" remembered Autry. "I looked at the clock. The union allowed you four numbers and three hours of recording time. I said, 'It's only that 'Rudolph' thing. Throw it in and let's go. Up to that moment I wasn't certain I'd even use it. But it was an only take, which was unheard of. This was before tape, meaning that you couldn't edit out your mistakes. I always prided myself on the quickness with which I admit I was wrong, especially when it turned out as well as 'Rudolph.'"[8]

In October 1949, the song was released to radio stations with "If It Doesn't Snow On Christmas" as its B-side. One month later "Gene Autry came to New York for a Madison Square Garden rodeo show," says Carlisle. "Johnny Marks went down to Autry's dressing room and asked him if he would sing 'Rudolph' on the last day of the rodeo. Gene said 'Rudolph? This is a rodeo.' But Marks convinced him, and Autry finally gave in. At the end of the show they threw a blue spotlight on him and a guy dancing around in a Rudolph costume with a huge red nose. Autry sang it for the first time in public, the audience went insane, and it was picked up by the national news media. That's when the song first took off."

During its first year alone, Rudolph's song sold two million records and helped resurrect and redefine Gene Autry's sluggish career. It entered Billboard's pop chart on December 3, 1949, went on to become the singing cowboy's first

Gene Autry with Rudolph

and only number one record, and consecutively re-entered the charts each Christmas from 1950 to 1954. Autry re-recorded the song in 1957 for his own label, Challenge Records, and that version eventually peaked at number seventy.

Sales of Autry's original single continued to skyrocket. By 1953, it reached the four million mark, and in six years time picked up an additional one million units sold, with "the electric success of it sparking a remarkable publishing operation for Johnny Marks," according to *Billboard*.[9] That year, to celebrate its tenth anniversary, Columbia Records re-released the record paired with a new version by Ray Coniff.

By now over 200 commercial versions of the song had been recorded, but Gene Autry's outsold them all, eventually growing to over eight million purchased. In time, it evolved into the second most successful Christmas record in pop music history, and the third largest-selling non-seasonal hit

Rudolph (1954)

ever. Other acts to have charted with it include The Chipmunks, The Melodeers and The Temptations, who helped push overall sales beyond 150 million units worldwide, for a song that has been translated into every language imaginable.

Autry segued his success into a number of subsequent children's holiday songs including two million sellers — "Peter Cottontail" and "Frosty The Snowman" — as well as dozens of other Christmas songs and albums. He recorded many other Johnny Marks songs through the 1950's like "The Night Before Christmas Song," a duet with Rosemary Clooney, "When Santa Claus Gets Your Letter" and "Nine Little Reindeer," which he co-wrote.

May, who died at the age of seventy-one in August 1976, told an interviewer that "in December 1949, Rudolph moved to number one on the hit parade and there was no kidding myself — I was working for a reindeer. After the song came out Rudolph officially joined Santa's team," he continued, "and I saw him everywhere: he glowed in store windows, he hung from street lights, I saw him in parks, I lit his nose to dedicate a new shopping center, and he found his way into letters to Santa. Rudolph took me to Santa Claus that year and I got the present of a lifetime — a very comfortable home in the suburbs for my family."[10]

The author placed a huge plastic replica of the famous reindeer on the front lawn of that suburban Chicago home every Christmas, and went on to write two reindeer sequels entitled, *Rudolph's Second Christmas* and *Rudolph Shines Again.* He quit his job at Montgomery Ward in 1950 for seven years to work full-time for his own Rudolph company. The royalties from his creation helped put Barbara and his five other children through college. They now hold the famous creature's copyright and operate their father's thriving legacy. In 1998, the Mays approved the release of an updated animated Rudolph feature movie, starring the voices of Whoopie Goldberg and John Goodman. It includes a new version of the title song, sung by country singer Clint Black.

"For me, the story has appeal that reaches every child," said May's daughter Virginia Hertz. "Rudolph didn't start as an incredible superhero with a big ego. His powers were undiscovered and nurtured by someone else. It's difficult for children to see how they can do well in a world dominated by experienced adults, but Rudolph is a guide."[11]

"My dad liked the story of the unrecognized child who finally proves himself," adds Barbara May Lewis. "He was teased and knew what it was like to be an underdog and a runt. He put a lot of himself into Rudolph."[12]

Rudolph (1976)

Rudolph (1998)

1959

AN INTERVIEW WITH GENE AUTRY'S CLOSE FRIEND ALEX GORDON, CONDUCTED SHORTLY BEFORE AUTRY PASSED AWAY

What is your relationship with Gene Autry?

I'm Vice President of Flying A Pictures, and I'm in charge of his old movies, his film archives and the restoration work for his old movies. I've known Gene Autry since 1939. When I was a kid in England in 1939, I became president of Gene's fan club. After the war, I emigrated to New York, and started working for him in 1951.

How did Gene and "Rudolph The Red-nosed Reindeer" songwriter Johnny Marks meet?

They met when Gene called him and told him he'd like to do the song. Johnny Marks had written to him, and had sent him a demo record of "Rudolph." Gene did some other songs of his through the years, and they were friends up until Johnny died.

Please talk about "Rudolph's" producer, Carl Cotner.

He was from Kokomo, Indiana, and he originally wanted to become a symphony violinist. He studied at Cincinnati College, but in the depression, things didn't look good for him, and he decided to make his fiddle pay his way. So he barnstormed around the country with small-time engagements for country dances. Gene Autry was also touring at that time and making appearances to boost his record sales. His fiddler got sick when he was playing in a small town in Indiana, and he asked people at a radio station there if they knew of a fiddler who could fill in. They recommended Carl Cotner. In 1945, Gene appointed him as his musical director, and he subsequently wrote all the arrangements for his TV shows and records. He also played the fiddle on his recordings and wrote his orchestrations.

Did he produce "Rudolph?"

Yes. He was in charge of that session. He did the arrangement and conducted the orchestra. He produced the recording but didn't pick the song. Carl also produced "Here Comes Santa Claus."

1955

How did Elvis Presley end up recording Gene and Oakley Haldeman's "Here Comes Santa Claus?"

Elvis knew Gene from his early days in the business, and he was a great admirer of his. He was greatly influenced by Gene and sang some of his song's on his early recordings. When Elvis heard "Here Comes Santa Claus," he invited me and Gene to a party and came to Gene and asked if he could record the song.

What kind of process did Gene Autry go through when he wrote songs?

Gene mainly worked on the words. He doesn't read music and would hum something and then call Carl Cotner and have him write it down. Other times he would just give him an idea. Gene never put himself on a record that he wasn't involved with some way.

Who came up with the title for Gene and Oakley Haldeman's song "Here Comes Santa Claus?"

Gene definitely came up with the title because he heard it at a parade that we were both at together. The kids were shouting, 'Here comes Santa Claus,' and afterwards, we went back to the office. Gene decided that it would make a good song and then called Carl. It was definitely Gene's idea.

How was "Rudolph" picked for Gene to sing?

Gene was getting a lot of submissions of songs of all kinds. By that time he had many gold and platinum records, and in 1933 a song he co-wrote called "That Silver Haired Daddy Of Mine" had sold a million copies. He received the first gold record ever given to anyone for it. When he was looking for a Christmas song after the success of "Here Comes Santa Claus," he received "Rudolph" from Johnny Marks, but at first didn't think it was suitable. He didn't like the song, but his wife Ina happened to see it and played the demo, which was also sent to Bing Crosby, Dinah Shore, and many others who all turned it down. Ina said, 'Gee I like that song. I think the kids will like it because it talks about the ugly duckling who nobody wants to play with, but goes on to succeed anyway.' Gene gave it some thought and decided at the tail end of a recording session to do it. They only had twenty minutes left and ended up doing it in one take. To this day it has sold over 25 million copies and is now the second largest-selling Christmas song ever.

M O N T G O M E R Y W A R D
C H I C A G O 7

August 27, 1948

Mr. Charles E. Widmayer, Editor
Dartmouth Alumni Magazine
Hanover, New Hampshire

Dear Charlie:

Recalling your previous interest in Rudolph, I am very happy to bring you up-to-date at this time on the many amazing things that have happened to the little red-nosed guy since my last letter to you. If this does not measure-up as a general magazine story, please be good enough to turn it over to the '26 class secretary.

I'm glad to say that if you do decide that Rudolph is news-worthy, you will be in good company. Two weeks ago I was called down to the offices of Coronet Magazine for a lengthy interview ... with the result that Rudolph and his old man will be the subject of a feature article in their December issue, on the news-stands November 24. A Photostatted "proof-of-claim" is attached. In addition, the December issue of House & Garden will illustrate and write-up a few of the Rudolph products. I attach two newspaper write-ups, typical of the many Rudolph received last Christmas season.

The Rudolph products last year were uniformly successful. RCA-Victor's album (Paul Wing narration, George Kleinsinger music) was their juvenile best-seller by better than 2 to 1. The publisher's 100,000 edition of the book was a sell-out. This year he is planning to sell 250,000 of the greatly improved edition enclosed. On the stuffed toy and slippers, Wards received orders for three times as many as the manufacturers were able to produce. (I have in front of me a want ad that ran last December in the Huron, South Dakota Daily Plainsman:— "WANTED TO BUY. One Rudolph the Red-Nosed Reindeer stuffed toy. Willing to pay double price.")

And so-on, down the line. This year there will be about thirty products ... list attached. About half of these will be sold nationally; the other half will be exclusive with Montgomery Ward. But when I tell you that Wards expects to sell 250,000 of the stuffed Rudolph this year, you'll realize that <u>exclusives</u> can still be <u>extensive</u> !

The most important development for this year is the Technicolor movie of Rudolph the Red-Nosed Reindeer, which will be shown this coming Christmas season in 1,500 theaters, 900 cities and towns, including 37 of the top 40. I hope you get a chance to see it, perhaps in Claremont. It's directed by Max Fleischer ... sympathetically and tenderly ... with narration by Paul Wing.

Mr. Charles E. Widmayer
Hanover, New Hampshire
August 27, 1948

The movie was sponsored by Wards, who expect to have it shown at Christmas-time year-after-year.

Another interesting development is that Rudolph has been cavorting in Ringling Brothers Barnum & Bailey Circus ... the chance result of my visit with Bob Edgar ('26) in Grosse Points, and to Bob's contacts with the owners of the circus. Rudolph cavorts as one of the story-book characters ... a small pony with special antlers (a specially wired nose, of course) and a blanket proclaiming his name. The clown who runs along-side Rudolph alternately flashes Rudolph's nose and his own. (I enclose a couple of stats on this subject.)

I have another little juvenile story being published this year ... Winking Willie (a dog story) ... but I'm afraid he'll have a hard time keeping up with his predecessor. I'll send you a copy as soon as it's off the press.

With Rudolph, it's the old story of nothing succeeding like success. Now that he's up there, more and more manufacturers (including some of the biggest) are scurrying to climb on the band-wagon. All very exciting ... to the point of being scarcely believable.

I'm still at Wards in my job of Retail Copy Chief. Sometimes there aren't enough hours in the day (or night) to keep up the Ward job and all my Rudolph activities as well. Fortunately, one of the most important parts of my Ward job today is directing and coordinating all phases of Wards tremendous promotion of Rudolph and Rudolph merchandise.

To show you the extent of Wards promotion ... I attach samples of the puzzle-toy we distributed as a give-away last year, in a quantity of 3,500,000 ... and the luminous-ink toy we will distribute in a 4,000,000 quantity this Christmas.

That should tell you the story ... and <u>then</u> some ! If by chance you wish any further information, please get in touch with me.

With kindest regards, and thanks again for your interest.

Cordially yours,

Robert L. May

RLM:djm

P.S. The various enclosures mentioned (except the Rudolph product list attached) in this letter have been sent you under separate cover. In addition, I am enclosing a copy of the catalog being sent out this year (by Rudolph's publisher) to book stores and department stores all over the country. Please note particularly the outside and inside front covers, and pages 8, 10 and 11.

RUDOLPH PRODUCTS FOR CHRISTMAS 1948

Slippers	**Pin**
Moccasin-Socks	**Pendant**
Sweatshirts	**Bracelet**
Riding-Stick Toy	**School-bag**
Bank (nose lights-up with each coin)	**Snow-suit**
Jig-Saw Puzzles	**Cap**
Playskool Puzzle Plaque	**Scarfs**
RCA-Victor Record Album	**Socks**
Book	**Underwear**
Projector and Rudolph Film	**T-Shirts**
Parker Brothers Game	**Ties**
Christmas-Tree Ornament	**Overalls**
Child's Plate-Bowl-Mug set	**Dungarees**
Watch (by Ingraham)	**Play-suits**
Ring	**Pajamas**

RUDOLPH PRODUCTS NOW BEING DEVELOPED FOR CHRISTMAS 1949

Umbrella	**Handkerchief Sets**
Flashlight	**Baby Silverware**
Pull-toy	**Candles**
Pencil-box	**Yarn Pictures**
Clock	**Mask (with nose that lights)**
3-Dimensional Film	**Unbreakable Tumblers**
Child's Divided Grill Plate	**Compacts**
Lamp	**Dart Game**
Rubber Boot (By U.S. Rubber)	**Rattle**
Radio	

On August 27, 1948, Robert L. May wrote this letter (facsimile above, continued from previous two pages)
to his alma mater, Dartmouth College.

RUDOLPH THE RED-NOSED REINDEER — SELECTED DISCOGRAPHY

SINGLES

ARTIST	FLIP SIDE	LABEL	YEAR
Paul Anka	I Saw Mommy Kissing Santa Claus	ABC-Paramount	1960
Gene Autry	If It Doesn't Snow On Christmas	Columbia	1949
Jimmy Boyd	The Little Match Girl	Columbia	1953
The Cadillacs	Shack-a Doo	Josie	1956
Cheech & Chong	Santa Claus And His Old Lady	Ode	1977
The Chipmunks	Spain	Liberty	1960
Perry Como	Rudolph The Red-nosed Reindeer	RCA Victor	1955
	B-side sung by The Three Suns		
Bing Crosby	The Teddy Bear's Picnic	Decca	1950
The Crystals	I Saw Mommy Kissing Santa Claus	Pavillion	1982
	B-side sung by the Ronettes		
Red Foley	Frosty The Snowman	Decca	1950
Alan Jackson	We Three Kings	Arista	1996
	B-side sung by Blackhawk		
Spike Jones	All I Want For Christmas Is My Two Front Teeth	RCA Victor	1950
Sammy Kaye	Winter Wonderland	Columbia	1951
Guy Lombardo	Christmas Tree At Home	Decca	1951
Dean Martin	White Christmas	Capitol	1992
Mitch Miller	The Twelve Days Of Christmas	Columbia	1961
Willie Nelson	Pretty Paper	Columbia	1979
Nancy Sinatra	Winter Wonderland	Elektra	1981
The Smithereens	A Girl Like You	Capitol	1994
The Temptations	Silent Night	Gordy	1968
Mel Tillis	Winter Wonderland	Elektra	1981
Ernest Tubb	Christmas Is Just Another Day For Me	Decca	1961
The Ventures	Depression	EMI	1994

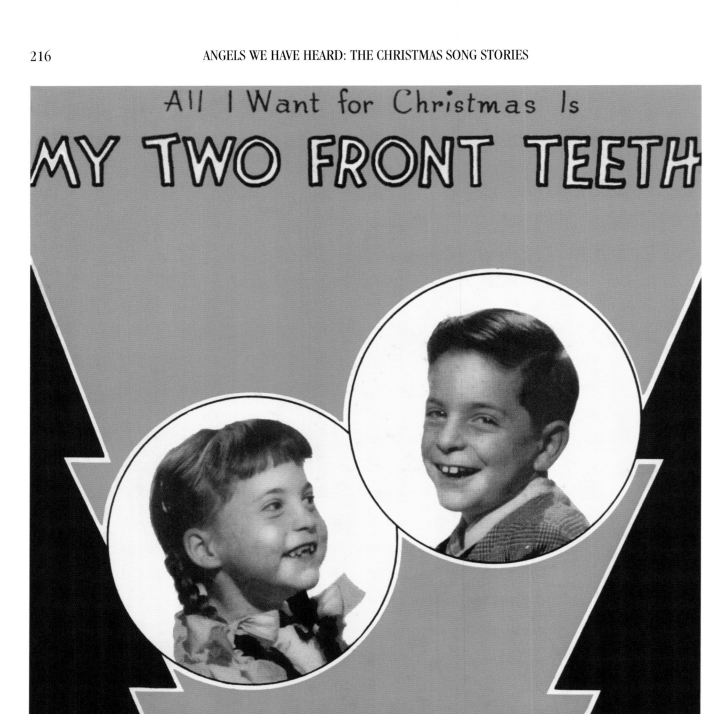

All I Want for Christmas Is

MY TWO FRONT TEETH

WORDS AND MUSIC BY
DON GARDNER

As Rudolph products continued to fly off Montgomery Ward shelves, this children's holiday novelty song, which was introduced on Perry Como's radio show, tickled the nation's funny bone when it was released in the late 1940's. The Nat King Cole Trio, with vocal group, The Starlighters, recorded one of the earliest takes on "Teeth." But it was novelty band leader Spike Jones who had the most success with it, selling over a million copies. He took it all the way to number one in 1948. Subsequently Jones rode the airwaves with his own version of "Rudolph" in 1950.

Price 50¢
in U.S.A.

Spike Jones' rendition of "Rudolph" comically shared vocal billing with the animated icon and his fellow reindeers. Jones went on to achieve a third children's novelty hit in 1952 with "I Saw Mommy Kissing Santa Claus." That same year, twelve-year-old Jimmy Boyd sang the tune on Frank Sinatra's TV variety show, and it soon became a number-one million-selling single. He followed this success the next year with his own version of "Rudolph." In 1954, he hoped lightning would strike twice when he recorded "I Saw Mommy Do The Mambo (With You Know Who)." A decade later The 4 Seasons rejuvenated Tommie Connor's "Mommy" when they released it as a single in 1964, backed with "Santa Claus Is Comin' To Town."

In the late 1940's, Leroy Anderson was busy arranging music for The Boston Pops Orchestra, which recorded his then instrumental "Sleigh Ride" in 1949. A year later Mitchell Parish added words to the song. "Sleigh Ride" would go on to become a Motown Christmas hit when The Ronettes recorded it in 1963 for the LP *A Christmas Gift For You From Phil Spector*. Parish is best known for co-writing the tin-pan-alley standard "Stardust," and penned a second holiday tune titled "Christmas Night In Harlem."

1950 was a tremendous year for Jay Livingston and Ray Evans, who saw Nat King Cole take their "Mona Lisa" all the way to number one. That same year, Bob Hope and Marilyn Maxwell sang the duo's "Silver Bells" for the first time in the movie *The Lemon Drop Kid*. Bing Crosby and Carol Richards soon followed with the first successful recording of it, and "Silver Bells" continued to gain popularity in the 1960's when versions were released by Earl Grant and Al Martino.

CAROLING, CAROLING — 1954

**WRITERS — ALFRED BURT
WIHLA HUTSON**

**ARTISTS —
THE COLUMBIA CHOIR &
THE RALPH CARMICHAEL
BRASS ENSEMBLE**

COLUMBIA RECORDS

Alfred Burt — 1942

*Anne Burt as depicted by
Melva (Copyright 1984
Augsberg Publishing)*

As thirty three-year-old Alfred Burt lay dying of lung cancer at his southern California home in the winter of 1954, his young wife Anne made a promise to him she would spend the rest of her life taking care of their baby daughter, Diane, and a diverse canon of Christmas songs he had been creating for over a decade — a musically rich and poetic tapestry including the warm-hearted whimsical ode, "Caroling, Caroling." Many of those tunes intimately represent the Burts' holiday seasons, since they were specifically written for annual Christmas cards they sent out to their own friends and family beginning in 1942. Although this music was never intended for commercial release, Anne Burt kept her promise of the heart by posthumously releasing her husband's songs as a "Christmas card to the world," ultimately giving him a gift of musical immortality.

The birth of "Caroling, Caroling," as well as all of Alfred Burt's soul-stirring holiday masterpieces, is as much a miraculous love story between him and his wife as it is a tale of family tradition, spiritual connections and the true meaning of Christmas giving. In 1922, Alfred's Episcopal minister father, Reverend Bates Burt, searched for a way to personally touch his Pontiac, Michigan, community during the holidays without giving in to the industrial world's materialistic gift-buying mentality. This was a practice he felt threatened to obscure the sacred message of Christ's arrival. Wishing to impart something of his spirit, he began a yearly tradition of composing a song at the piano in early autumn to mail out with his hand-made Christmas cards in December. As the tradition grew, it became a much-cherished symbol of hope for his parishioners, and people eagerly looked forward to learning a new song and then singing it throughout the days leading to the Holy Child's birth.

"My father-in-law thought that Christmas was getting too commercial," recalls Anne Burt, "and so he decided to create something personal to send to his parishioners and family. He started this tradition when my husband was two years old, and it continued until Al took over in 1942. He said, 'Now you're the musician — you've been through the university — you furnish the music and I'll furnish the words.'"

Reverend Bates' son, Alfred Burt was born on April 22, 1920, in the tiny town of Marquette, Michigan, a place of breathtaking natural beauty situated upon the pine-covered shores of Lake

Rev. Bates Burt

Many years after Rev. Bates Burt first collaborated with his son, the Alfred Burt Carols would go on to appear on countless projects, including "The Wonderful World Of Christmas" (above, 1975), which contains Tennessee Ernie Ford's "Caroling, Caroling."

Superior. Two years later, his family moved to Pontiac where young Al's musical and spiritual life became largely influenced by his father's All Saints' Episcopal Church ministry. As a child he wrote his first musical compositions for Easter and Christmas church festivals, studied piano, played trumpet, and later established a jazz dance band that played at religious functions — all with his father's enthusiastic guidance and permission.

Along with several teachers, Reverend Bates was able to establish a strong creative bond with Alfred, and Anne remembers how they were the driving force behind the dawning of her husband's unique ability to freely experiment with different musical styles: "They didn't put him in a box like so many teachers do. They didn't tell him to paint the leaves green when he wanted to paint them purple. And his father really allowed his creativity to flourish, encouraging him to play in his jazz band and even letting him set up a drum set in the rectory attic. He was considered to be a young genius, and that band ended up winning many competitions."

Alfred also sang in his father's church choir with Anne, his hometown sweetheart, a natural-born singer who would one day unknowingly help manifest his awe-inspiring musical destiny. "I went to All Saint's Episcopal Church," she says. "Al and I sang together there in what was known as The Young People's Choir — the church was the center of our activities when we were growing up and it was there that I got to know Al as an individual."

"We both went to Pontiac High School," she continues. "In 1937, after a school basketball game, we went down to a local ice cream parlor with all of our friends. One of the girls I was with liked Al, and after talking with him for awhile, he offered us a ride home but dropped her off first. From then on we started dating."

During this time another powerful church/choir connection of synchronicity helped shape the creative direction of Alfred Burt's life. In 1929, a woman by the name of Wihla Hutson became the organist for All Saint's Church, later taking on the additional duty of directing The Young People's Choir. Born on April 29, 1901, in East Gary, Indiana, Hutson divided her time between the church and working as a secretary for the Detroit Board of Education. One day she would go on to write the lyrics for "Caroling, Caroling," as well as

Alfred Burt leading the Junior Choir at All Saint's Church in Pontiac, Michigan (1936)

seven other Alfred Burt Christmas songs, assuming Reverend Bates' role after he passed away.

"Wihla had been part of our life and family at the church and we adored her," says Anne. "She wrote poetry for our choir dinner parties, and since she lived over forty-five minutes away, she would stay over night with the Burts whenever there was a winter storm." During those times, the family became intimately aware of Wihla's talent for writing when she joined along in their tradition of penning poetry to accompany their stocking presents. "We all learned that she had a wonderful gift for putting words into poetry, and she became very close to Al — before his voice changed he would walk in his pajamas from the rectory to the church when she needed him to replace a sick soprano. He would stand by the organ, sing and then go back to bed."

With all of these compelling influences under his belt, Alfred Burt went off to study music at the University Of Michigan.

Wihla Hutson

After graduating in 1942, he unknowingly became involved in a race against time.

In November of that same year, the first of the fifteen Christmas card carols he left behind immediately began to take shape. Reverend Bates found the lyrics for it in a Roman Catholic carol book, and they named their primary collaboration, "Christmas Cometh Caroling." It was one of seven consecutive carols the son/father duo would write and jointly send out to their Pontiac, Michigan, church community. "I was there that eventful day," remembers Anne, "when Al's father reminded him of the deadline for the printing of the

card. He hadn't set the lyrics to music and asked me if I minded waiting, then went to the family Steinway and in fifteen minutes wrote the music."[1]

World War II strongly influenced the Christmas card carols they wrote and sent out over the next three years, with their lyrics pondering a need for peace and offering Christianity as a solution to the conflict.

Ironically, it was his 1944 card entitled "Jesu Parvule" that convinced Anne to reunite with Al after a long separation. Since then an eye injury had redirected her life, causing her to leave behind her plans to become an elementary school teacher and instead join the navy as a surgical nurse. She received "Jesu Parvule" while stationed in San Diego. "We didn't see each other during the war and I was dating other people," she recalls, "but then he sent me a Christmas card that he and his father had created. In it he wrote a note saying that he didn't know what had transpired in my life, but he would like to hear from me. I came in shaking and thinking that I had to do something with this man — he seemed to be getting to me."

During the war, Al wrote arrangements and played in a base dance band, while Anne won a singing contest in New York City. The prize was a war bond, and she fondly remembers a woman handing it to her and whispering in her ear, 'What the hell are you doing in the navy with a voice like that!' "When I got to San Diego, I joined a dance band myself and I can still remember the boys' faces when I walked in that day and said, 'Hi, there, I'm a new W.A.V.E. on the base and I sing.' I did a radio show with Bob Crosby from the naval station that was broadcast all over the world in 1944. We sang the duet, 'Put Your Arms Around Me Honey.'"

In 1945, with the war almost over, the Christmas card Al sent Anne convinced her to visit him in Texas. He hitchhiked to see her in Fort Worth, met her train, and ended up proposing to her in church upon bended knee with "Rosa Madre," a favorite song of hers, playing in the background. Soon after, Reverend Bates married the engaged couple at his Michigan church, and at once the newlyweds decided to couple their musical talents, creating a professional dance band they called "The Hal Richards Orchestra." It toured across the country for fifteen months.

Alfred Burt

Bob Crosby (1937)

"Al wrote all of the arrangements, played the trumpet, and I sang pop standards like "Honey Keep Your Mind On Me" and "Apple Blossom Time." At times we even shared the spotlight together as vocalists."

After the band's demise, they decided to move to New York City, the place where Alfred Burt began to make the music industry connections Anne would desperately need to continue his work following his tragic death.

His career came to a critical juncture in 1949 when he became jazz trumpeter and arranger for a commercially popular act called "The Alvino Rey Orchestra," featuring the well-known King Sisters on vocals. By 1948, Rey's group racked

up six top-ten hits, reaching number one with "Deep In The Heart Of Texas." Married to one of the King Sisters was James Conkling, soon-to-be president of Columbia Records, who later became instrumental in helping Anne record the carols. Conkling would also help get their work to one of the most successful singers of the time — Nat King Cole.

By then, with Al on the road promoting his career, Wihla and Anne decided to begin working together on his carols. "Dad Burt had died and I was expecting our first child," says Anne. "I went back to Michigan for six months, and Wihla and I went out to dinner one November night. She asked me what she should write about for the carol that year, and I told her that we should do a song for our baby — Al wants to write a lullaby." They sent this collaboration with their 1949 Christmas cards, aptly naming it "Carol of the Mother." That night the two women also had a conversation concerning race, with Anne espousing her belief regarding the "universality of Christ," and the fact that "children have no color line and must be taught to hate." Wihla would incorporate this idea into the words she wrote for the 1951 carol, "Some Children See Him."

"I shall never forget when Al, after his father's death, asked me to write words for further carols so that the family custom might be continued," recalls Wihla Hutson. "I was deeply touched and could hardly believe that this great honor was mine."

"As to the subject matter," she continued, "a few times the themes were jointly agreed upon before hand. When Diane

The King Sisters

was on the way we wrote "Carol of the Mother." One or two of the texts had personal overtones: "Come, Dear Children" and "We'll Dress The House" were the happy and busy Burt household at Christmas time. To know that Al asked me for the words was all the urging I needed. I still wonder if I really wrote the texts myself or whether an angel was pushing the pen!"[2]

In 1950, Al and Anne decided to buy a home in California and began settling down with their new baby. For the next few years they continued to create the carols with Al writing the music, Wihla mailing her lyrics from Michigan and Anne editing those words, as well as choosing original artwork for

This 1965 holiday LP contains four Alfred Burt carols and was recorded with The Alvino Rey Orchestra and Ralph Carmichael under the vocal direction of Jimmy Joyce.

the cards. Their Christmas card list had grown from fifty to four hundred fifty, and with Anne now expecting a second child, she and her husband were experiencing the happiest times of their lives.

To top it off, in 1952, as Alfred Burt began writing music for television, he experienced one of the biggest breaks of his career when a choral group known as The Blue Rays performed "Come, Dear Children" at the King Sisters' annual holiday party. It was a significant event — the first time the Hollywood community heard one of the Burt carols sung live — and it exposed his music to industry executives who soon helped Anne introduce them to a world-wide audience. "It was the hit of the party," she says. "People were thrilled to death because the harmonies and style were so new."

The moment was bittersweet — little did the guests at that festive gathering know they were listening to one of the last songs Alfred Burt would ever write.

"In 1953, our whole life would change," wrote Anne. "Al came down with a virus flu that left a lingering cough. Entering the hospital for tests, he was still optimistic that it was a simple problem. Neither of us were prepared for the results. He had lung cancer."[3] Due to the stress from this chilling diagnosis, Anne ended up losing her baby.

That year, as she used her nursing skills to care for Al at home, Anne made sure a pad of paper for writing music was always kept by his bedside. Columbia Records' James Conkling now felt an urgent need to act upon his desire to work with the Burts on a demo tape for a future record, and

asked if a few more tunes could be written for the project. As Al wrote the music from his bedside, Wihla was immediately contacted, and swiftly wrote the words to "O Hearken Ye." At this time she also composed lyrics for two other songs never sent out as cards — "We'll Dress The House" and "Caroling, Caroling."

For the demo tape "a volunteer chorus of the finest singers in Hollywood met in the North Hollywood Mormon Church," recalls Anne Burt, "and Al's wheelchair could easily enter from the parking lot into the auditorium where he led the session. In our home, over a cup of hot chocolate, Al reviewed the taping, thrilled at the turnout for him, the lovely voices, and the fact something he had written would be released. 'This is the happiest day of my life,' he remarked."[4]

Tennessee Ernie Ford titled his 1958 Christmas album after Alfred Burt's last written carol. The set also contains two other Burt compositions — "Some Children See Him" and "O Hearken Ye."

That batch of demo songs also included "The Star Carol," a song Alfred Burt wrote the day before he died. Anne vividly remembers this time of what she believes to be his finest creation: "When I heard the 'Star Carol,' that's when I knew Al was dying. His legs were in traction, he was down to fifty-five pounds, and I hadn't cried because Al wanted the household to be happy for Diane. But I was getting weary of the disease and had to get out of the house. That's when I looked up at the stars and heaven and said, 'God if you're going to take him, take him now, the end is near.' That song was so pure, but life gets so simple when death gets so close."

"When I came back in he said, 'Honey I'm getting so tired.' I said, 'I know, if you're holding on for Diane and me, don't. I'll take care of her.' He relaxed and was ready to let go, and that's the moment I promised him I would also take care of his music. I took that promise seriously — when it comes to the Burt carols I have always made sure they were kept pure."

Anne and Diane Burt as depicted by Melva (Copyright 1984 Augsberg Publishing)

Alfred Burt died on February 6, 1954. An hour after his death a signed contract from Columbia Records to record his carols was delivered to the Burts' doorstep. That same year, upon the first Christmas without her husband, Anne published the carols, released the record, and sent "The Star Carol" out as the last Christmas card carol to friends and family. It was signed by her and Diane, and included a small note "telling of the end of their tradition," and the beginning of the Chistmas legacy of love Alfred Burt unknowingly gave to the world.

Alfred Burt

Nat King Cole

A CONVERSATION WITH ANNE BURT

Were you with your husband on the day he wrote "Caroling, Caroling?"

Yes — it was written in November of 1953, three months before he died, so he was very ill at the time — it took an awful lot out of him to get it done.

Where was it written?

He wrote it at our home in southern California because he didn't like hospitals. I had a medical background and took care of him. I put a hospital bed in our bedroom and moved in a little table and chair for my daughter to share dinner hour with him.

How long did it take him to write it?

The music was written spontaneously. My husband had that talent — he could sit down at the piano when guests were over and instantly whip off a few arrangements for us to sing. He heard and wrote "Caroling, Caroling" in his head, as with all of his music — he never needed a piano to write anything. That's why I would leave a pad of paper at his bedside so that he could write anytime he got inspired. Jimmy Joyce, a friend of ours, who would later work with me on a second album of Alfred's carols, came over and played it on the piano, and that's the first time I heard it.

Did you ever send "Caroling, Caroling" out with your Christmas cards?

No. When we found out that Al was dying, Jimmy Joyce contacted our friend Jim Conkling, who was president of Columbia Records. He had already heard one of the carols sung at a Christmas party, so he was aware of Alfred's talent, but he had no idea that this young man would die at the age of thirty-three. When he heard of Al's condition though, he wanted us to immediately make a demo tape of Alfred's carols, and subsequently realized we needed more music. Al quickly wrote four more songs with Wihla Hutson, one of which was "Caroling, Caroling."

Nat King Cole's "The Christmas Song" LP was released in 1962, and included Alfred Burt's "Caroling, Caroling." This followed Cole's earlier release of Burt's carol on his first Christmas set entitled "The Magic Of Christmas."

The Christmas Song
MERRY CHRISTMAS TO YOU

WORDS AND MUSIC BY

Mel Tormé and Robert Wells

"It was so damn hot today. I thought I'd write something to cool myself off. All I could think of was Christmas and cold weather." Those were the words of Robert Wells, who co-wrote "The Christmas Song" with Mel Torme on a hot day in July 1945 at his home in California. In June of the following year, the Nat King Cole Trio went into a New York studio to record a simple piano version of it without strings. Cole's wife Maria, along with his manager, convinced him to go back into the studio two months later to re-record it with strings and a full orchestra, in order to make it more commercial. That version debuted in November 1946 as a Capitol Records single backed with "In The Cool Of The Evening," and went on to sell over a million units.

BURKE AND VAN HEUSEN, INC.
MUSIC PUBLISHERS
1619 BROADWAY   NEW YORK, N. Y.

CHRISTMAS WITH...
BING CROSBY
NAT KING COLE
DEAN MARTIN

SL-6925
STEREO

1973

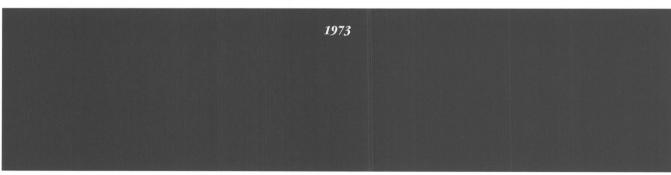

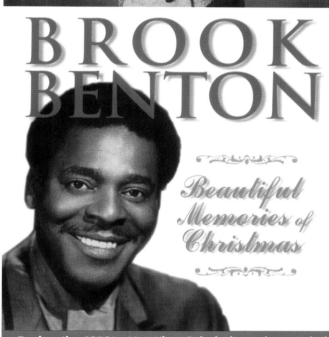

During the 1950's, Nat King Cole led a quiet revolution when he shattered mainstream culture's silent color barrier. Among the African-American performers who followed him, and became important interpreters of holiday music, were Mahalia Jackson (upper left), Charles Brown (upper right), Harry Belafonte (lower right) and Brook Benton (lower left). A year after Cole's "Caroling, Caroling" was introduced, Mahalia Jackson's first Christmas LP, *Sweet Little Jesus Boy*, debuted. And in 1956, Aladdin Records released Charles Brown's self-written "Merry Christmas Baby," which was later recorded by many other artists including Elvis Presley. That same year, Harry Belafonte recorded the calypso gem, "Mary's Boy Child," written by his colleague, Jester Hairston. "Child" was first launched as a single and later included on Belafonte's 1958 album, *To Wish You A Merry Christmas*. Brook Benton began releasing Christmas singles in the late 1950's, and in 1963 he achieved a top-five holiday hit on Billboard's Christmas singles chart with the song, "You're All I Want For Christmas."

Nat King Cole was one of the first popular singers to record "Caroling, Caroling" — how did he become involved?

It was through James Conkling and Ralph Carmichael, Nat's producer at the time. He was a personal friend of ours, and he played "Caroling, Caroling" for Nat King Cole after Al died. Nat's manager asked Ralph Carmichael about the song, and he told him it was a new American Christmas carol written by a friend of his who was now deceased. His reply was that his client wasn't doing any new carols for his upcoming Christmas album, just old standards. Well, at that time Nat King Cole walked into the office, heard it playing and insisted on including it, letting everyone know that he was in fact recording another new song for the project called "A Cradle In Bethlehem." Eventually, Nat's recording ended up bringing new attention to all of the Alfred Burt carols.

Did Nat King Cole admire your husband's work?

Yes, and sadly they both died from the same disease, lung cancer. I went to see Nat in the hospital shortly before he died and gave him a Burt Carol Christmas album. He ended up giving it to his clergyman at his church and told him that it was his favorite Christmas album.

When was "Caroling, Caroling" first recorded?

In April of 1954 for my husband's first Christmas album entitled *The Christmas Mood — The Alfred Burt Christmas Carols*, which included only nine out of fifteen of the carols. I used the royalties from it to record a second album in 1964 that contained the entire canon.

Who sang on that first album?

A group we named The Columbia Choir, and it was made up of about twenty of the finest Hollywood backup singers of the time. They did the whole thing a cappella, and it became commercially available in November 1954. Alfred worked with them on the demo tape while he was in a wheelchair.

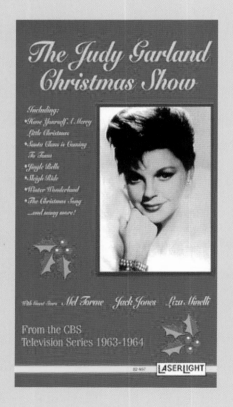

The Sinatra Family (upper left) recorded Alfred Burt's "Some Children See Him" in 1969. Nat King Cole's daughter, Natalie (upper right), recorded "Caroling, Caroling" for her 1994 "Holly & Ivy" disc. That song was also a part of "Christmas Eve With Johnny Mathis" (lower left), as well as Judy Garland's 1963 Christmas television show, which was later released on video (lower right).

When did you find out from Columbia Records that they would make an album of your husband's songs?

The contract for the recording arrived the day Al died, so the end of his mortal life became the beginning of his musical life.

Is it true that George Winston was inspired by this album?

Yes. In fact he included one of my husband's unreleased songs on his 20th anniversary album. It was another lullaby he wrote for our daughter, called "Sleep Baby Mine." George also recorded two other Burt carols for his Christmas album.

Who else has recorded "Caroling, Caroling?"

Many people have recorded it since 1954. Mel Torme, The Osmond Brothers, The Sinatra Family, Natalie Cole, Maureen McGovern, Johnny Mathis, and even The Dalmatians. Disney did a parody on it to promote the new movie of *101 Dalmatians* before it opened. They played it for me beforehand to see if I liked it, and I noticed that they had taken out the words, 'caroling, caroling.' They felt that everyone knew it, but I insisted that they keep the words in there. On our way to a party, my daughter asked me if her father would have wanted animated dogs singing one of his songs. I said, 'Honey, it's secular, besides we're going to a party where you're going to see old film of a show your father was in where he was in drag, wearing a wig and apron, and singing falsetto. I think Mother can OK a Dalmatian singing the carol.'

What did you think of Natalie Cole's version of the song?

I was thrilled to death with it — she's one of the greatest singers that ever came down the pike. I love her interpretation.

How does "Caroling, Caroling" thematically fit into the whole canon of Christmas songs your husband wrote?

I don't think it has the emotional quality of his song "Some Children See Him," or the haunting aspects of "The Star Carol," because it's an up-tune and it's secular. And I keep telling people that they shouldn't sing it too fast because of the way Al wrote it — it's supposed to have the feel of a sleigh ride — and that's the tempo he wanted for it. A lot of people try to do it too fast and it's not that way at all. It has to be relaxed.

When did Wihla Hutson write the lyrics?

At the end of 1953, the same time its music was composed. We told her we needed a secular song, and the idea came from her past experiences with Michigan and Indiana snows.

What has been your specific role with the music after Alfred died?

Well, first of all, I know Al's story because I lived it with him. When the contract arrived, I went to New York and gave them that story so they could include it with the carols. I allowed the carols to grow, and have been involved in all of the legal aspects from the beginning. I won't legally consent to anything anyone tries to do with the carols that takes away from their purity. I knew that there was a need in the world for Al's music, and after the first album came out with only part of the canon, I reinvested the money from it into a second recording. I later spent my own money to put both of these out in CD format, since I was getting a lot of calls from people whose vinyl had worn out.

Did you personally finance the second recording of your husband's work?

Yes, I paid for the recording session. It was released in 1964 and we titled it *This Is Christmas.*

When you say there is a need out there for your husband's music, what exactly do you mean?

Well, it's the same reason my father-in-law started the carols to begin with. Christmas has become too commercial, and we've lost the essence and real meaning of it. Alfred's carols give people a new outlook on life, and they offer people a tradition from the past. This music is as inspirational to me as it is to other people. When I went into surgery for a mastectomy, I used my husband's carols to relax me before going in, and they brought me back out of it afterwards.

Why do people still listen to these songs?

Al was very much ahead of his time. People like Nelson Riddle have told me that he took an accepted form of a Christmas carol and put the new jazz innovations into that form.

Was he fusing jazz with Christmas music from the beginning?

Yes, because he loved jazz, and we would go to all of the jazz clubs in Michigan and wouldn't leave until the last note was played at two in the morning. We would also frequently go to Motown to hear African-American jazz.

Why aren't there many good Christmas songs written today?

The problem is that the songs aren't coming from the heart. They're made up depending on the commercial need. Our carols came from the heart — they're the natural outgrowth of our life, and life is so much more interesting than anything contrived.

The above compilations were released in the 1960's and included an Alfred Burt carol. Pictured from left to right are: Grants Department Store's "A Very Merry Christmas," "The Sound Of Christmas" & "The Sound Of Christmas Vol. 2."

THE ALFRED BURT CAROLS

CHRISTMAS COMETH CAROLING — 1942

WHAT ARE THE SIGNS — 1943

JESU PARVULE — 1944

AH, BLEAK AND CHILL THE WINTRY WIND — 1945

ALL ON A CHRISTMAS MORNING — 1946

NIGH BETHLEHEM — 1947

CHRIST IN THE STRANGER'S GUISE — 1948

CAROL OF THE MOTHER — 1949

THIS IS CHRISTMAS — 1950

SOME CHILDREN SEE HIM — 1951

COME, DEAR CHILDREN — 1952

O HEARKEN YE — 1953

CAROLING, CAROLING — 1953

WE'LL DRESS THE HOUSE — 1953

THE STAR CAROL — 1954

Each of the above albums contains one or more Burt carols (see discography). Shown clockwuise are: Kenny Loggins' "December," Aaron Neville's "Soulful Christmas," Liz Story's "The Gift," Andy Williams' "Merry Christmas," George Winston's "December," Mannheim Steamroller's "Christmas Extraordinaire," The Lennon Sisters' "Noel," Peggy Lee's "Christmas Carousel," Perry Como's "Greatest Christmas Songs" and The Boston Pops' "We Wish You A Merry Christmas."

THE ALFRED BURT CAROLS — SELECTED DISCOGRAPHY

ARTIST	BURT CAROL	ALBUM
Julie Andrews	This Is Christmas	1990 Hallmark Sound Of Christmas
Debby Boone	Some Children See Him	Home For Christmas
The Boston Pops	*Various*	*Various*
Diahann Carroll	Some Children See Him	*Various*
Nat King Cole	Caroling, Caroling	*Various*
Natalie Cole	Caroling, Caroling	The Holly And The Ivy
Columbia Choir	**All Burt Carols**	**The Alfred Burt Christmas Carols**
Perry Como	Caroling, Caroling	The Perry Como Christmas Album
	Some Children See Him	Greatest Christmas Songs
Harry Connick, Jr.	Some Children See Him	A Jazzy Wonderland
Bing Crosby *(with Jack Halloran &* *The Voices Of Christmas)*	*Various*	A Time To Be Jolly
Dino	Caroling, Caroling	A Wonderful Time Of The Year
Tennessee Ernie Ford	*Various*	*Various*
Dave Grusin	Some Children See Him	A GRP Christmas Collection
Hollywood Pops Orchestra	Caroling, Caroling	The Sound Of Christmas, Vol. 2
The King Family	*Various*	*Various*
Peggy Lee	The Star Carol	Christmas Carousel
The Lennon Sisters	The Star Carol	Noel
Kenny Loggins	Some Children See Him	December
The Manhattan Transfer	Caroling, Caroling	The Christmas Album
Mannheim Steamroller	Some Children See Him	Christmas Extraordinaire
Johnny Mathis	Caroling, Caroling	Christmas Eve With Johnny Mathis
Maureen McGovern	*Various*	Christmas With Maureen McGovern
Aaron Neville	The Star Carol	Soulful Christmas
Simon & Garfunkel	The Star Carol	A Very Merry Christmas
	The Star Carol	Old Friends
Frank Sinatra, Jr.	Some Children See Him	The Sinatra Family Wish You A Merry Christmas
Liz Story	We'll Dress The House	The Gift
The Voices Of Jimmy Joyce	**All Burt Carols**	**This Is Christmas**
Fred Waring	*Various*	*Various*
Andy Williams	Some Children See Him	Merry Christmas
George Winston	Some Children See Him	December (20th Anniv. Ed.)
	Sleep Baby Mine	

SIMPLIFIED ACCORDION SOLO

IT'S BEGINNING TO LOOK LIKE CHRISTMAS

Words and Music by MEREDITH WILLSON

Among the many artists who recorded Alfred Burt's carols was Perry Como, whose soothing voice was a perfect match for holiday music. Within a thirty-year period, Como released over twenty Christmas singles, and his bubbly, Crosby-esque style helped make Meredith Willson's "It's Beginning To Look Like Christmas" an immediate favorite upon its arrival in 1951. Willson penned it while he was writing *The Music Man*, which opened on Broadway the week of Christmas, 1957. Like his hit musical, this yuletide classic addressed the innocent charm of small-town America, a theme Perry Como revisited when he recorded "(There's No Place Like) Home For The Holidays," released in 1954 (see right page). It would debut five months before Bill Haley & The Comets' "(We're Gonna) Rock Around The Clock" became the first number-one rock record.

50¢

PLYMOUTH MUSIC CO.
1270 SIXTH AVE., NEW YORK 19, N. Y

RECORDED BY PERRY COMO ON RCA-VICTOR RECORDS

(There's No Place Like)
HOME FOR THE HOLIDAYS

Lyrics by AL STILLMAN

Music by ROBERT ALLEN

PRICE
1.50
IN U.S.A.

SALES AND SHIPPING:
8th FLOOR — 17 WEST 60th STREET
NEW YORK, N.Y. 10023

RONCOM MUSIC COMPANY

jingle-bell rock

Words and Music by JOE BEAL and JIM BOOTHE

CHET

ATKINS

PLATTERS

BOBBY HELMS

PAUL and PAULA

CHUBBY CHECKER

PARADISE ISLANDERS

BOBBY VEE   CHIPMUNKS

BOBBY RYDELL   THREE SUNS

TERESA BREWER   EDDY ARNOLD

LENNIE DEE   JOHNNY DORELLI

JIMMY MAKULIS   MAX BYGRAVES

JAN GARBER   BABY BELL   LOR CRANE

THE ABERBACH GROUP
Sole Selling Agent:
Hill and Range Songs, Inc.
241 West 72nd Street
New York, N.Y. 10023

$1.50

Distributed by

JINGLE BELL ROCK — 1957

WRITERS: JOSEPH BEAL
JIM BOOTHE

PRODUCER: OWEN BRADLEY

ARTIST: BOBBY HELMS

DECCA RECORDS

Even though its roots are firmly planted in Nashville, Tennessee, its lyrics have nothing to do with rock music, and its charismatic singer came from a country-western world, "Jingle Bell Rock," released in December 1957, is considered to be the very first rock and roll Christmas song to gain mainstream acceptance. Like Brenda Lee's "Rockin' Around The Christmas Tree," Bobby Helms' hit shot the relatively new star to unparalleled heights of holiday immortality. Likewise, it was an exciting extension of the then-burgeoning Nashville scene, and represented an experimental 'country-politan' sound that cleverly merged various musical styles of the time.

A Hoosier native, Bobby Helms was born on August 15, 1933, and began singing at the age of nine on his father's *Monroe County Jamboree* radio program in Bloomington, Indiana. As a teenager, he started appearing on *The Hayloft Frolic* television show and caught the ear of country-music maven Ernest Tubb, who recognized his natural talent and invited him to Nashville. It was Helms' big break, and he subsequently landed a record deal with Decca Records' country music division in 1956.

At this time, the country music world was in serious trouble. Its record sales were quickly dwindling, and it was desperately struggling to redefine itself as it began to face stiff competition from a daring new style of music best symbolized by a trend-setting newcomer named Elvis Presley. To regain its audience, it needed to recreate its rural past by turning it into something that sounded more like the city.

Ernest Tubb (1948)

In 1957, when 23-year-old Bobby Helms released "Fraulein," his first single, he unknowingly found himself caught between the rugged Ernest-Tubb-country of his youth and the unruffled Nashville territory newly architected by his producer Owen Bradley, and his vocal arranger Anita Kerr. Together with guitarist/producer Chet Atkins, and a slew of talented Nashville session players, they set out to polish, commercialize and gentrify country music. They made it less twangy by eschewing fiddles. They made it jazzier by adding horns. They made it 'popier' by replacing steel guitars with violins, and nasal yodeling with cooing, inoffensive background choral harmony. And they wound up creating a brand new style of country music called The Nashville Sound.

Bobby Helms' "Fraulein" well epitomized this awkward transitional period from old country to new country, since it started out with a lively fiddle yet included Kerr's candied vocals. It was played simultaneously in the autumn of 1957 at pop and country radio stations across the nation, and became an important bridge to Helms' immediate follow-up

smash, "My Special Angel." This top-ten pop record contained all the glossy elements of the new Nashville Sound, and set the stage for the entrance of what would become Bobby Helms' most enduring signature song, "Jingle Bell Rock."

That song's producer would be Owen Bradley, a proficient musician who developed an ear for both pop and country music early on in his career as he simultaneously played around Nashville with his own Big Band orchestra. He also spent time working in various positions at WSM, one of the largest country radio stations in the USA. He moved over to Decca Records in 1947, where he went on to guide the careers of singers like Patsy Cline, Burl Ives, Loretta Lynn and Brenda Lee. Later in his career, he would help develop a new sound for country-pop star k.d. Lang.

In 1955 Bradley opened up Music City's first recording studio in an old home situated on a quiet street in Nashville. It was located on 16th Avenue South, and marked the beginning of Music Row. At the time it had what was considered to be one of the best acoustic environments in the world, and it quickly became the recording birthplace of scores of hit

1957

Owen Bradley (c. 1970)

records including Gene Vincent's "Be-Bop-A-Lu," Brenda Lee's "I'm Sorry," and three of Bobby Helms' top-selling singles.

One of those singles would be "Jingle Bell Rock," which according to Bradley "was recorded on very inexpensive equipment around September 1957." In addition to producing the session, Bradley played piano on the song as well, and remembers it was one of his "earlier sessions done in a little studio downstairs. It was a very small room where a whole bunch of hits were cut including 'Fraulein' and 'My Special Angel.'"

"It was a little bitty room in this real old house," remembers Anita Kerr, Grammy-award-winning vocalist and lead backup singer on Helms' holiday hit. "It was the only studio on the whole street, and it was right after Owen had bought it, so he was still experimenting, moving microphones around and moving the rhythm section in this corner or that corner to find the best place to get the best sound."

Kerr grew up in Memphis, Tennessee, and formed her own singing group in 1949. Known as the Anita Kerr Singers, the group gained enormous popularity in the 50's and 60's, singing backup on dozens of pop and country records including Roy Orbison's "Only The Lonely," Eddy Arnold's "Make The World Go Away," and all of Brenda Lee's early hits. Her close-harmony vocal arrangements helped define the seminal Nashville Sound, and she is credited with co-creating a brand new style of crossover music.

Back in the late 50's, Anita Kerr and her singers were in hot demand as they worked with Owen Bradley on a regular basis. Since they had sung on two of Helms' previous hits produced by Bradley, he hired them once again for "Jingle Bell Rock."

Remembering that recording session, Kerr recalls she had very little time to prepare for the groundbreaking event: "I didn't even hear the song until we walked into the studio that

day and we rehearsed it quite a few times. We arranged it on the spot, which is unheard of today. In those days we used to do four or six songs in three hours, now it takes months or years to do one album."

"That day we sang everything at the same time together and we all performed live with the band and went straight to tape. We were on our own microphone and Bobby Helms had his own, and we stood around our mike and kind of faced him. We were three feet away from him and could see him and mouth the words with him so that we would phrase everything together when it was our turn to sing."

"On average we had about forty-five minutes to work on the song and didn't have time to analyze it," admits Bradley. "'Jingle Bell Rock's' arrangement was done on the spot and everybody in the room contributed to it. Bobby didn't read music, so we just gave him a piece of paper with the words on it and had him memorize the melody that day. The Anita Kerr Singers had their own way of making up their arrangements, and the band the same thing. This song was done in the same spontaneous manner that we did most everything and this was one that we were lucky on."

"In those days we only had mono," he continues. "We didn't have stereo, so we had only one track. When we finished the record, we walked out of the studio and that was it, so we had only one shot at it. We couldn't change the content of the record after it was done. Now you can change anything on the record afterwards, you can alter one part without affecting the others."

Before entering the recording studio, Bradley's boss sent him a demo of "Jingle Bell Rock" from his office in New York City. He requested that Bobby Helms "learn and record it" since he was "coming off two hit songs." Immediately, Bradley knew the unique musical chemistry he shared with Kerr would be perfect for a certain sound he hoped to create.

"I used the Anita Kerr Singers when I wanted a choir sound," he says. "I'm an old musician and arranger, and I sort of looked at this from a musical standpoint. I wanted this choral sound, and I think that set it up as a Christmas song. It just so happened that Anita's group had what I was looking for. They had female voices, which gave it a choral sound rather than a male quartet sound."

"I think we're a big part of the record," adds Kerr. "We're a big part of the sound. And I think because of the way we sounded and because of the harmonies that we used, which were fairly modern for that time, it made it more of a pop song than if we hadn't been on it. And we were tickled to death that it became a hit. I'm surprised that it's lasted so long but I can see why. It's a catchy Christmas song. Even though it was recorded so many years ago in mono, to this day it still sounds good."

A key ingredient of this Nashville Sound was a core group of Nashville session musicians who worked with Kerr and Bradley regularly, and were used to dabbling in many different styles of music. Since the recording of "Jingle Bell Rock" was done in an old-fashioned way (the singers performed live with the musicians, making things up as they went along), it was important that everyone be on friendly territory conducive to creativity.

Among these innovative players known as the "Nashville Cats" was Hank "Sugarfoot" Garland, a brilliant jazz guitarist who played on other Bobby Helms records, and just about every Nashville session in the late 50's. He's credited with creating the bell-like guitar lick on the opening of Patsy Cline's "I Fall To Pieces," and came up with the jazzy electric guitar part at the beginning of "Jingle Bell Rock." It's hard to imagine what the song would sound like without the guitar riffs he came up with the day of the recording, riffs heard throughout the song's two-minute-plus playing period.

"We were all a part of that Nashville Sound," says Kerr. "We were still a small group of musicians and singers that played together regularly."

"Actually, when they talk about the Nashville Sound, it was not so much a sound but a method," adds Bradley. "The players would contribute not only their playing but their ideas as well. If you have an orchestra or a huge band you just can't do that."

And he remembers this tight-knit group approached "Jingle Bell Rock" with the same passion they brought to all their endeavors: "The only difference was this time we had a Christmas song that was a novelty, so we just gave it the best shot we could. And it was a helluva good song, let's face it when you've got a good song you have to do a lot to mess it up."

"Jingle Bell Rock" was a Christmas song with a radical sound, and that worried both producer and singer. Owen

Hank "Sugarfoot" Garland

Bradley didn't know if "the public would buy it," and was unsure of "mixing rock with Christmas music," because to do so was highly unusual for the time period. "Everybody had been doing more or less the traditional type things. People thought rock was sort of evil, so there was some reluctance to do it. But I don't think we were consciously trying to make a rock sound. We were all going through a transitional period of trying to cope with rock and roll. We had lots of hit country records, but some of us were coming out of the pop music world, the kind of music Frank Sinatra did. And some of the musicians in our little group had played in the staff orchestra at WSM country radio, where I worked."

Bobby Helms, like everyone else, was straddling two separate musical worlds. "'Fraulein' had a country fiddle on it but we had a semi-rock-and-roll piano and drum sounds as well," says Bradley. "At the time Bobby wasn't that anxious to

Chet Atkins, co-creator of the Nashville Sound (1958)

record 'Jingle Bell Rock,' he had something else in mind, and might have thought it would ruin his image since he started out as a country artist."

"But none of us knew what we were doing and were just trying to hang on. We weren't really into rock and roll, and we didn't look at 'Jingle Bell Rock' as a real rock and roll song. But rock music at that time included pop, r&b, and country music elements, and a lot of this stuff sort of just happened. I don't think anyone was smart enough to sit down with a pencil and paper and figure out how to do it."

"At the time I thought Bobby was awfully country to be singing such a pop song," adds Kerr. "But the musicians were playing country and pop, and we did loads of country sessions, and then turned around and sang pop songs on *The Arthur Godfrey Show*. So 'Jingle Bell Rock' was ultimately merging pop with country, and its rhythm section or its drums are what in that day turned it into rock."

The song's writers, Joseph Beal and James Boothe, weren't writing about rock music when they penned what would become the first rock and roll Christmas song. In an interview Beal granted to *The Press of Atlantic City*, published on May 18, 1958, he was certain that his song would become "a Christmas annual," and said that "the rock in the title does not come from Rock and Roll, but from an idea acquired during a New England winter. It's about the rocking of the sleigh as it is pulled by a horse through snow, setting alive several sets of jingle bells." He admitted that this misunderstanding ultimately boosted the record's sales to rock-loving teenagers. "It's the kids now who make the hits," he said. "The adults have nothing to do with it."

Beal was born in Braintree, Massachusetts, on June 25, 1900. After graduating from Boston University, he joined *The Boston Evening Transcript* and became its youngest editor. He served time in World War II, and later made a career change when he moved over to television as director of programming at WDSU-TV, New Orleans. He broke the deep

Joseph Beal

south media's color line when he controversially chose to televise a four-character African-American drama.

In 1954, a friend invited him to co-write the ballad, "Unsuspecting Heart," which singer Sunny Gale released the following year. Three years later, on December 23, 1957, "Jingle Bell Rock" entered Billboard's pop singles chart, ultimately peaked at number six and sold close to 500,000 records in its first year alone. It would become only one of seven Christmas songs in history to crack that chart's top ten, and the songwriter's only lifelong hit record. Oddly enough, as successful as it was, Decca Records only released it as a single and never included it on a Bobby Helms album.

In 1965, Bobby Helms re-recorded his trademark evergreen for Kapp Records. By 1967, "Jingle Bell Rock" had sold more than three million copies, and had been recorded by many other artists including a Chubby Checker/Bobby

Rydell duet, and versions sung by Chet Atkins, the Chipmunks, Hall & Oates, and Bobby Sherman. Yet Beal considered his incredible success to be a mere fluke. "It's just a streak of luck," he said. "There are guys who have been wearing out shoe leather for years who probably write better songs than we do. It's a matter of coming to the right publisher at the right time with the right type of song."

The timing was right for an artistic collaboration to develop between Beal and "Jingle Bell Rock's" other half, James Boothe, a Sweetwater, Texas, native born on May 14, 1917, who shared a similar past with his partner. Boothe was educated at the University Of Southern California, spent time working as a newspaper reporter and served in the Second World War. He was also a poet, whose work won university honors, and he was published regularly in *Poetry*, a national magazine of verse.

His future occupation was foreshadowed in a hometown newspaper interview he gave during his last year at USC. "The best training in the mechanics of the art of poetry writing can be obtained in the study of music," he said, "especially in writing song lyrics." And when putting together a book of his aunt's posthumous poems after he returned from the war, he wrote: "The most important thing about writing song lyrics was to do poetry and to become aware of the rhythm of life and the technique of rhyming."

According to Maud Jennings, a cousin of Boothe's and executor of his estate, "Jingle Bell Rock," was his only commercial success, even though he penned many songs after moving to New York City in the early 1950's. Jennings re-

members Boothe as an "exceedingly kind and generous" man "different from his family," who regularly sent home presents and demo records of his songs. Boothe originally set out to write music for the movies, yet found Hollywood stifling to his sensitive nature.

In conversations Jennings had with her cousin, she remembers him talking about the songwriting process he shared with Beal: "I remember on one occasion talking to Jim and asking him how he did his work with Joe and he said we do it together. I will come up with a tune and he might have a theme for it, and then we'll work it out on the piano. It was really very much a cooperative thing."

Although Beal composed many songs without Boothe, including a holiday tune called "Winter Champagne," the pair wrote together through the mid-60's and penned a second seasonal jingle called "Christmas In The Country." In addition to other pop songs like "The Heavens Cried," they created a piece for the US Marine Band entitled *The USA March*, as well as "Welcome Conventioneer," the one-time official song of Atlantic City.

As for "Jingle Bell Rock," Jennings remembers that when she asked him about its creation in 1958, Boothe said he and Beal were just "fooling around with an idea for a Christmas song, and that he wished he had written 'How Much Is That Doggie In The Window,'" since he didn't realize at the time how big the song had already become.

While it is unclear whether Beal and Boothe ever shared a romantic relationship, some close to them speculate about their sexuality. Shortly before passing away on October 19,

1967, after having been ill for several years, Beal married a woman who had been caring for him, but shared his life with a male companion before then. Boothe remained a bachelor up until he died in New York City on December 29, 1976. The song's royalties for both respective writers were left to various family members.

As for Bobby Helms, in 1997, the year "Jingle Bell Rock" turned forty, sadly he lost his battle with emphysema and died on June 19 in Martinsville, Indiana. His son, Robert Helms II, remembers how much the song meant to his father. "It could be the middle of summer, but dad always ended his shows with 'Jingle Bell Rock,' " he says. "He performed a lot at Christmas time, even the year before he died when he wasn't feeling well, he went out with his oxygen and performed it."

Upon the song's fifth decade of popularity, Robert Helms believes "Jingle Bell Rock" gave his father a legendary legacy, and is amazed people still want to hear the version he recorded almost a decade before he was born. A musician himself, who played regularly with Bobby Helms' band, he understands why it has lasted for so long.

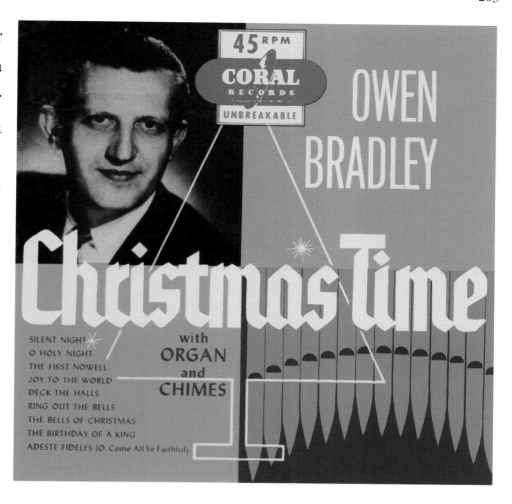

"We recorded the song one more time before dad passed away, and we sat and listened to the original recording because we wanted to replicate it. We noticed how incredible that initial session was, how perfect the voices were even though they were singing live into two mikes. And we talked about how 'Sugarfoot' worked on that guitar lick that went down in music history, and how the snare drum they used was the coolest sounding snare drum ever for the 50's. There were a lot of magical things that happened that day. It had to be magic."

Bobby Helms (1957)

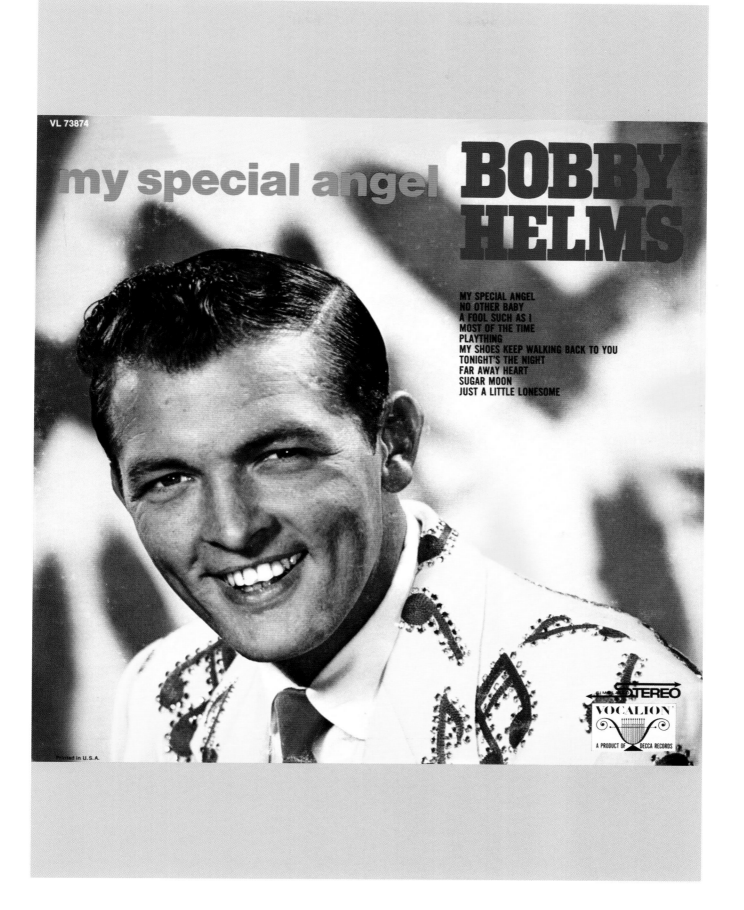

"Jingle Bell Rock" was one of three Christmas songs included on the 1961 Bobby Rydell/Chubby Checker LP (upper left & right). Chet Atkins (lower left) and Brenda Lee (lower right) also released their own versions of the tune in the 1960's.

Bobby Sherman (upper left, 1970) and Hall & Oates (upper right, 1983) both recorded Beal & Boothe's "Jingle Bell Rock," which appeared on the Chipmunks' 1963 holiday set (lower left). The helium-voiced animated critters were the brainchild of Ross Bagdasarian, AKA David Seville, and to this day their "Chipmunk Song" holds the unique honor of being the only number one Christmas record in rock history. That nugget was released as a single in 1958, and subsequently included on "Let's All Sing With The Chipmunks," their first Christmas LP (lower right).

SELECTED CHRISTMAS DISCOGRAPHIES

BOBBY HELMS

SINGLES

LABEL	TITLE	YEAR
Decca	Jingle Bell Rock/Captain Santa Claus	1957
Kapp	Jingle Bell Rock/The Bell That Couldn't Jingle	1965
Little Darlin'	Jingle Bell Rock/I Wanta Go to Santa Claus Land	1967
Certron	Jingle Bell Rock/The Old Year Is Gone	1970
MCA	Jingle Bell Rock/The Bell That Couldn't Jingle	1973
MCA	Jingle Bell Rock/Captain Santa Claus	1973
Mistletoe	Jingle Bell Rock/Jingle Bells	1970's

ALBUMS

Forum	Jingle Bell Rock	1974
Mistletoe	Jingle Bell Rock	1970's
Pilz	Jingle Bell Rock	1993
Collectables	Christmas Album	1998
KRB	Jingle Bell Rock	2000

OWEN BRADLEY

SINGLES

LABEL	TITLE	YEAR
Coral	Silent Night/Oh Holy Night	1950
Coral	The First Nowell/Joy To The World	1950
Coral	Deck The Halls/Ring Out The Bells	1950
Coral	O Come All Ye Faithful/The Birthday Of The King	1950
Coral	Uncle Mistletoe/Merry Christmas Rhumba	1951
Coral	Santa Claus Looks Like My Daddy/Uncle Mistletoe	1951
Coral	O Come All Ye Faithful/Blest Be The Tie That Binds	1952

ALBUMS

Coral	Christmas Time	1950
Coral	Organ and Chimes	1956
Decca	Joyous Bells Of Christmas	1957

THE ANITA KERR SINGERS

SINGLES

Sesac	On This Holy Night/Bring A Torch Jeanette Isabella/ Sleep, Sweet Jesus, Sleep/The 12 Days Of Christmas	1960's
Sesac	Deck The Halls/All Through The Night/ Rise Up Shepherds And Follow/Christmas Is The Day	1960's
Ampex	Shine, Shine/O Come All Ye Faithful/Noel	1970
Ampex	Oh Holy Night/Angels We Have Heard On High/ What Child Is This/Joy To The World	1970

ALBUMS

Sesac	On This Holy Night	1960's
Ampex	A Christmas Story	1971

As rock & roll eclipsed the Big Band era, Christmas novelties like "The Chipmunk Song," "Santa Baby" and "Nuttin' For Christmas" became quite popular in the 1950's. Eartha Kitt's slinky interpretation of "Santa Baby," released on RCA Victor Records, capriciously seduced the nation in December 1953, and the sultry chanteuse is still closely associated with it. In 1954, Kitt capitalized on her lucrative love affair with "Santa" by releasing a simlar ditty entitled "(This Year's) Santa Baby." Like "I Saw Mommy Kissing Santa Claus," Kitt's "Baby" sexualized Saint Nicholas, turning him into an adult fantasy figure ripe for a repressed post-World War II audience. Over thirty years later, this naughty notion would be resurrected by Madonna, who recorded "Santa Baby" in 1987 for the album *A Very Special Christmas*.

NUTTIN' FOR CHRISTMAS

Words and Music by SID TEPPER and ROY C. BENNETT

PRI
75
(In U.S

Beginner's Edition
(*First Grade*)

As recorded by STAN FREBERG on Capitol Record No. 3280

ROSS JUNGNICKEL, INC.
Sole Selling Agent:
HILL AND RANGE SONGS, INC.
1619 BROADWAY
New York 19, N. Y.

"Nuttin' For Christmas" debuted in 1955, and among the first to record it was Eartha Kitt, who released it that year with the B-side "Je Cherche Un Homme (I Want A Man)." Her version, however, faced stiff competition, since Stan Freberg (pictured above), The Fontaine Sisters, Barry Gordon and two other acts all charted in 1955 with their own "Nuttin.'" The race for consumers' hearts was won by seven-year-old Barry Gordon, who introduced "Nuttin'" on *The Milton Berle Show*. It peaked at number six on the charts, higher than any others, and went on to sell over a million records.

ROCKIN' AROUND THE CHRISTMAS TREE — 1958

WRITER: JOHNNY MARKS

PRODUCER: OWEN BRADLEY

ARTIST: BRENDA LEE

DECCA RECORDS

During a midnight session on October 19, 1958, thirteen-year-old Brenda Lee stepped into a studio to record "Rockin' Around The Christmas Tree," a song that boldly merged the nascent Nashville Sound with the new and controversial rock-and-roll style of the Eisenhower Era. It eventually sold over 8 million singles, and has woven Lee's wholesome voice into the red and green tapestry of American pop culture. Johnny Marks' song was groundbreaking for Brenda Lee, since it made her the first woman to have a hit with this kind of Yuletide hybrid, and the second person in music history to achieve this kind of Christmas-rock success. (SEE JINGLE BELL ROCK)

Born in Atlanta, Georgia, on December 11, 1944, Brenda gave her first performance in church at the age of five, and a year later awed judges of a local talent contest with her grand-voice version of "Take Me Out To The Ball Game." She nabbed first prize, and embarked upon a professional singing career that began at a local radio station and led to regular television gigs in Atlanta. By the time she was sixteen, Brenda Lee was catapulted to international stardom.

The early years of her career saw her shattering a variety of barriers and stereotypes at a time when few women were allowed to experiment in the somewhat taboo and newly emerging sound of rock and roll music. Yet it was apparent from the start that the little girl with the big, hiccuping Elvis Presley-esque voice, had the strength to take on such a monumental task, since as a child she helped support her family when her father died in a tragic accident, and her mother was forced to work sixteen-hour days in a cotton mill.

BRENDA LEE

including:

I'M SORRY

SWEET NOTHIN'S
WEEP NO MORE MY BABY

DL 4039   Printed in U.S.A.

1960

At the age of twelve, she made her national television debut on a talent show called *Ozark Jubilee*. Her voice was striking for someone so young, and it wasn't long before Paul Cohen, head of country talent at Decca Records, discovered the adult-sounding child prodigy, later known as "Little Miss Dynamite." Brenda Lee was signed to his label on May 21, 1956. By 1963 Little Miss Dynamite had racked up a dozen top-ten hits, including classics like "I Want To Be Wanted," "Break It To Me Gently" and her biggest non-holiday standard, "I'm Sorry."

Ironically, her first recording session at that label included a pair of country-flavored Christmas songs — "Christy Christmas" and "I'm Gonna Lasso Santa Claus." They featured Paul Cohen's assistant, Owen Bradley, on piano, who would soon inherit his boss' position and go on to produce all of Brenda Lee's hits.

An important architect of the Nashville Sound, Bradley began his career at the age of fifteen by playing piano at road houses, lodges and local clubs. Five years later, he gained a job at Nashville's legendary WSM radio station, and remained there for over two decades, where he performed with his own act — The Owen Bradley Quintet. His tenure at Decca Records lasted close to thirty years, a span of time that would see him produce musical giants like Buddy Holly, Patsy Cline and Loretta Lynn. One of his other talents was producing Christmas songs like "Jingle Bell Rock," "A Holly Jolly Christ-

1962

mas" and of course, Brenda Lee's "Rockin' Around The Christmas Tree," a song tunesmith Johnny Marks wrote in the middle of summer while vacationing in Vermont.

By 1960, Marks had earned close to a million dollars in royalties from another Christmas hit he wrote, "Rudolph The Red-nosed Reindeer," and was eager to follow this success with a song appealing to a new generation of listeners.

Two other famous tunes he wrote, "A Holly Jolly Christmas" and "I Heard The Bells On Christmas Day," as well as the entire score for the 1964 *Rudolph* television special, established him as one of the most successful holiday songwriters of all time.

According to Marks' son Michael, it wasn't unusual for his father to be thinking of winter in the middle of summer, since

he actually wrote many of his Christmas songs during the warmest months of the year. The inspiration for Brenda Lee's tune came while he was sunbathing on a Vermont beach, gazing at the majesty of the surrounding fir trees. Pondering nature's beauty, he noticed some nearby teenagers kicking up sand while dancing to the beat of the radio.

The result of this daydream, in which sunny pine trees mingled with kids moving to rock and roll music, was "Rockin' Around The Christmas Tree," and Marks sent a simple piano composition of it to Owen Bradley, who immediately recognized its appeal. Intuitively, he imagined its style might be just right for his new rising star, given the huge success of Bobby Helms' "Jingle Bell Rock" a year earlier.

Brenda Lee (1961)

Johnny Marks' two-minute opus, which tells the giddy story of a sentimental Christmas party hop full of pumpkin pie and new-old-fashioned dancing, was cut in the largest room of Owen Bradley's self-owned Nashville recording studio. Known as the "Quonset Hut," it was located upstairs from a smaller studio where Bobby Helms recorded "Jingle Bell Rock."

That evening, during a marathon session stretching well beyond midnight, little Brenda Lee recorded another holiday song — "Papa Noel" — as well as her version of the familiar standard, "Bill Bailey Won't You Please Come Home." Familiarity was left behind however, when she moved up to the mike to belt out Johnny Marks' daring new jingle.

A sound like this was still unusual for the time period, especially for an adolescent female singer, but Bradley was try-

ing to find a new pop niche for Brenda outside the country music world. "Jingle Bell Rock" gave him the confidence "Rockin' Around" could work for her. "We had great success with it and felt like we had a chance with Johnny's new song for her," recalls Bradley. "Both were recorded at my studio on 16th Avenue in Nashville, and we used the same band, except for the addition of Boots Randolph for a short sax solo, which made it rock right along."

Before entering the studio, Bradley came up with an idea for the song that would unite the soft sounds of country and pop with the edgier more daring sounds of rock and roll. He had commissioned The Anita Kerr Singers, a small choral group of male and female voices, to sing background vocals on "Jingle Bell Rock," as well as previous Brenda Lee records. He hired them again for his upcoming session. "I wanted to keep the voices pure," he says. "To start off with a choir and then have Brenda rocking with the sax and guitars."

This live instrumental accompaniment was provided by the same group of musicians he had worked with in all of his recording sessions. They were experimental artists who were used to improvising with and fusing pop, r&b, jazz and country elements. In the end, they would unknowingly create a catchy new "countrypolitan" sound.

For the session's live vocal accompaniment, Anita Kerr recalls she added two singers to her normal four-singer backup group, which offered a more lush and balanced harmonic cushion.

Kerr thinks of this time fondly, clearly remembering Brenda Lee's rambunctious charm and remarkable talent. "I couldn't

Boots Randolph

get over that big voice coming out of such a little girl," she says. "She was a cutie, and would talk to our group when the engineers were fooling around with the microphones. Here she was a child, and she would come over and tell us jokes that we couldn't believe."

Brenda remembers that even though Christmas was two months away, a mood was deliberately set in place making it easier for her to perform. "Owen had the studio all decorated for Christmas, so I could get in the holiday spirit, and it was just a lot of fun." She also recalls how the whole thing was done very spontaneously: "Back then when we recorded, we went in without arrangements and everyone sang and played together because there were no overdubs. The demo was played and we all got together and decided what we wanted to do. All of the instrumental and vocal arrangements were done that night right there on the spot."

Bradley admits this after-hour autumn meeting went along very smoothly: "We didn't spend a lot of time doing it because it just sort of fell into place, and that's the real fun kind of creativity. Brenda was very much a professional. She learned the songs before she came in and then got the hell out of there. She wasn't a prima donna."

Despite the fluidity of this gathering of great talent, the road to the song's success was not very merry.

In November 1958, Decca Records released "Rockin' Around The Christmas Tree" as a single paired with the Cajun Yuletide ditty, "Papa Noel." It failed to enter the charts and ended up selling abysmally. "The same record that eventually sold millions of copies only sold 5,000 the first Christmas it was out," says Bradley. "Nobody really knew who Brenda was."

All of that would change within two years' time when a whispery love song called "Sweet Nothin's" propelled Brenda into the top five of Billboard's Pop Singles chart in the spring of 1960. Her summer would be even hotter with the release of "I'm Sorry," another tender ballad, that became her first number-one record. It included something extremely unusual for a late 1950's Nashville recording session — a string section — brought in by Bradley to enhance Lee's mature vocals.

With this newfound success, Decca didn't waste any time and re-released "Rockin Around" for the 1960 holiday season. It immediately shot into the top twenty, returned to the charts for twelve years, and went on to become the fourth-

1966

largest selling Christmas single of all time. In 1964, the song became part of the album, *Merry Christmas From Brenda Lee*, which charted for six non-consecutive seasons, peaking at number seven in 1972 on Billboard's Christmas Album chart. It contained four other holiday tunes released that winter including her own version of "Jingle Bell Rock."

"Rockin' Around The Christmas Tree" is a reminder of what music sounded like in the 1950's, and its popularity has spread across four decades of time. Over the years it's been featured in the movie *Home Alone,* recorded by Darlene Love and Ronnie Spector for 1992's *A Very Special Christmas 2,* and sung by a range of other acts like Three Dog Night, The Partridge Family and Amy Grant.

Brenda Lee and Owen Bradley (c. 1980)

The tune has become a cherished evergreen for Lee, who admits Christmas is her favorite holiday: "After eating and talking I always wind up in the living room with friends and family at the piano singing "Rockin' Around The Christmas Tree." It's very precious to me because actually it's as much my signature as 'I'm Sorry.'

"Every time I go on stage," Lee continues, "I sing it no matter what time of year it is. And it's so astounding because I have people come up to me today and say, 'You know Christmas isn't Christmas unless we play your song.' That still amazes me, because I always dreamt of becoming a part of people's lives and emotions, but I never thought it would happen on such a large scale."

It seems as though "Rockin' Around," will always be identified with Brenda Lee, and Bradley believed it was because he found a perfect union between song and artist. "Johnny Marks had a great idea," he said, "and Brenda knew how to communicate it, how to make us understand what it was about. To this day, it's still not Christmas to me until I hear her sing it."

In 1999, MCA/Decca released "Brenda Lee Rockin' Around The Christmas Tree," which included, for the first time, all of her Decca Christmas recordings. The eighteen-track set also contains three songs previously unreleased in the US — "White Christmas," "Jingle Bells" and "Silent Night."

B R E N D A   L E E

MORE WITH BRENDA LEE

How did you meet Owen Bradley?

Well, we met when he was working with Paul Cohen at Decca Records. After Paul died, Owen became my producer and produced me from about 1957 on. He's been a big influence in my life, not only professionally, but personally. He's a dear, dear man and a genius at what he does.

Why did you begin your recording career with two Christmas songs?

When you're eleven years old, you're looking for songs to record because a lot of people won't submit them to a child. Those were two that were submitted that we liked.

Do you remember who brought "Rockin' Around The Christmas Tree" to you?

Owen Bradley brought it to me. It was sent to us by Johnny Marks, who sent me a lot of songs through the years. I loved it, and thought it was a great Christmas tune with a fabulous arrangement. And it's a well-produced song.

What kind of a relationship did you have with Johnny Marks?

Johnny was a great guy. We used to talk to each other several times a year before he passed away, and he was just a very gentle, kind man who became my friend.

How did "Rockin' Around" help your career?

It helped my career immensely because of its record sales. When it came out again in *Home Alone*, there was another big resurgence of popularity for it. But it has never lost its place at Christmastime in the forty years since I recorded it. And the original recording has been played every year.

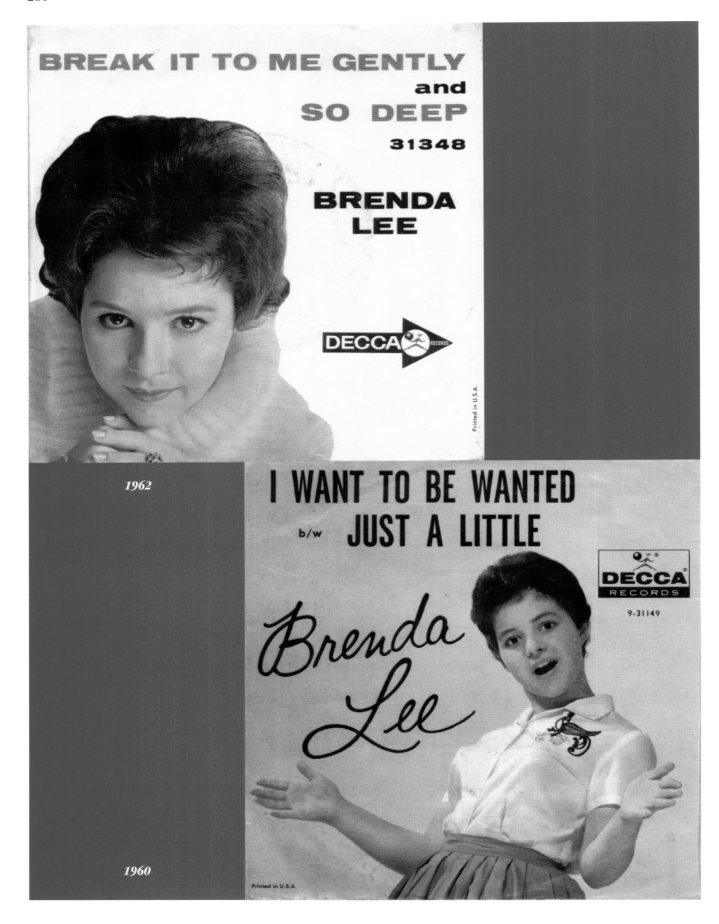

1962

1960

How were you able to create such an impressive musical legacy?

I had people like Owen Bradley, and the wonderful musicians and arrangers that we used. A lot of ingredients went into what Brenda Lee put out on the market. I'm very lucky that I was able to work with those kind of people at such an early age. All the people like Floyd Cramer and Boots Randolph, who played on those records and added their own talent, helped make Brenda what she was.

At the time did you think it was unusual to record a Christmas rock song?

I actually didn't think of it as a rock song. Of course, we used Boots Randolph on sax, and he played a mean sax solo. But we all got together and thought, "What would make this song good, and how could we give a Christmas song a different slant?" We all came up with it.

Why has "Rockin' Around" survived for so long?

I think all of my songs have withstood the test of time because they are all well-crafted. They would have been hits by other people, and I feel very blessed that I was able to record them.

When you hear it are you swept back in time?

I listen to it if it comes on when I'm in the car, and I get really nostalgic. I think of all the musicians on the sessions who are no longer here with us, and I remember the day we went in and recorded it. I have a lot of great memories.

Brenda Lee with Johnny Marks (c. 1960)

IN JUNE 1997, OWEN BRADLEY DISCUSSED HIS INVOLVEMENT WITH "ROCKIN' AROUND THE CHRISTMAS TREE." HE PASSED AWAY ON JANUARY 7, 1998.

How did you get involved with Brenda Lee's career?

I worked with Paul Cohen, who was in charge of the country music department at Decca Records, and Brenda was an artist that he signed. I was Paul's assistant, and then he was promoted to head of Coral Records. When he took that job, since I was an apprentice at Decca for about ten years, they moved me up and gave me the position of producing the country music people. Brenda was one of those artists. I also signed Loretta Lynn and Conway Twitty, and worked with Patsy Cline, who I inherited from another label.

Were you a part of Brenda's first recording session in 1956?

Oh yes, I played piano on those. I quit playing on most of the sessions in 1958 when I became a full-time A&R person. Up until then I used to do both.

How did "Rockin' Around" come to your attention?
Johnny Marks used to pitch mostly Christmas songs in Nashville. He sent me the song on a little acetate record and a lead sheet. We made it up right in the studio with no music, and I just did it again recently for Brenda on another record. We did it as close to the original as we could.

Owen Bradley and Brenda Lee (c. 1960)

What did you think when you first received it?
We weren't really into rock and roll a whole lot because we had lots of country acts, but at that time we were trying to get Brenda into that. Actually that's sort of the secret of making records anyway — finding the right material and getting it to

My sincerest thanks to everyone who helped make the past 10 years so memorable! Brenda

PERSONAL MGT.
PENTHOUSE
1808 WEST END BLDG
NASHVILLE, TENN

the right person. And it seemed like the right song for her, so I gave it to her and she learned it. Then we came into the studio. Boots Randolph was on it, and I'm pretty sure Floyd Cramer played on it with Hank Garland, Brady Martin and my brother Harold.

Was a Christmas rock song unusual for that time period?

Yeah, a little bit. I didn't know if the public would buy it. But I shouldn't have worried about it — they've been buying it for forty years. I talked to Johnny Marks shortly before he passed away, and he told me it sold millions.

Had merging a Christmas song with a rock beat ever been done before?

We did "Jingle Bell Rock" a year before, and it was with the same band. The only difference was we had Boots Randolph the saxophonist on "Rockin' Around," and we didn't have him on "Jingle Bell Rock." We got a little bolder as time went along. "Jingle Bell Rock" was a monster record, and it gave us the reason to do "Rockin' Around."

Was the version you created close to Johnny Marks' idea?

No. I think he just had a piano. It wasn't close to that, it wasn't that way at all. He just gave me a lead sheet. It was a very sparse kind of demo and not very elaborate. Sometimes the demo is better than the record, but in this case it wasn't anything like the demo.

Why did "Rockin' Around" fail to catch on at first?

It wasn't Brenda's fault. Nobody knew her when it first came out, and this was really a problem with the recording companies. You only have a window of about two to three weeks to sell a Christmas record, and so the record company has to have confidence. In order to have that confidence, they have to have somebody that's real hot. If the singer's hot and you've got a great record, then you can press up a million. If you only sell six or seven hundred thousand, you're still all right, 'cause maybe you'll get rid of them next year. But when you have an unknown singer you can't do that. It's too much of a risk.

"Sweet Nothin's" (UK sheet music)

What was it about Brenda's voice that made the people eventually buy her Christmas song?

I like the way she sings. I tried to figure out how to give her different songs, and she did some pretty neat ones during that time. You know, you hear Teresa Brewer sing "Music! Music! Music!" and it just fits. If somebody else does it, it don't sound right. Brenda was the right age, and it just had enough rock and roll to give it excitement but not be offensive.

What's the secret of your financial success?

I was really lucky. I'm not really an expert at picking songs, but I learned a lot from Paul Cohen, who was pretty good at it. He taught me that you couldn't look at the writer or publisher. You just had to listen to the song on its own merit. And of course, you have to be as lucky as hell.

After all these years, what are your final thoughts on "Rockin' Around?"

You know, I get a big charge out of it when I hear it on the radio. I'm not going to turn it off. I keep listening to it because over the years, a hit like that keeps sounding better and better.

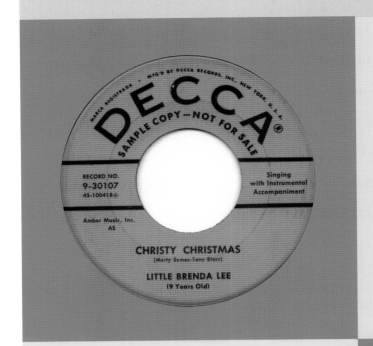

*Shown clockwise: "Christy Christmas" along with its B-side, "I'm Gonna Lasso Santa Claus" (1956),
"Rockin' Around The Christmas Tree" and its B-side, "Papa Noel" (re-issue 1960).*

BRENDA LEE'S SELECTED CHRISTMAS RECORDING HISTORY

SINGLES

LABEL	TITLE	YEAR
Decca	Christy Christmas/I'm Gonna Lasso Santa Claus	1956
Decca	Rockin' Around The Christmas Tree/Papa Noel	1958
Decca	Rockin' Around The Christmas Tree/Papa Noel	1960
Decca	Jingle Bell Rock/Winter Wonderland	1964
Decca	This Time Of The Year/Christmas Will Be Just Another Lonely Day	1964
Decca	This Time Of The Year/Blue Christmas/Jingle Bell Rock/	
	Rockin' Around The Christmas Tree/Marshmallow World/Winter Wonderland	1964
MCA	Rockin' Around The Christmas Tree/Papa Noel	1973
MCA	Jingle Bell Rock/Winter Wonderland	1973

ALBUMS

Decca	Merry Christmas From Brenda Lee	1964
MCA	Merry Christmas From Brenda Lee	1973
Warner Bros.	A Brenda Lee Christmas — In The New Old Fashioned Way	1991
MCA	Jingle Bell Rock	1993
MCA/Decca	Rockin' Around The Christmas Tree	1999

Written in 1949, "A Marshmallow World" became quite popular in the 1950's. Among the first to record it were Vaughn Monroe and Bing Crosby, who both released single versions of it in 1950. The capricious ditty, which Brenda Lee included on her first Christmas album, was written by Carl Sigman and Peter De Rose. De Rose co-wrote "The Lamp Is Low," with "Sleigh Ride's" lyricist, Mitchell Parish, while Sigman co-penned Andy Williams' 1970 hit theme to the movie, *Love Story*.

Monument Records released Roy Orbison's "Pretty Paper" in 1963, a song written by country singer Willie Nelson, whose own version of it debuted the following year. Two interpretations of Orbison's "Paper" were cut in London on September 11, 1963. Hank Garland, Boots Randolph, Chet Atkins, The Anita Kerr Singers, as well as Owen Bradley's brother Harold, were most likely on board that day, since virtually all of Orbison's Monument recording sessions included them. Shown above is the UK version of "Pretty Paper's" sheet music.

A HOLLY JOLLY CHRISTMAS — 1962

WRITER: JOHNNY MARKS

PRODUCERS:
  OWEN BRADLEY
  MILT GABLER

ARTIST: BURL IVES

DECCA RECORDS

If any song could fully capture the essence of a joyous, wayfaring stranger like Burl Ives, a man poet Carl Sandburg once called "the mightiest ballad singer of any century," it would have to be the frolicking folk-oriented "A Holly Jolly Christmas." Johnny Marks, a master of Christmas pop music, wrote the tune for the phenomenally successful 1964 *Rudolph The Red-Nosed Reindeer* television special. In that charming perennial favorite, Ives plays benevolent Sam The Snowman, who cheerfully waddles while warbling "A Holly Jolly Christmas." It's one of three gems his frozen character sings as he narrates this tale telling of animated misfits longing to belong, and the dangerous heartfelt journey they must face in order to fight discrimination and find self-acceptance.

Ives' own life was a similar episodic journey leading him to a colorfully unique and spiritual place. In 1929, the twenty-year-old Illinois native had early aspirations of becoming an evangelist, but he dropped out of college, and boldly left the comfort of his rural small-town existence to discover America and learn more about himself. He departed with fifteen cents in his pocket, a banjo, and a yellow suitcase labeled "I'm just a vagabond lover." It was a quixotic quest that ultimately saw the earthy artist endear himself to generations of fans, in roles which cut across myriad genres of communication including radio, theater, books, movies and television.

Big Daddy (Burl Ives) advises his son Brick (Paul Newman), "Truth is pain an' sweat an' payin' bills an' makin' love to a woman you don't love anymore."

M-G-M
Presents
Cat on a Hot Tin Roof
in
METROCOLOR

Burl Ives and Paul Newman in "Cat On A Hot Tin Roof " (1958)

The natural-born folk singer learned over 300 narrative ballads from his barefoot pipe-smoking grandmother, and took these simple tunes with him as he whimsically hitchhiked thousands of miles across forty-six states, Canada and Mexico. He gleaned many more songs as he went along from coal miners, cowboys, hoboes and preachers.

During this time, he was living in places like freight trains and haylofts, making a meager itinerant living performing the unpretentious repertoire of traditional folk music that had become a part of his soul. These were naive childlike songs seeking to soothe a depression-era between-war nation struggling for a more promising future. It wouldn't be long before he sparked an urban folk revival and introduced this down-home blend to millions of people around the world.

How he went from the ephemeral life of an unknown wanderer, to the immortality of celluloid and recorded fantasy, is probably just as miraculous as Rudolph's spectacular escape from Bumble, the Abominable Snow Monster. Remarkably, after moving to New York City in 1937, his rustic charm seemed to appeal to sophisticated Greenwich Village nightclub audiences. He soon found himself debuting on Broadway and appearing on his own CBS radio show appropriately titled *The Wayfaring Stranger*.

Burl Ives arranged the folk gem, "I Wonder As I Wander," for his above 1953 set, *Folk Songs Dramatic And Humorous*. Folk singer John Jacob Niles (1882 — 1980) is credited with publishing "Wander" in 1934, and claimed to have discovered it in Cherokee County, North Carolina. The song's creator and the exact date it was written remain unknown.

An autobiographical book and his entrance into movies followed, with roles in a number of important films like *East Of Eden*, *Cat On A Hot Tin Roof* and *The Big Country*, for which he won a Supporting Actor Academy Award. He was signed to Decca Records in 1948.

The 1950's saw him at the peak of his singing career as he released a slew of popular albums and carefree singles like "Blue Tail Fly," "Lavender Blue (Dilly Dilly)" and "On Top Of Old Smoky." During that decade he also recorded two full-length holiday albums, *Christmas Day In The Morning* and *Christmas Eve with Ives*.

DL 78391
STEREO
Christmas Eve
DECCA
with Burl Ives
TWELVE DAYS OF CHRISTMAS
OH, LITTLE TOWN OF BETHLEHEM
IT CAME UPON THE MIDNIGHT CLEAR
KING HEROD AND THE COCK
SILENT NIGHT
THE SEVEN JOYS OF MARY
THE FRIENDLY BEASTS
JESOUS AHATONIA
WHAT CHILD IS THIS?
DOWN IN YON FOREST
THERE WERE THREE SHIPS
Printed in U.S.A.

1957

1952

"Rudolph The Red-Nosed Reindeer" (Copyright 1964 Rankin/Bass Productions)

Over the next decade Burl Ives' popularity continued to grow. By 1961, the man who at one time was told his music was too hillbilly for mainstream audiences, had sold over five million albums. The following year found him winning a Grammy Award for his top-ten hit, "Funny Way Of Laughin'."

It was a perfect time for producers Jules Bass and Arthur Rankin to hire the hot, grandfatherly folk balladeer for an exciting new Christmas project they were working on with writer Romeo Muller, starring a beloved stop-motion reindeer with a tremendous nasal problem.

Rankin/Bass had never worked with a star like Ives before, and although it's now common practice, hiring a celebrity to provide a voice for an animated figure was uncommon back then. But according to Rick Goldschmidt, author of *The Enchanted World Of Rankin/Bass,* the show's sponsor, General Electric, most likely requested Ives in the middle of producing it in hopes of selling it to a large television network. "It seems as though they added in Sam The Snowman later," he says. "He's generally not in any scenes with the characters except toward the very end. So apparently, Burl came into the picture a little later."

Evidently two of Ives' most famous nuggets from it, "Silver And Gold" and "A Holly Jolly Christmas," were originally intended for the miner character of Yukon Cornelius, played by Canadian actor Larry Mann. "All of the songs for the show were probably recorded long before Burl Ives' songs were done," says Goldschmidt. "In fact, they just took the actual music from those previous recording sessions and wiped Larry

Mann's voice off 'Silver and Gold,' 'Holly Jolly Christmas,' and probably 'Rudolph The Red-nosed Reindeer.' Burl didn't perform his part with the other actors. He went into the studio with those songs already recorded, and just added his vocals and dialogue to Johnny Marks' music."

While Marks wrote all of the music for *Rudolph,* "Holly Jolly Christmas" is the only song from it to have been given a 1962 copyright. The rest of the material was registered with the Library of Congress in 1964, and it may be that it was the first song he wrote for the special, or that he initially penned Burl's classic evergreen for a different project.

The prolific New York City songwriter was destined to somehow be involved in Rudolph's filmic saga since he was the

JOSEPH E. LEVINE
ARTHUR RANKIN, JR.'S

THE ORIGINAL
SOUND TRACK
RECORDING

THE DAYDREAMER

STARRING THE TALENTS OF

TALLULAH BANKHEAD
VICTOR BORGE
PATTY DUKE
JACK GILFORD
MARGARET HAMILTON
SESSUE HAYAKAWA
BURL IVES
BORIS KARLOFF
HAYLEY MILLS
PAUL O'KEEFE
CYRIL RITCHARD
TERRY-THOMAS
ED WYNN
RAY BOLGER

MAURY LAWS
JULES BASS
ARTHUR RANKIN, JR.
JOSEPH E. LEVINE
JULES BASS

HANS CHRISTIAN ANDERSEN

"Daydreamer"
Theme Sung by
ROBERT GOULET

ANIMAGIC ... EASTMAN COLOR
VIDEOCRAFT INTERNATIONAL
EMBASSY PICTURES

Burl Ives played Father Neptune in the 1966 Rankin/Bass motion picture "The Daydreamer."

brother-in-law of Robert L. May, creator of the children's book the special is based upon. Marks also lived next door to Arthur Rankin, and at first was reluctant to get involved with his production. "He didn't want to make the special," says Goldschmidt. "From everyone I've talked to, Marks was quite a character and very protective of his song. Arthur had to convince him to bring Rudolph to television."

The pair must have hit it off though, since they collaborated on a number of subsequent shows including *The Ballad Of Smokey The Bear*, and two more stop-motion productions starring that most famous reindeer — *Rudolph's Shiny New Year* and *Rudolph And Frosty's Christmas in July*. Rankin and Bass reunited several more times with Burl Ives

as well, who played Father Neptune in their 1966 live-action/stop-motion movie *The Daydreamer*, and G.B., the Great Easter Bunny, in their 1976 animated special *The First Easter Rabbit*. He also made an appearance in their film, *The Bermuda Depths*, released in 1978.

One of the reasons "A Holly Jolly Christmas" has survived so long has a great deal to do with the overwhelming success of Sam The Snowman's wintry fairy tale, which NBC first aired on December 6, 1964, as part of its *General Electric Fantasy Hour*.

The show cost 500,000 dollars to make and was contracted to run for only two years. Because its original broadcast won fifty-five percent of the audience share for its time slot, it subsequently went on to air for over three decades, and eventually became the longest running, highest rated television special in the history of the medium. This grew into a financial windfall for Ives, since his lawyers were able to work out a way for him to get paid every time the show aired, a practice uncommon back then. To this day, Ives' estate receives a royalty check every year it runs, and each time a *Rudolph* video is purchased.

Yet Decca Records apparently wasn't aware of how in demand *Rudolph* would become, since a store version of its soundtrack competed with a General Electric promotional version viewers could receive through the mail for a small amount of money, along with proof of a product purchase.

Burl Ives and Owen Bradley at Bradley's "Quonset Hut" recording studio in Nashville, Tennessee (1961)

In 1965, that giveaway campaign was halted, and Decca re-issued *Rudolph's* soundtrack shortly before the special's sophomore debut.

Although all of Burl Ives' songs were on those original releases, Rudolph and Hermey the Elf's duet, "Fame And Fortune," was left off, since its sequence was added to the second airing of *Rudolph*. MCA Records re-released the *Rudolph* soundtrack minus Johnny Marks' "Fame and Fortune" in 1973 and 1995.

The show's original soundtrack included other songs written by Johnny Marks, tracks used as hidden background music for the special. "I Heard The Bells On Christmas Day" was played at the beginning when Sam first slides onto the chilly scene. "Rockin' Around The Christmas Tree" was heard while Santa's elves gaily prepared for Christmas Day. Instrumental versions of these chestnuts, as well as additional Marks creations like "When Santa Claus Gets Your Letter" and "The Night Before Christmas Song," (two tunes earlier popularized by Gene Autry) were all contained on the B-side of *Rudolph's* first commercial soundtrack.

The phenomenal 1964 ratings of *Rudolph* galvanized Decca Records into not only rushing the soundtrack out for the following holiday season, but releasing an entire Burl Ives Christmas album as well, aptly titled *Have A Holly Jolly Christmas*. Oddly enough, both albums contained different versions of one of Ives' most requested songs. "I think Burl was immediately associated with Christmas after doing that special," says Goldschmidt. "And I think Decca wanted to cash in on

it and had to have Burl re-record 'Holly Jolly,' because otherwise General Electric would have gotten a cut of the royalties."

Milt Gabler (right) with Branford Marsalis (1990)

The two "Holly Jolly" soundtrack cuts (one with Ives alone and one with him joined by a chorus) were produced by Maury Laws, and in keeping with the cheerful nature of the show, he gave them a "poppy," happy-go-lucky treatment. Ives' own album version, co-produced by Owen Bradley, was interpreted in a country/folk style with background voices provided by The Anita Kerr Singers. It was the latter version only that Decca Records released as a single in 1964, and it peaked at number thirteen on Billboard's Christmas Singles chart.

On February 5, 1964, Owen Bradley met Milt Gabler (producer of Bill Haley's 1955 groundbreaking hit "Rock Around The Clock"), Burl Ives, The Anita Kerr Singers, and a talented bunch of session musicians (including Bradley's guitarist brother Harold) at Columbia Recording Studio in Nashville. That day they recorded "A Holly Jolly Christmas," as well as "Beautiful Anna Bell Lee" and "Hobo Jungle," two non-Christmas Ives songs that appeared on later albums.

Burl Ives in the 1963 film "The Brass Bottle"

1964

Owen Bradley and Burl Ives (c. 1965)

"On that day I was responsible for the band, the music and its arrangement," recalls Owen Bradley. "During the rehearsal I sat around the piano and played the song for everyone. It was another Johnny Marks song. He had a lot of Christmas hits and was making a fortune off of them. Evidently he ran into Milt Gabler and they gave 'Holly Jolly Christmas' to Burl earlier in New York City."

Bradley further explained that Milt Gabler's involvement revolved around the fact that he had become a legendary producer and songwriter at Decca Records, who had worked with everyone from Ella Fitzgerald to Nat King Cole. "Milt brought Burl down to Nashville and we all had lots of fun," adds Bradley, who worked with Ives for many years on close to thirty songs. "I also did his last album before he died in 1995. We were good friends and Burl was a real colorful person."

"Burl was a sweetie to work with," offers "Holly Jolly's" background vocalist Anita Kerr. "I really liked him very much, he was very funny and he seemed to always show up with a bottle of Jack Daniels and take a little swig every so often. He'd end up clowning around and breaking up everybody in the room in the middle of the take. We'd always look forward to him coming to Nashville."

Kerr and her group began singing regularly on Burl Ives' records in the early 50's, and helped create a mainstream country/folk pop sound for him. They worked along with Bradley, and a group of experimental musicians known as the Nashville Cats. Both Gabler and Bradley gave her a great

Burl Ives' "Children's Favorites" LP (c. 1950)

deal of autonomy, and she's credited with creating "Holly Jolly's" catchy vocal-bell harmony. Her voice can also be heard on two other classic Christmas songs she worked on with Bradley — "Jingle Bell Rock" and "Rockin' Around The Christmas Tree."

According to Burl's wife, Dorothy Ives, "A Holly Jolly Christmas" best represents her husband because "it gives the feeling and the verve of the man. It's an up song and it's very much like Burl because he had an up spirit. He was synonymous with Christmas, and somehow his image and what he stood for was Christmas.

"And Burl loved the same things that children loved," she adds, "presents and surprises, unusual toys, bugs and bees and dogs and cats. Christmas, of course, encompasses all of that. It's very much a part of nature and it's very much a part of the spiritual life of Christians, so of course he loved it."

Owen Bradley and Burl Ives (c. 1985)

And obviously his legendary performance in *Rudolph* is also something Burl held close to his heart. "When I tour the country, I am recognized as Sam The Snowman by everyone from the airline stewardesses down to the smallest of children," he said shortly before his death. "I loved that special so much that we had wood figures of the Rudolph characters made and we decorate our front lawn with them every Christmas. The popularity of that special overshadows my Oscar performance and my role as 'Big Daddy' in *Cat On A Hot Tin Roof* and I'm grateful to have been a part of it."[1]

"In the last years of his life we always started the holiday watching *Rudolph*," recalls Dorothy Ives. "We worked for fifteen years with the President's Committee for the Handicapped through three administrations, and we recognized that the land of misfit toys were the handicapped toys which Santa rescued. That was symbolic for us because we believed that really, there are no misfit toys or misfit anything. Our slogan used to be: 'In the arts there are no handicaps.'"

"The mind controls the heart of the matter," once concurred Burl. "If your mind says you are handicapped then you are. It's largely a matter of thought."[2]

Burl also believed that like Christmas, his soul was immortal and would survive long after his wayfaring, vagabond life on earth was over. "Our hearts are the eternal part of us that goes on and on," he stated. "And as another man said, 'The longest journey any man will ever take is from his conscious mind to his heart.' I feel very strongly that I am a part of the

1949

entire cosmos, not something apart from this pulsating universe. If a piece of wood will never die, this bouncy thing called Burl will never die as well."[3]

"Even though he's gone, it's still like our two worlds are touching," concludes Dorothy Ives. "Now during the holidays when I go shopping, I hear him singing 'A Holly Jolly Christmas' and it seems to be played more than anything else. He's out there and he's saying, 'There is a verve and joy to life, attach yourself to it, and let your religion be the doctrine of the heart.'"

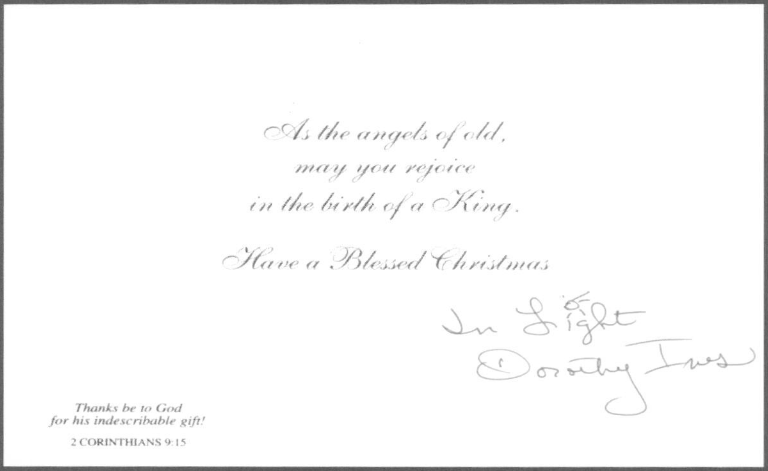
As the angels of old,
may you rejoice
in the birth of a King.
Have a Blessed Christmas
In Light
Dorothy Ives
Thanks be to God
for his indescribable gift!
2 CORINTHIANS 9:15

Christmas greetings from Dorothy Ives

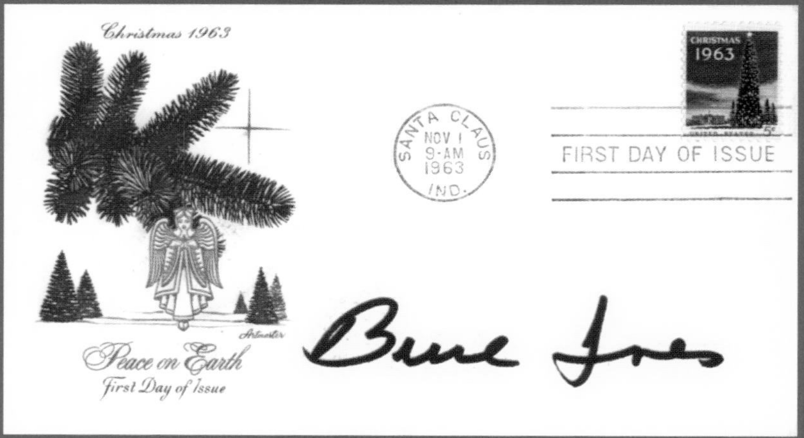
Christmas 1963
CHRISTMAS
1963
SANTA CLAUS
NOV 1
9-AM
1963
IND.
FIRST DAY OF ISSUE
Peace on Earth
First Day of Issue
Burl Ives

This First Day of Issue was signed by Burl Ives and postmarked at Santa Claus, Indiana, in 1963.

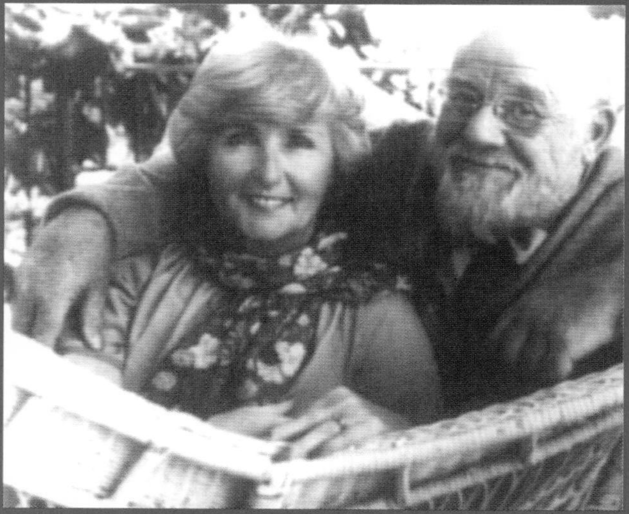

Dorothy and Burl Ives

MORE WITH DOROTHY IVES

Was Christmas music always a part of Burl Ives' life?

Burl was a child of an evangelistic singer, and he thought that he learned many of the Christmas hymns in his mother's womb. She would go Wednesday nights to prayer meetings when she was expecting. When he was very young, his father bought a pump organ for his sister, and Burl at the age of two or three was the only one who sang on pitch and knew all the lyrics. So he felt like it was always part of him.

Were Burl and Johnny Marks friends?

Burl knew Johnny very well and loved him. And he adored Burl. Every Christmas he called and they would talk then, but outside of that we didn't hear from him. He was an interesting man and a bit of a loner.

What kind of a man was Burl Ives?

He never had bad press and everybody felt the gentle side of his nature. And he lived the spiritual life. Once we started traveling that path of compassion, tolerance and non-judgment, his life was invigorated, and he came to represent the spirit of Christmas of ancient days. As he got older, he would walk into a room and have the magnificent appearance of his inner being that came from studying world religions for over thirty years. You have no idea how we miss him. When he died at 3:30 in the morning, an amazing rainbow appeared. The sky lightened. People called me and said, 'Dorothy, look out the window!' This to me was a manifestation, not just a coincidence.

What's your favorite *Rudolph scene?*

Of course, my real favorites are when Sam The Snowman is on the scene. But I love the scene with the misfit toys, and when Santa says the first stop will be to rescue them.

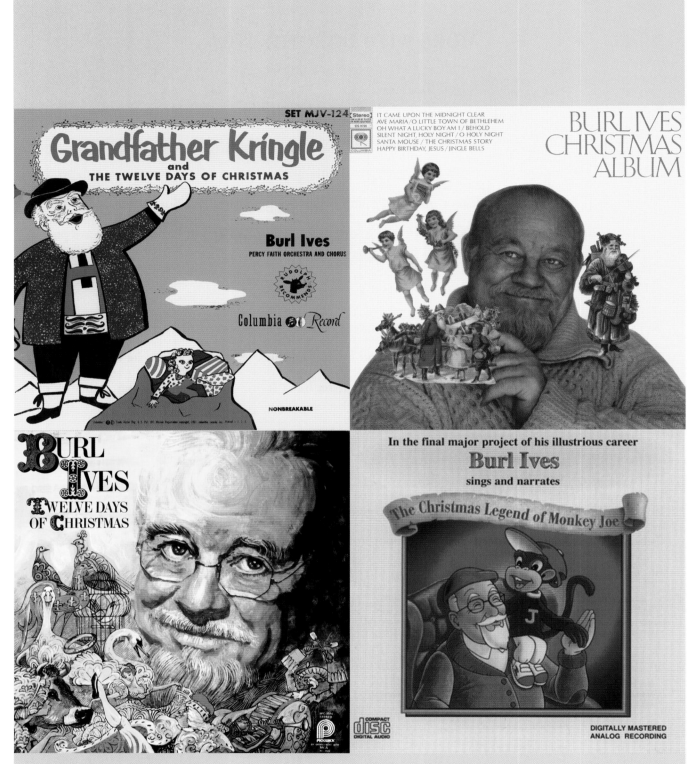

Burl Ives' "Twelve Days Of Christmas" was released in Canada on Pickwick Records

"The Christmas Legend of Monkey Joe" was narrated by Burl Ives and is believed to be his final major project before his death in April 1995.

BURL IVES' SELECTED CHRISTMAS RECORDING HISTORY

SINGLES

LABEL	TITLE	YEAR
Columbia	Grandfather Kringle/The 12 Days Of Christmas	1951
Decca	The Friendly Beasts/There Were Three Ships	1952
Decca	Jesous Anatonia/What Child Is This?	1952
Decca	The Seven Joys Of Mary (Pt.1)/The Seven Joys Of Mary (Pt.2)	1952
Decca	King Herod And The Cock/Down In Yon Forest	1952
Decca	A Holly Jolly Christmas/Snow For Johnny	1964
Columbia	Santa Mouse/Oh What A Lucky Boy Am I	1968
MCA	A Holly Jolly Christmas/Snow For Johnny	1989

ALBUMS

Decca	Christmas Day In The Morning	1952
Decca	Christmas Eve With Burl Ives	1957
Decca	Rudolph The Red-nosed Reindeer	1964
Decca	Have A Holly Jolly Christmas	1965
Columbia	Burl Ives Christmas Album	1968
MCA	Have A Holly Jolly Christmas	1973
MCA	Rudolph The Red-nosed Reindeer	1973
Columbia	Burl Ives Christmas Album	1995
MCA	Christmas Eve With Burl Ives	1998
Decca	The Very Best Of Burl Ives Christmas	1999
Monkey Joe	The Christmas Legend Of Monkey Joe	1999

Burl Ives (left) with Johnny Marks (c. 1964)

JOHNNY MARKS' SELECTED SONGOGRAPHY

SONG	PERFORMER	YEAR
Address Unknown *(written with Carmen Lombardo/Dedette Lee Hill)*	The Ink Spots	1939
A Caroling We Go	**Fred Waring**	**1966**
Anyone Can Move A Mountain *(From "The Ballad of Smokey Bear")*	Kate Smith	1966
Cane Bottom Chair	Ray McKinley	1950
Don't Cross Your Fingers Cross Your Heart *(written with Al Donahue/Larry Shay)*	Kay Kyser & His Orchestra	1938
Don't Let The Parade Pass You By *(From "Rudolph And Frosty's Christmas In July," written with Larry Conley)*	**Ethel Merman**	**1977**
Everyone's A Child At Christmas	**Gene Autry**	**1955**
Ev'rything I've Always Wanted *(From "Rudolph And Frosty's Christmas In July")*	**Porter Wagoner**	**1977**
Free	Tommy Leonetti	1956
A Holly Jolly Christmas *(From "Rudolph The Red-Nosed Reindeer")*	**Burl Ives**	**1962**
How Long Is Forever?	Gene Autry	1950
I Can't Find Anything To Suit My Mood *(written with Dedette Lee Hill)*	Guy Lombardo	1938
I Heard The Bells On Christmas Day *(Based on the poem "The Christmas Bells," by Henry Wadsworth Longfellow)*	**Bing Crosby**	**1956**
I Wouldn't Know Where To Begin	Eddy Arnold	1953
Is It Only Cause You're Lonely	Porter Wagoner	1979
Joyous Christmas	**The Beneficial Singers**	**1969**
Minuet For Clarinet *(From "The Tiny Tree")*	**Guy Lombardo**	**1975**
The Moving Finger Writes *(written with Joe Davis)*	Red Skelton	1973
Neglected	Fats Waller	1937
The Night Before Christmas Song *(adapted from Clement C. Moore's poem, "'Twas The Night Before Christmas")*	**Gene Autry & Rosemary Clooney**	**1952**
Rockin' Around The Christmas Tree	**Brenda Lee**	**1958**
Rudolph The Red-nosed Reindeer	**Gene Autry**	**1949**
She'll Always Remember *(written with Eddie Pola, co-writer of "It's The Most Wonderful Time Of The Year")*	Glenn Miller	1942
Silver And Gold *(From "Rudolph The Red-Nosed Reindeer")*	**Burl Ives**	**1964**
Summer Holiday *(written with Larry Conley)*	Eddy Duchin	1936
To Love And Be Loved *(From "The Tiny Tree")*	**Roberta Flack**	**1956**
We Speak Of You Often *(written with Dedette Lee Hill)*	Guy Lombardo	1938
What've You Got To Lose But Your Heart *(written with Carmen Lombardo)*	Frankie Carle	1946
When Autumn Comes *(From "The Tiny Tree")*	**Roberta Flack**	**1958**
When Santa Claus Gets Your Letter	**Gene Autry**	**1950**
Who Calls? *(written with Dedette Lee Hill)*	Bing Crosby	1941

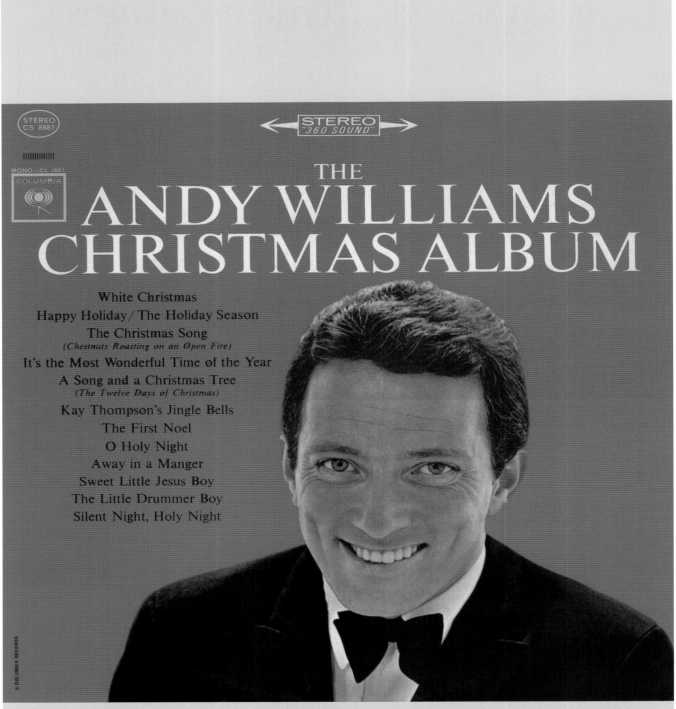

If there is a quintessential Andy Williams Christmas song, it would have to be "It's The Most Wonderful Time Of The Year," which was part of the popular singer's 1963 gold-certified holiday collection (above). In 1968, Columbia Records issued it as the B-side of the Williams' single, "The Christmas Song," and due to the tune's growing popularity, it was given a new release in 1976. The songwriting duo, Edward Pola and George Wylie, whose biggest hit had been the 1950 ditty, "I Said My Pajamas (And Put On My Pray'rs)," penned "Wonderful." Other songs of theirs were recorded by Doris Day, Bing Crosby and Peggy Lee. In addition to his surviving holiday hit, Wylie is also known for a second pop-culture coup — he co-wrote the theme song to the kitschy 1960's television show, *Gilligan's Island.*

Few successful Christmas songs originate from Broadway musicals. One exception is "We Need A Little Christmas," written by Jerry Herman for the 1966 production, *Mame*, starring Angela Lansbury. In 1974, Lucille Ball took over for Lansbury as leading lady for a film version of it, in which she sang Herman's holiday chestnut. Since then many artists have covered the classic, and in 1995, Andy Williams cut it for his Christmas disc, appropriately titled *We Need A Little Christmas*.

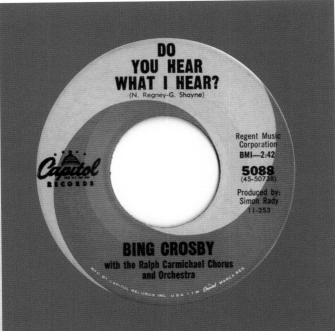

Even though his holiday appeal remains timeless, by the 1960's, new Bing Crosby Christmas releases began slowing down. Among the handful that received his Midas touch then was 1963's "Do You Hear What I Hear?," written by Noel Regney and Gloria Shayne. The following year, Decca Records launched *Bing Crosby's Favorite Songs Of Christmas*, and among that collection was Johnny Marks' evergreen, "I Heard The Bells On Christmas Day." Marks' lyrics for the tune, which was orignally released by Crosby in 1956, were adapted from the 1861 Henry Wadsworth Longfellow poem, *The Christmas Bells*.

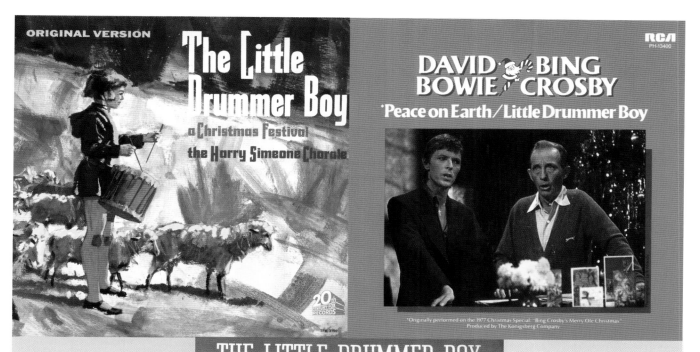

Harry Simeon co-wrote "The Little Drummer Boy" with Katherine Davis and Henry Onorati in 1958, and his chorus, made up of twenty-five voices, was the first act to record it. A graduate of The Julliard School Of Music, Simeon was for many years an arranger for Fred Waring, and he arranged the music and conducted the orchestra for his "Drummer Boy" recording. In 1963, his chorus became one of the first to record "Do You Hear What I Hear?" Five years later, Rankin/Bass would build an entire television special based upon "Drummer Boy." In 1977 it became a Bing Crosby/David Bowie duet. Released posthumously, Simeon's song was one of the last to have been recorded by Crosby, who performed it for his 1977 Christmas television special. Bing Crosby died on October 14, 1977.

As traditional holiday music continued to captivate listeners, the new rock/funk/Motown sounds of the 1960's gave birth to the modernization of the Christmas carol. Shown clockwise are: "Another Beatles Christmas Record" (1964), "The Beach Boys' Christmas Album" (1964), "The 4 Seasons' Christmas Album" (1966), "A Christmas Gift For You From Phil Spector" (1964), "A Merry Christmas — The Supremes" (1965) and "Jackson 5 Christmas Album" (1970). "James Brown's Funky Christmas" (1995, center) is a compilation of songs from both "James Brown And His Famous Flames Sing Christmas Songs" (1966) and "Soulful Christmas" (1968).

The Modern Carol

II

The Carpenters on the cover of "Rolling Stone" magazine (July 4, 1974)

MERRY CHRISTMAS DARLING — 1970

WRITERS:
  RICHARD CARPENTER
  FRANK POOLER

PRODUCER:
  JACK DAUGHERTY

ARTIST: CARPENTERS

A&M RECORDS

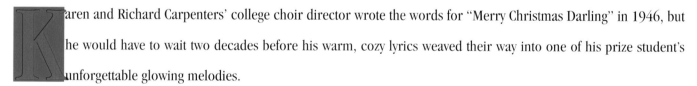

Karen and Richard Carpenters' college choir director wrote the words for "Merry Christmas Darling" in 1946, but he would have to wait two decades before his warm, cozy lyrics weaved their way into one of his prize student's unforgettable glowing melodies.

In 1964, while his sister Karen was still in high school pursuing her new-found passion of drum playing, seventeen-year-old Richard Carpenter eagerly prepared to begin musical studies at California State University, Long Beach. Shortly before enrolling, he tagged along one day with a friend already studying voice there, and they quickly came to the attention of Frank Pooler, then head of the university's division of choral studies. He immediately noticed Richard's impressive vocal acumen and invited him to sign up for the choir: "I gave him an on-the-spot vocal audition," he recalled, "and his ear, one of the best I'd ever heard, absolutely astounded me."[1]

As a way of encouraging sixteen-year-old Karen to sing, Richard decided to bring her to him on Saturday mornings for vocal instruction, and Pooler became one of the first musical professionals to recognize her unique voice. Later, when she had joined Richard at the university (and in the choir), Pooler, now the pair's influential mentor, vehemently defended Karen's natural talent when she was briefly suspended for poor academic performance.

1970

He was also consistently supportive of and enamored with Richard's musical achievements, so much so that in 1966, he asked him to pen the music for "Merry Christmas Darling's" romantic lyrics, words that had been sitting around without a satisfactory setting since the Second World War.

Karen, Frank Pooler and Richard in Sydney, Australia (1972)

"In 1966, Frank Pooler asked me to set music to a lyric that he had written twenty years earlier," remembers Richard in the 1991 liner notes for *Carpenters — From The Top*. "We were all pleased with the result, and for the next several years Karen and I would perform the song at different Christmas parties for which we were hired."

Right before the decade closed, with the Vietnam War violently raging, the smooth-sounding Carpenters were signed to A&M Records, and the sweet innocence of their majestic choral harmonies provided a soothing balm for a country broken in half.

The following year, on November 16, 1970, four months after they landed their first number-one record with "Close To You," they completed the final mixdown of "Merry Christmas Darling," and it was officially released as a single four days later with the non-holiday "Mr. Guder" as its B-side.

Production credit for Richard and Karen's holiday classic would be given to Jack Daugherty, once a trumpeter for Woody Herman's band, who helped bring the duo to the attention of Herb Alpert, co-owner of A&M. According to some sources however, Richard played a major role in that production, as well as all of the Carpenters' early work, even though Daugherty was given top billing for it.

Weeks after its debut, "Darling" shot to number one on Billboard's Christmas Singles chart, and returned to that position in 1971 and 1973.

Now knowing there was a tremendous Christmas market out there for them, the Carpenters began sowing the seeds for their first seasonal set — 1978's *Christmas Portrait*. The rock invasion of the 60's and 70's, however, suddenly made their plan seem old-fashioned to many in the music industry, including the sibling's record label. After work was initiated

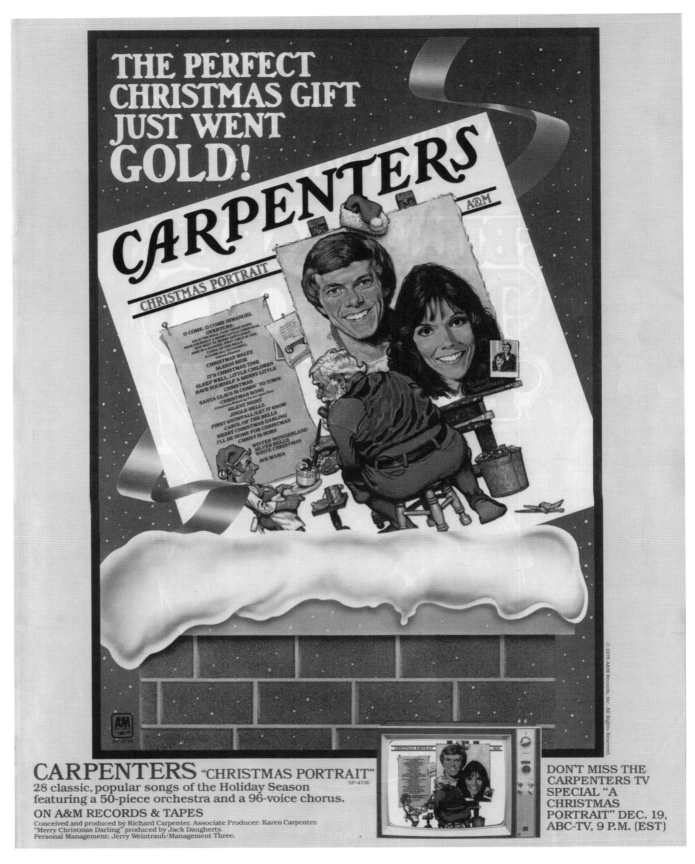

on it, A&M became even more reticent, since at that point the cost of the long length of time spent recording, along with the price of a full orchestra and choir, made it the most expensive Carpenters' album to produce.

Since Karen had always been unhappy with her original vocal, some of that time went into cutting a new version of "Darling": "The lead vocal was re-recorded at Karen's request in 1978," stated Richard in *From The Top*'s liner notes. Fortunately her 1970 interpretation has been preserved on disc as part of that boxed set.

Record company problems continued to plague the pair, with *Portrait* receiving little attention from A&M, leaving Karen at one point confused by her label's lack of promotion. "*Christmas Portrait* assumed its own momentum however,

and has sold more than two million units, demonstrating that when they found their niche, their audience was waiting."[2]

Over time, that fan base continues to grow, making *Portrait* one of the rare holiday albums to remain in the top ten throughout the 70's, 80's, 90's and beyond.

In 1984, one year after Karen's tragic death due to complications from *Anorexia Nervosa*, Richard decided to give those fans an unexpected gift by releasing a second Carpenters' holiday album entitled *An Old Fashioned Christmas*. It served to resurrect Karen's voice by including unused recordings from her *Christmas Portrait* sessions. It also contained the haunting track, "Little Altar Boy," a song Richard claims to be his unsurpassed favorite vocal performance ever achieved by his sister.

Celebrating the Carpenters' first gold album — "Close To You." From left to right: Jack Daugherty, Richard Carpenter, Jerry Moss, Karen Carpenter and Herb Alpert (1970)

Karen Carpenter (c. 1970)

CARPENTERS' CHRISTMAS DISCOGRAPHY

SINGLES

TITLE	B-SIDE	YEAR
Merry Christmas Darling	Mr. Guder	1970
Santa Claus Is Comin' To Town	Merry Christmas Darling	1974
The Christmas Song	Merry Christmas Darling	1977
Do You Hear What I Hear?	Little Altar Boy	1984

ALBUMS

TITLE	YEAR
Christmas Portrait	1978
An Old-Fashioned Christmas	1984
Christmas Portrait — The Special Edition	1990
Christmas Collection (*Two disc set containing both Carpenters' Christmas Albums*)	1998

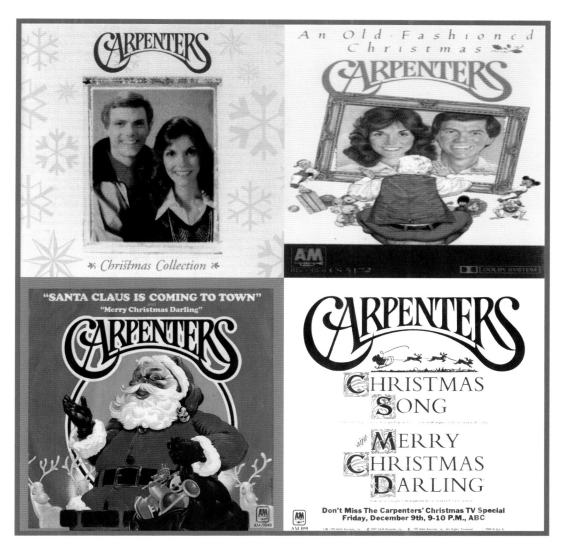

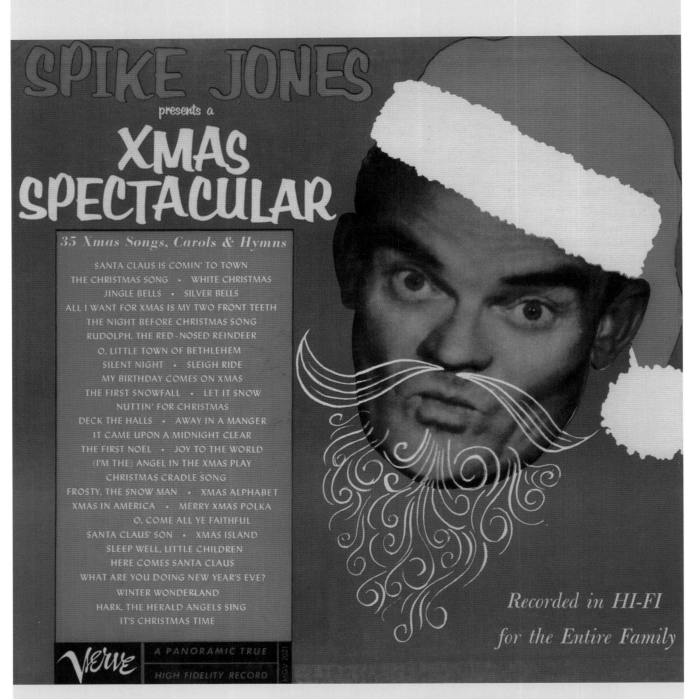

According to Karen Carpenter, much of "Christmas Portrait" was modeled after the above 1956 Spike Jones holiday LP.

KAREN CARPENTER INTERVIEW — RADIO STATION KIQQ
LOS ANGELES — DECEMBER 24, 1978

On *Christmas Portrait:*

"To sing these songs is something that gives me more pleasure than I can really put into words. We've taken a lot of the material off of this album from the original Spike Jones Christmas album, which is, in our opinion, practically the best Christmas album ever recorded. I enjoy doing this music all year round, which has been proved, because it took us fourteen months to cut this album, and while people were walking down the aisles saying, 'What in heaven's name are you doing Christmas stuff in the middle of August?' it never occurred to me, because I could do it anytime of the day or night, anytime of the year."

On *"Merry Christmas Darling:"*

"'Merry Christmas Darling' I think is a little special to both of us, because Richard wrote it, and the lyrics were written by the choral director at Long Beach State choir, where we went to school, Frank Pooler. Frank was very helpful in our college days, when we were trying to get a contract and constantly missing classes and everything. He was the only one down there who actually understood what we were after, and he stood behind us all the way. We just did a benefit at Long Beach State, for a scholarship fund, and we did it with the choir, and the whole thing, and we did 'Christmas Darling,' and he just glows every time we do it. I think it's my favorite, because it's really close to me."

Richard Carpenter on *Christmas Portrait:*

"For years after the release of 'Merry Christmas Darling,' Karen and I talked about recording a Christmas album. By early 1978, we finally got under way. I wanted the arrangements to be in the traditional vein. I wanted the album to play almost as a continuous performance and to feature some lovely lesser known tunes as well as the standards. Since the two of us liked so many Christmas songs, we were soon into a marathon of sessions. Ultimately we had recorded almost enough to fill two albums. Karen outdid herself vocally, particularly on 'Have Yourself A Merry Little Christmas,' and Bach/Gounod's 'Ave Maria.'"

"Merry Christmas Darling" was the follow-up release to "We've Only Just Begun," which debuted in September, 1970, and peaked at number two on Billboard's Hot 100 Singles chart.

AN INTERVIEW WITH FRANK POOLER

During the time Karen's voice was turning Richard and Frank Pooler's collaboration into what would become a rare post-1960's Christmas hit, he remained a cherished confidant. They invited him to direct choirs for their 1977 Christmas television special, and for the album track "Because We Are In Love," which became Karen's wedding song. In Long Beach, California, on June 25, 1983, Pooler also directed the choir for a concert that honored his beloved student shortly after she passed away.

Did you write "Merry Christmas Darling's" 1946 lyrics for anyone in particular?

I was going with a girl at that time — I was a teenager — and we had just started going to college. We split at Christmas time for the usual holiday, and I wrote the song for her. However, we broke up shortly after that, and I had wondered for fifty years whether or not she actually knew that was for her. About three years ago, I found out where she was, where she was living, and we met for the first time. I said, 'Did you ever know that I'd written that song for you?' And she said, 'I had no idea.' And I said, 'Well, it's true.' I gave her a copy of the song, records and stuff like that. And she said, 'Well, now I have a treasure!' Fifty years, and she didn't know it. But it was just written because I missed her during a Christmas holiday. It was really wonderful to renew old acquaintances and to finally get it off my chest that the piece had really been written for her. That's really how the thing came into existence.

Was it unusual for you to write a song for someone back then?

I've always been dabbling in music, in fact I've spent my life in music. I was writing back then and used to write charts for the big band in the high school I went to. I used to write a lot of songs. In fact, I still do.

Where did you write the lyrics?

I wrote them at a summer home that my family had in northern Wisconsin. I grew up in Wisconsin, in a little town on the border of Minnesota. I wrote "Merry Christmas Darling" when I was a freshman at college and she was a sophomore.

March 1971

Did you just write the lyrics for the song?

I wrote words and music at the same time. The song was performed a lot back then, and it was actually published. I remember there was a young group made up of three guys in Boston that performed it a lot. Then a lot of junior high school kids picked up on the thing and sang choral arrangements of it.

Has the original version ever been professionally recorded?

No, I don't think so. It was recorded often but not professionally, just by amateur groups and singers.

How was that music different from the music Richard Carpenter wrote?

It's just a completely different melody. Richard has never heard the original melody. I never gave that to him, I just gave him the words.

Did the words go through any changes since you wrote them?

I don't think so.

What was the song's connection to the Persian Gulf War?

During the Persian Gulf War crisis, it was played a lot as part of some kind of greeting-card commercial on Los Angeles radio. One of the local disc jockeys was playing it every twenty-five minutes, because he thought it was very appropriate for people at that particular time. The sentiment was expressive of what he thought a lot of the guys in the Gulf were thinking about.

Can you talk about some of the other songs you've written?

I haven't written any other popular songs that have been recorded except for a new song I just wrote for my hometown. Most of the other music I've written has been more of a classical nature, and there's hundreds of those, which all have been published. I have over 600 publications of choral music. That's really how I've spent my life. The work that I did with Carpenters was kind of on the side from my academic work.

How did you end up working at California State University at Long Beach?

Well, they offered me a job. I was teaching in a town north of Chicago, Illinois, when I got a telephone call one night. It was about twenty below zero. Someone asked me if I'd be interested teaching in Long Beach.

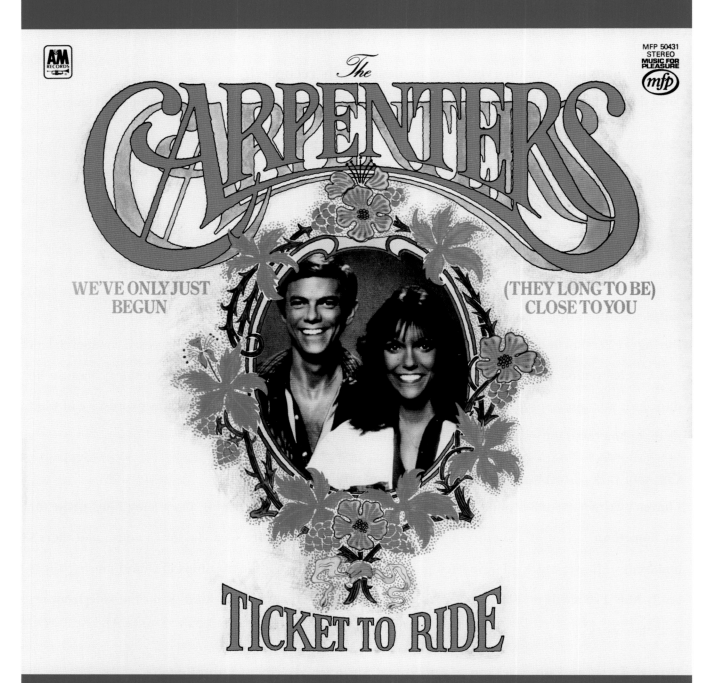

Following their string of successes in 1970, A&M Records re-released "Offering," the Carpenters' first album, in 1971, and renamed it "Ticket To Ride." A UK version of it is shown above.

I asked what the temperature was out there, and was told it was eighty-two degrees. I said, 'I'll take the job.' They said, 'Don't you want to know what it is or how it pays?' I said, 'No, get me out of here!' I started working there in 1960, about four years before I met Richard Carpenter.

How did you meet Richard?

He brought up a young man to audition for my choir. I thought the young man was very good, but Richard, who was playing piano for him, just knocked me out. He had such a superb musical ear. I played patterns of increasing difficulty on the keyboard and asked him to sing them back for me. He could do anything. When Richard started school the following year he joined my choir, and was in it until "Close To You." He used to bring Karen up when she was still in high school, and I would give her voice lessons every Saturday morning. He would then cart her off to Hollywood for drum lessons. He was very careful to nurture her musical education. She later enrolled at Long Beach State and was there for a few years too. The two of them were both in my choir at the same time for two or three years. I have great pictures of them in the choir.

Did you single them out for solo work when they were in your choir?

Oh, Richard was my piano accompanist and Karen did a lot of solos. A lot of the things that they later recorded were first introduced in our choir. I featured Karen a lot back then. Later, the choir recorded with them under different names. I think my girls sang back-up on "I Need To Be In Love."

What did you think of Karen's voice when you first heard it?

Well, it knocked me out. She could do anything with her voice, and it was phenomenal. It was low, it was high. The way we used to work Karen's lessons is that she would do the usual classical stuff, Schubert and Brahms, and then we would usually end the lesson with something that Richard had written. So it was kind of a classical/pop orientation, which is really how Long Beach State was organized at that time. We did an awful lot of popular music and jazz, as well as the traditional material. This attracted a lot of people like Karen and Richard, and many others.

Did you ever think her voice would go on to do what it did?

The first time I met her I never dreamed that it would ever get to that stage, because it's not just talent and voice that does that — it's luck. I had no idea, but I knew that they were both great, and that something was going to happen, particularly with Richard, because he was so determined. I mean the guy was working and auditioning for everything constantly. Events and timing worked out just right for them. Karen's voice though was a natural gift. And I think musicality is a gift from God, you either got it or you haven't got it. If you haven't got it, no amount of training is ever going to give it to you.

Did Karen learn anything from you that she later brought to her recording sessions?

One of the things about being a good teacher is knowing when to leave somebody alone. I think too much education can be a bad thing.

Why did you defend Karen when she was academically suspended?

So often there are these really superb talents that don't fit the mold of the curriculum, and if you don't fit it can be hard on you. I always fought hard for them and felt they were special. I spoke up for a lot of kids who weren't interested in taking music education courses and that kind of crap, and were thrown out because of it.

How did Richard end up writing new music for your song?

Richard was in one of my voice classes. At the time he and Karen had been playing at little clubs and restaurants around town, and it was the Christmas holiday season. He said, 'I'm so sick of "White Christmas" and the other Christmas songs,' and asked me for something else. Frankly, I had forgotten about my Christmas song, but when he asked it triggered something, and I told him I had a song that I wrote a long time ago that he might want to look at. I went home and dug out the old sheet music that had a picture of these lay brothers from Boston on the cover. I played the tune through, and I didn't like it particularly anymore, so I just gave him the words.

Do you know anything about the process Richard went through to write "Darling's" music?

He once said that this was the first song he ever wrote a melody to where the song was complete. He had the complete lyric, and then he wrote the tune up in the practice room at Long Beach State. When he works with another songwriter he might have a tune, and the person might supply the words later. Or there might be bits and pieces of both as they worked together. But he acknowledged that "Merry Christmas Darling" was the first tune he had written music for that was brought to him complete in itself. And he recalled that I had given it to him, and he had gone upstairs to a practice room and wrote the music.

Do you think Karen and Richard took some of what they learned in your chorus and integrated it later on?

I wrote an article about that in *The Choral Journal* in 1972 called *The Choral Sound of the Carpenters*. The choir training helped shape the Carpenters' music, especially on such earlier recordings as "Invocation" and "Mr. Guder." Richard once described the Carpenters' emerging sound as a choral approach to pop.

What was it about Karen's voice that made it such a perfect match for Christmas music?

Her voice was a voice that had instrumental implications. She could sound like a tenor sax, or a flute. It was a voice that was capable of so many different colors. These weren't colors that were taught, they sprang from her heart. She could move from one kind of instrumental timbre to another. That's what made Karen really unusual. She had another side to her that very few people ever saw — she was a very funny girl. She could be marvelously funny.

What's your opinion on her ability to interpret a lyric?

She was like Sinatra. Karen didn't make music, Karen was music.

Were you a part of the actual recording session for "Merry Christmas Darling?"

That was the second or third single that they ever made. I had heard that they were performing it live around various places. In early November 1970, I got a call from Richard and he said, 'Would you come up to A&M studios? I have a surprise for you.' I went up there and he said, 'Sit down.' He then flipped a switch. All of a sudden this sound started coming out, and it was "Merry Christmas Darling." I had never heard the music, and it took me a couple of seconds to identify what it was. Suddenly, it occurred to me

Richard and Karen with Frank Pooler in California (1967)

that I wrote those words when I was a kid. That was a Christmas surprise for me. I had not known it was recorded, and didn't know what he had done with it. I was overwhelmed with the sound, and moved to tears. I could not believe that those words had come back to life after all those years.

Would Karen be surprised that her voice is still relevant today?

I think that she would be very pleased and very happy to know that the legacy keeps going on. I don't think it would surprise her. When you've got something, you know you've got something, regardless of what anyone says about it. The stuff that Richard picked out for her to sing is timeless, isn't it? Their music is eternal, and is miniature three-minute art. Like the operas of Puccini, it will go on forever.

John Lennon and Yoko Ono on the cover of "Rolling Stone" (January 22, 1981)

HAPPY XMAS (WAR IS OVER) — 1971

WRITERS:
JOHN LENNON
YOKO ONO

PRODUCERS:
PHIL SPECTOR
JOHN LENNON
YOKO ONO

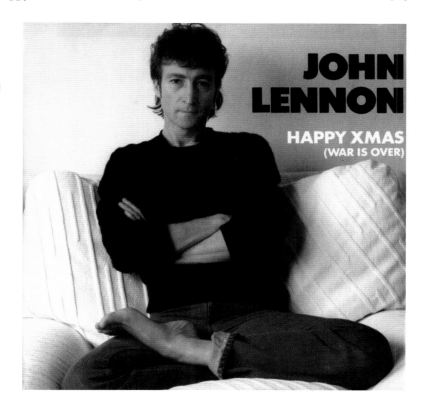

ARTISTS: JOHN & YOKO/PLASTIC ONO BAND WITH THE HARLEM COMMUNITY CHOIR

APPLE RECORDS

In 1968, over 500,000 American troops were stationed in Vietnam, and a tragic record had been set for the devastating quagmire in Indo-China — more than 12,000 US soldiers had lost their lives that year. To protest, John Lennon and Yoko Ono initiated a long peace campaign, defined by dramatically staged symbolic events designed to capture quick media attention.

First they planted two acorns at Coventry Cathedral in London, which they felt ideally represented East (Yoko) meeting West (John). The following year, as the death toll continued to rise, the newly married couple decided to turn their Amsterdam honeymoon into a peace rally "bed-in," and invited reporters to watch as they stayed in bed for seven days straight. At a second Montreal "bed-in," they actually recorded the song, "Give Peace A Chance," in bed. "The least Yoko and I can do is hog the headlines and make people laugh," said John at the time. "We're willing to be the world's clowns if it will do any good. For reasons known only to themselves, people print what I say. And I say, 'Peace.'"[1]

One of the pair's most famous peace stunts occurred just before Christmas 1969, the time when they rented billboards in eleven high-profile locations around the world, like New York City's Times Square and London's Piccadilly Circus. They now decided to raise awareness by plastering huge signs on these boards declaring: "War is over if you want it. Happy Christmas from John and Yoko." A second poster followed simply stating, "We Want It," and in December they threw a *Peace For Christmas* concert in London. John later spoke about the public's response to their performance-art pranks saying, "We got

John and Yoko's Montreal "bed-in" (1969)

just thank-you's from lots of youth around the world — for all the things we were doing — that inspired *them* to do something. We had a lot of response from other than pop fans, which was interesting. From all walks of life and age."[2]

As the killing in Southeast Asia continued to rage, The Beatles disbanded, and a newly solo Lennon moved from England to New York City. The public outpouring felt in the late 60's most likely inspired John and Yoko to turn their billboard anti-war event into what has since become an enduring Yuletide modern classic called "Happy Xmas (War Is Over)." It wasn't the first time Lennon recorded a holiday tune though — during his days with The Beatles, he made special Christmas records for the band's fan club every year, and had once expressed a desire to pen his own seasonal song. "I always wanted to write a Christmas record," he told reporters, "something that would last forever."[3]

"Billboard" magazine ad for "Phil Spector's Christmas Album"

"Happy Xmas" represented John Lennon's first New York recording, and like his recent hit "Imagine," it once again

Paul McCartney was the third solo Beatle to have a Christmas single in the 1970's. In 1974, Apple Records yielded George Harrison's "Ding Dong, Ding Dong." McCartney's "Wonderful Christmastime" (upper right) was issued in 1979 and re-released twice by Columbia Records. Several re-releases of "Happy Xmas (War Is Over)" have been launched over the years, including one put out by Geffen Records two years following Lennon's death (upper left). The CD shown above is a 1997 promotional-only release. Shown below McCartney and Lennon are two discs which contain a rare cover of "Happy Xmas." The Alarm recorded it in 1996, and their version appears on the 1997 various artists set, "Rockin' In Your Stockin'" (lower left). In 1998, Celine Dion included it on "These Are Special Times," her first holiday album (lower right).

called upon people to visualize the ideal. During his first full month as an American resident, he went into the studio in October, 1971, to create it with Yoko Ono and producer Phil Spector, then famous for his "wall of sound" technique. Spector had previously produced Lennon on "Instant Karma (We All Shine On)," and worked as a re-mixer for The Beatles' *Let It Be* soundtrack. His own classic 1963 holiday set, *A Christmas Gift For You From Phil Spector,* featured Motown-sounding artists like The Ronettes and The Crystals. It was re-issued on The Beatles' Apple label in 1972.

Lennon requested that Spector imitate the background of George Harrison's "Try Some, Buy Some," which had recently been recorded by his wife Ronnie Spector, lead singer of The Ronettes. He later referred to the session for "Happy Xmas" as "beautiful." Part of the beauty he remembered could have been associated with the children from the Harlem Community Choir, who were brought in by Spector to give the tune a community touch.

On December 1, 1971, "Happy Xmas (War Is Over)" was released in the USA with the B-side, "Listen, The Snow Is Falling." It was postponed in England until the following year due to rumors of a publishing feud over Yoko's co-credit writing contribution. It went top five there, peaked at number three stateside on Billboard's Christmas Singles chart, and re-entered on four subsequent occasions. In 1975, the song was included on the Apple album, *Shaved Fish.*

John Lennon was murdered on December 8, 1980, and miraculously, much of the work he left behind, including his classic holiday evergreen, continues to inspire peace in new generations of listeners. "As long as people imagine that someone is doing something to them and that they have no control, then they have no control," he once told a reporter. "We're just as responsible as the man who pushes the button."[4]

French release of "Happy Xmas (War Is Over)" (1972), with the B-side, "Listen, The Snow Is Falling" (facing page)

Christmas single releases began to steadily decline in the 1970's. Among the handful of new holiday hits spawned then were "Feliz Navidad" (1970), written and recorded by Jose Feliciano (center), and Elton John's 1973 opus "Step Into Christmas" (upper right). The Eagles' 1978 cover of "Please Come Home For Christmas" (lower left), a song penned and recorded by Charles Brown, became a widely-popular interpretation of this 1960's classic. Even though they failed to powerfully penetrate the mainstream, two Christmas songs that aptly represent 70's musical trends are Wayne Newton's '76 Disco bauble "Jingle Bell Hustle" (included on Rhino Records' *Have A Nice Christmas — Holiday Hits of the 70's*, upper left), and The Kinks' punk-rock "Father Christmas," released first as a single in 1977, and later included on the album, *Come Dancing With The Kinks* (lower right).

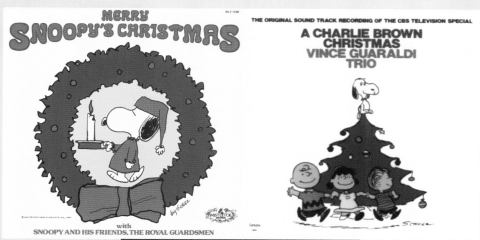

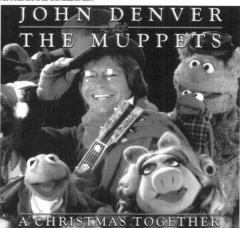

The 1970's saw the debut of the Vince Guaraldi Trio's soundtrack to Charles Schultz's children's television special *A Charlie Brown Christmas* (upper right). Launched in 1965, the perennial TV favorite contained the now-standard "Christmas Time Is Here," a tune created by Vince Guaraldi and Lee Mendelson. Another yuletide nugget based on a Peanuts character is "Snoopy's Christmas" (upper right), recorded by the Royal Guardsmen, and issued as a single in 1967. During the kitschy decade of the 70's, Miss Piggy competed with Snoopy for worldwide attention, and in 1979 John Denver joined voices with her and other Muppets to create *A Christmas Together* (center). In the early 70's The Partridge Family (lower left) and The Brady Bunch (lower right) were also honored with their own holiday sets.

It Must Have Been The Mistletoe

(OUR FIRST CHRISTMAS)

Words and Music by JUSTIN WILDE and DOUG KONECKY

Barbara Mandrell

Recorded on MCA Records

 Exclusive Selling Agent for
the United States and Canada
WARNER BROS. PUBLICATIONS INC.
265 Secaucus Road • Secaucus, N.J. 07096 2037
A Time Warner Company

$3.50
in U.S.A.

IT MUST HAVE BEEN THE MISTLETOE (OUR FIRST CHRISTMAS) — 1980

WRITERS:
JUSTIN WILDE
DOUG KONECKY

PRODUCER:
TOM COLLINS

ARTIST:
BARBARA MANDRELL

MCA RECORDS

(left to right) Doug Konecky & Justin Wilde

War was finally over, pop-punk raged, and near the heat and haze of "Beverly Hills, LA," former marketing major Justin Wilde convinced his Jewish songwriting partner Doug Konecky to collaborate with him in 1979 on something outrageously bizarre — writing a dreamy Christmas song long after it had become fashionable or easily profitable to do such a thing. The pair met two years before in a UCLA songwriting workshop, and quickly began collaborating on sentimental tunes with Big Band titles like "There's Magic In My Love." Little did they know what they were in for, however, when Wilde mistakenly believed that making money from a traditional holiday melody built around romantic images of mistletoe and falling snow, would be as easy for them as it had been for Bing and Berlin.

But if anyone could perform such a Herculean task at a time when the country took pride in declaring the death of anything musically old-fashioned or corny, it would have to be Justin Wilde, known in the yuletide music industry as "Mr. Christmas," and owner of Christmas and Holiday Music publishing company. "Mr. Christmas" credits his parents, Ruth and Jerry Volomino, with instilling in him a phoenix-like determination he called upon to single-handedly turn "Mistletoe" into an evergreen classic.

BARBARA MANDRELL

CHRISTMAS AT OUR HOUSE

MCA-5519

1984

In the early eighties, Wilde worked relentlessly at sending their song to any popular singer he thought might be the first to record it and fulfill his dream of making it a timeless standard. It was a difficult enterprise, since in order to save money, record companies were no longer eager to invest in new Christmas music.

"Before I got the first record on it, I had sent the song out 376 times," says Wilde. "Back in the 40's, 50's and early 60's, when it was fairly much of a singles market, it was very commonplace for labels to release Christmas singles. By the time I was promoting 'Mistletoe,' it was now an album-oriented market, and they were hardly ever releasing singles from the albums anymore."

With this new record-label trend taking place, which sacrificed the Christmas single for the holiday LP, it became easier for companies to recycle old standards, and made it more difficult for a new song like Wilde's to pierce the nation's collective consciousness.

Despite all these obstacles, Wilde continued to independently promote "Mistletoe." After four years, his big break finally arrived when Dolly Parton turned it down in favor of her own material.

"In 1984, when I heard that Dolly Parton and Kenny Rogers were doing a duet Christmas album, I was in seventh heaven, and thought it was the answer to my prayers," remembers Wilde. "I gave tapes to everyone involved in the project, but all of a sudden, Dolly came in just before the recording session started with about six original Christmas songs she had written, which just about eliminated all other original material. I was devastated, but I picked myself up, because I knew that Barbara Mandrell was also getting ready to record a Christmas album. So I marched myself home, made another

My sincere thanks to all the people involved with the making of this album. I'm especially proud of the songs and the really gifted people who wrote them, the unique and lovely arrangements of Bergen White, the incredible performances given by the musicians and singers and the excellence with which they are presented by Tom Collins and my engineers. My thanks also to my sisters Louise and Irlene for singing with me on the song, "From Our House To Yours." Music has always been such an important part of Christmas at our house. My sisters and I would put together a Christmas program at home when we were little girls and have our parents sit and listen. As much as I love Christmas and its music, being able to record this album makes it the best Christmas present I've ever received and I thank you. From our house to yours we send our love . . .

Merry Christmas,

Barbara Mandrell

Kathie Lee Gifford

tape, and Fed-Exed it to Barbara's producer at the time — Tom Collins. They got the tape on Friday, and Barbara began cutting my song on Monday."

Soon after Barbara Mandrell recorded "Mistletoe" for her 1984 *Christmas At Our House* set, she was involved in a serious car accident, and MCA Records halted plans to send any of the album's songs to pop radio stations. A promotional vinyl 45, with "Mistletoe" as its B-side, had been issued to country radio only.

That didn't stop him from quickly coming up with a plan in which he and Konecky would diligently hand deliver "Mistletoe" for five days straight to pop stations in their home state of California during the holiday season of 1984.

"Because of her horrible car accident, Barbara Mandrell was out of commission for the next nine months and wasn't able to do any promotion on the album," recalls Wilde. "At that point I took over the promotional campaign myself, gathered those records, and turned 'Mistletoe' into the A-side by

using a nail to scratch off the other two songs on it so only our song could be played. Doug and I then left for five days to deliver them ourselves by car to over 100 stations in California. I surveyed all of them the following January and found that most played it, and that I had received a great listener response."

Over the next ten years, Wilde continued to independently mail Mandrell's version to radio stations each Christmas. During that time, he sent the song out to a thousand other artists, hoping to land new covers of it. Attaining new recordings had always been an important factor in turning a holiday tune into a classic, but Wilde discovered that unlike

Vikki Carr

the past, most artists were now reluctant to record a song someone had already released.

"Some of the major standards of the golden era of songwriting in the 1940's and 50's had been cut fifty to seventy or more times," explains Wilde. "Someone like Perry Como or Patti Page didn't care whether forty-five people recorded a song before they were led to do their own version of it. But after the Beatles, few people wanted to record a song someone else had already recorded."

Despite facing these new challenges, Wilde persevered, and was successful in getting two other artists — Vikki Carr and Kathie Lee Gifford — to include it on their own Christmas projects. Over the years he would also single-handedly get Mandrell's "Mistletoe" onto fourteen compilation holiday discs, thirty-five sheet music folio books, a soap opera, a TV

movie, various choral arrangements, and even a music box. "I left no stone unturned," he says. "Any place I could find to put the song in order to expose it to the public, I pursued."

"Mr. Christmas" finally knew his exhaustive decade-long effort to make his song a familiar standard was paying off when he was out holiday shopping one December day at a Hallmark greeting card store in California. "I was in one of the malls doing my Christmas shopping," he recalls, "and suddenly I heard 'It Must Have Been The Mistletoe' playing on their speaker system. I was actually paying the cashier at the time, and I stopped dead in my tracks, hardly able to speak. Finally I screamed out, 'They are playing my song, they're playing my song!' She thought I was nuts, until I explained to her I had co-written it, and that it was the first time I had ever heard it played in public."

After hearing the demo of "It Must Have Been The Mistletoe" in her car, Barbra Streisand fell in love with it. She recorded the song for her second holiday set, "Christmas Memories," released in 2001.

CHRISTMAS and HOLIDAY MUSIC
SONGCASTLE MUSIC

"IT MUST HAVE BEEN THE MISTLETOE"
(Our First Christmas)

By:
Justin Wilde
Doug Konecky

Verse: It Must Have Been The Mistletoe
          The lazy fire, the falling snow
          The magic in the frosty air
          That feeling everywhere
          It must have been the pretty lights
          That glistened in the silent night
          Or maybe just the stars so bright
          That shined above you ...

Chorus: Our first Christmas
          More than we'd been dreaming of
          Old St. Nicholas
          Had his fingers crossed
              that we would fall in love

Verse: It could have been the holiday
          The midnight ride upon a sleigh
          The countryside, all dressed in white
          That crazy snowball fight
          It could have been the steeple bell
          That wrapped us up within its spell
          It only took one kiss to know
          It Must Have Been The Mistletoe

Chorus: Our first Christmas
          More than we'd been dreaming of
          Old St. Nicholas
      ** Must have known that kiss
              would lead to all of this

MAKES A GREAT
SOLO or DUET

Verse: It Must Have Been The Mistletoe
          The lazy fire, the falling snow
          The magic in the frosty air
          That made me love you
          On Christmas Eve a wish came true
          That night I fell in love with you
          It only took one kiss to know
          It Must Have Been The Mistletoe

Copyright Secured By: SONGCASTLE MUSIC

1984 Southern California Radio Survey: "IT MUST HAVE BEEN THE MISTLETOE"

The 42 stations which reported playing the song included:

KWDJ	Riverside	KDIG	San Bernardino (FM)	KWRM	Corona
KCKC	San Bernardino	KGUD	Riverside/Banning	KGFM	Bakersfield
KCBQ	San Diego	KGGI	San Bernardino	KNJO	Thousand Oaks
KNOB	Anaheim	KNTF	Alta Loma/Ontario	KGEO	Bakersfield
KQLH	San Bernardino	KAVL	Lancaster	KEZY	Anaheim
KAPV	Apple Valley	KOTE	Lancaster	KWVE	San Clemente
KAVR	Apple Valley	KDOL	Mojave	XETRA	San Diego
KIOT	Barstow	KAFY	Bakersfield	KSON	San Diego
KBPK	Buena Park	KUZZ	Bakersfield	KAVO	Fallbrook
KRUZ	Santa Barbara	KHAY	Ventura	KPSI	Palm Springs
KBLS	Santa Barbara	KCSN	Northridge	KDES	Palm Springs
KBBQ	Ventura	KRTH	Los Angeles	KCMJ	Palm Springs
KSRF	Santa Monica	KZLA	Los Angeles AM & FM	KMEN	San Bernardino
KVVQ	Victorville	KLAC	Los Angeles	KDIG	San Bernardino (AM)

The songwriters' independent effort to turn "It Must Have Been The Mistletoe" into a timeless classic began in 1984 when Justin Wilde and Doug Konecky visited the above forty-two radio stations to personally deliver Barbara Mandrell's recording of their song.

MORE WITH JUSTIN WILDE

How did you end up writing a Christmas song?

I was a marketing major in college and was always quite adept at the business side of the music industry. Doug and I had written two or three non-Christmas songs, but In 1979, I told him that I really wanted to write a holiday song, because if you ever have a Christmas standard, it will be around forever. So he agreed, and I threw the title, "It Must Have Been The Mistletoe," at him, which he liked. He started twiddling around with the music, taped some of the chorus and first verse, which I took home. We got together for maybe four sessions, at the most, at his house in Glendale, California, before it was finally in its completed form.

When did you know you had a potential hit on your hands?

As soon as we finished the song, we played it for some songwriters in one of Doug's workshops in LA, so that we could get some feedback on it. These people didn't pull any punches. They were very critical of any weak spots in songs they critiqued. Doug played the song on the piano, and I sang the melody for them. They loved it the way it was. Nobody thought it needed any changes.

Why did you decide to publish "Mistletoe" yourself?

Because I could never find a publisher willing to work my songs as hard as I was. My philosophy has always been that nobody wants to see me succeed more than I do, so I knew that I was going to have to do my own publishing from day one if I was ever going to launch any of my songs.

Did anyone show interest in "Mistletoe" prior to Barbara Mandrell?

Actually, the song had a history before it ever got recorded. In 1979, Doug and I created a demo, and the guy who played drums on it worked with Glen Campbell, and got it to him. Campbell liked it so much that he immediately decided to sing it as a duet with Tanya Tucker for a CBS show he was taping called *A Country Christmas*. It aired during the 1980 holiday season.

Other than Glen Campbell and Tanya Tucker, did anyone else perform your song for television?

In 1982, on *An NBC Family Christmas*, which was a special composed almost entirely of actors from various television series, David and Meredith Baxter Birney sang the song as a duet.

What was it like promoting Mandrell's record to radio by yourself in 1984?

I was on the road for five days driving to every big and little radio station in California, giving them copies of the single along with a bunch of mistletoe. It was interesting because I'd go into some larger cities like San Diego, and couldn't get past the front desk. But in some of the smaller areas, I remember going to stations where there were only two people working there, and they were so happy to see anybody in the music business. After five minutes, I had head phones on and was in front of a microphone doing a half-hour radio interview about "It Must Have Been The Mistletoe."

Why did you have to continue to promote the song for close to ten years?

I had to go out there and beat radio to death for the next seven holiday seasons. Every year I would call 400 stations up and convince them to play it — fortunately they really liked it and received a really good listener response. And I just continued to carry the ball year after year, because in order to establish a song as a hit in the listener's mind, it takes anywhere from ten to eighteen weeks to go up and down the chart. Well, with a Christmas record, you only get a chance for a few weeks of airplay each season, because no one plays that kind of music until after Thanksgiving. I realized if I wanted to turn "Mistletoe" into a standard, I would have to get that one or two weeks of airplay every year for nearly ten years.

What kinds of other songs have you written?

Mostly country album cuts — I had a single released by Loretta Lynn called "Heart Don't Do This To Me." I've written about five other Christmas songs, but after my experience with "Mistletoe," I wanted to do something different, and collaborated once again with Doug to write "Happy Hanukkah, My Friend," the first pop Hanukkah song, which we hoped would become the Jewish answer to "White Christmas." Doug, who's Jewish, thought it was a horrible idea, but I insisted it was a good move. When we released it in 1986, we got such an amazing response that we released an entire album of Hanukkah songs the following

"Happy Hanukkah, My Friend," written by Justin Wilde & Doug Konecky (1986)

year. The CD is called *Happy Hanukkah, My Friend*, and includes five of our original songs along with a few traditional tunes like "I Have A Little Dreydl."

Why did you create your own company, Christmas and Holiday Music, which exclusively publishes holiday music?

With "Mistletoe," I learned the Christmas market inside and out, and how to promote holiday material better than anyone else in the industry. It became my niche to the point where I decided to name myself "Mr. Christmas," and be the source for original Christmas songs. For example, when Melissa Manchester needed a fresh holiday song to sing during her *Colors of Christmas* tour in 1995, I found one for her. I knew however, that I couldn't write all of the songs myself, so I started signing songs by other writers, and now have close to 160 original Christmas songs. The first tune I signed was a song called "What Made The Baby Cry," written by William J. Golay, and it's been recorded by The Platters, Toby Keith and Vikki Carr.

When did you finally realize that "It Must Have Been The Mistletoe" had become a modern carol standard?

In 1995, *Newsweek* did a little piece on various celebrity weddings that had taken place during the Christmas holidays. There were pictures of women in their wedding gowns along with the headline, "It Must Have Been The Mistletoe." I realized that the title had enough recognition that it could be cited away from my song, and said to myself, 'I think we've finally arrived!'

Justin Wilde (center) with his parents (1976)

DO THEY KNOW IT'S CHRISTMAS? — 1984

WRITERS:
BOB GELDOF
MIDGE URE

PRODUCER:
MIDGE URE

ARTIST: BAND AID

COLUMBIA RECORDS

Midge Ure

After Bob Geldof sat down to watch a harrowing television documentary about the hundreds of thousands of people dying from a drought-induced famine plaguing Ethiopia, his conscience immediately urged him to do something about it. At once, he began planning a star-studded Christmas recording event that would raise money to feed the starving victims of this horrible African tragedy. "I feel enraged and disgusted by the TV scenes from Ethiopia," Geldof told reporters. "If we don't do something, then we are participants in a vast human crime."

The former lead singer of the post-punk Irish band The Boomtown Rats first took action by uniting with longtime friend Midge Ure, once front-man for the Brit-rock quartet Ultravox, to write "Do They Know It's Christmas?" In the fall of 1984, he called upon close to forty successful pop acts of the day like Boy George, Duran Duran, Jody Watley and George Michael, who came to London from different parts of the world for one day to quickly record the unique holiday charity single.

The mostly British super-group would be called Band Aid, and within months of that recording session, their song, whose chorus included a touching "feed the world" vocal plea, would go on to raise 11 million dollars for emergency Ethiopian famine relief. On December 3, 1984, "Do They Know" was released first in England, and

"Do They Know It's Christmas?" was the second seasonal song George Michael (upper left) was involved with in 1984. That year, he and his Wham! cohort Andrew Ridgeley (lower right) released something highly unusual — "Last Christmas" — a holiday ditty people could dance to in nightclubs. Shown above is the artwork from the first issue, a UK 12-inch import, which contained the B-side "Everything She Wants." Both were written by George Michael.

then throughout the world on Phonogram Records. Columbia Records issued a 45 record of it in the US one week later, where it rapidly soared to number thirteen on Billboard's Hot 100 Singles chart. Soon after, a hugely popular 12-inch single, containing two versions of the song, was distributed as well. Its success spawned similar philanthropic efforts for Ethiopia in twenty other countries, along with USA for Africa's "We Are The World" fund-raising single, and 1985's

Live Aid, a sixteen-hour live summer celebrity concert simultaneously performed in London and Philadelphia, and broadcast to a worldwide audience of 1.5 billion. It ended up bringing in approximately 56 million charity dollars for the Ethiopian crisis. In 1989, a new version of "Do They Know It's Christmas?" was recorded by what was now known as Band Aid II, but remained unreleased in the US due to legal reasons.

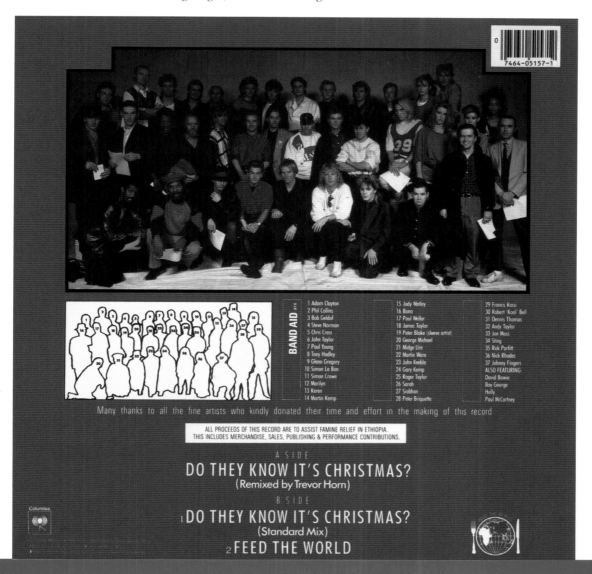

BAND AID (SHOWN ABOVE) WAS COMPRISED OF BAND MEMBERS FROM: U2, The Boomtown Rats, Spandau Ballet, Ultravox, Duran Duran, Heaven 17, Bananarama, Kool and the Gang, Culture Club, and Status Quo. It also included Phil Collins, Paul Young, Marilyn, Jody Watley, Paul Weller, George Michael, Sting and David Bowie, among others.

Wookiees, wacky reindeer, rappers, rockers, teen heartthrobs, Christians and country artists crossing over to the popular mainstream helped define Christmas music in the 1980's. Shown clockwise are: *Amy Grant — A Christmas Album* (1983), Bryan Adams (promotional ad for the 1985 single "Christmas Time"), "What Can You Get A Wookiee For Christmas (When He Already Owns A Comb?)" (1980 single release), *Kenny & Dolly — Once Upon A Christmas* (1984), *Merry, Merry Christmas — New Kids On The Block* (1989), *Christmas Rap* (1987) and "Another Lonely Christmas" (B-side for Prince & The Revolution's "I Would Die 4 U" — 1984). Elmo & Patsy's novelty "Grandma Got Run Over By A Reindeer" (center), was first locally released in California by the husband and wife team of Elmo Shropshire and Patsy Trigg. It became a national hit in 1983.

A paucity of new Christmas standards continued to be the trend in the 1990's. One rare exception was "Grown-up Christmas List" (upper left), written by David Foster and Linda Thompson Jenner (1990). Amy Grant and Barbra Streisand both covered this touching plea for harmony and world peace, which was first recorded by Natalie Cole. In 1997, the Trans-Siberian Orchestra addressed the threat against world peace with "Christmas Eve (Sarajevo 12/24)," taken from their *Christmas Eve And Other Stories* collection (center). Shown clockwise are other top-selling Christmas projects of the 1990's and 2000: *Christmas Interpretations — Boyz II Men* (1993), *Mariah Carey — Merry Christmas* (1994), *Dr. Seuss' How The Grinch Stole Christmas* soundtrack (2000), *Garth Brooks & The Magic Of Christmas* (1999) and *'N SYNC — Home For Christmas* (1998).

The Nineteenth Century's Sacred American Carol

III

O LITTLE TOWN OF BETHLEHEM — 1868

WRITERS:
PHILLIPS BROOKS
LEWIS REDNER

Phillips Brooks (1857)

Phillips Brooks gained instant fame after delivering an elegiac sermon to honor Abraham Lincoln, as his slain body lay in state at Independence Hall, Philadelphia. He went on to become one of the most famous preachers of the nineteenth century's Victorian Gilded Age, and wrote the timeless lyrics of "O Little Town Of Bethlehem" as an 1868 Christmas gift for the children of his Philadelphia church. The divine inspiration for his Episcopalian hymn came from a powerful spiritual awakening he experienced during an 1865 pilgrimage to The Holy Land, and his church organist Lewis Redner (1831 — 1908) composed its melody on Christmas Day, claiming to have been "roused from sleep late in the night hearing an angel strain whispering" in his ear. From then on Redner would always refer to the tune as his "gift from heaven."

During his time, Brooks was known as the "prince among preachers," a poetic orator who could passionately deliver over a thousand words a minute to fervent standing-room crowds. So sacrosanct were his words, that one of his most famous followers said after hearing him speak through an interpreter, she "had always known there was a God, but now she knew his name." Her name was Helen Keller, and she maintained a correspondence with him from the time she was ten until the end of his life.

As a child, Brooks expressed himself quite naturally through poetry, later referring to it as the "creator-power of making a world of beauty in the soul." A great-grandson of Samuel Phillips, founder of Phillips Academy in Andover, Massachusetts, he was born in Boston on December 13, 1835, graduated from Harvard in 1855, and subsequently failed as a school teacher. This was an important turning point that led him to the theological seminary, and a lyrical life of religious devotion.

His missionary life began in 1859 when he became rector at The Church Of The Advent, an Episcopalian house of worship in Philadelphia. Three years later he moved over to Holy Trinity, located in that city's Rittenhouse Square. The church, still in existence today, thrived under his ministry,

and there he would go on to achieve his most lasting contribution to mankind after his parish donated the money to send him on a yearlong trip abroad. That journey was an important one, for it was a rebirth which found him discovering the

O little town of Bethlehem,
How still we see thee lie!
Above thy deep and dreamless sleep
The silent stars go by

heart of Jesus Christ at the place of the Savior's developing consciousness, highest announcement of truth, and most complete mental and physical suffering.

On August 9, 1865, Brooks left New York City for a ten-day voyage on a ship destined for the British Isles. Landing in Ireland on August 18, he traveled on horseback for months to various European countries with a small party of fellow travelers. They reached Damascus on December 3. Almost immediately, he began to seek Jesus Christ in the actual places the spiritual leader had touched. Later, on his way to Bethlehem, he wrote in his journal of drinking the water of the river Jordan, remembering the area was "the first spot he has touched where Christ himself has been."

Holy Trinity Church, Philadelphia (2001)

He continued to retrace the footsteps of Jesus, arriving in Nazareth on December 13, his 30th birthday. Thoughts of the Messiah seized his soul as he noted that "it was a strange feeling to ride down through Nazareth, and look in the people's faces and think how Christ must have been about these streets just like them." He climbed the hill on which the city was built and thought about "how often Jesus must have climbed up here and enjoyed it." He gazed at the view, which to him was "perhaps the finest in Palestine," imagining what it looked like through Christ's eyes. "The west plain

A view of the Sea of Galilee

Yet in thy dark streets shineth
The everlasting Light:
The hopes and fears of all the years
are met in Thee tonight

is closed by the long dark line of Mt. Carmel stretching into the sea," he pondered. "And the sight that Jesus' eyes saw farthest off was that line of the Mediterranean over which his power was to spread to the ends of the world. It is a most noble view."

It was only a week before Christmas, and the young preacher was still experiencing a series of religious epiphanies. He went on to glimpse the Sea of Galilee as it "lay in the soft afternoon light, blue among the purple hills," a place which he felt embraced "the waves he walked, the shores where he taught, the mountains where he prayed. The whole country, every hill and valley seemed marked with his footprints. It was a site not to be forgotten."

On that same day, he visited the place of the Annunciation, where the angel Gabriel told Mary she would give birth to the holy child.

A portrait of Phillips Brooks (taken from the 1897 book, "Rising In The World or Architects Of Fate")

"We entered the Church Of The Franciscan Monastery," he wrote. "A monk took us down under the altar into a cave where there was black marble cut to mark the place where Mary stood. Opposite it are two stone pillars between which the angel came. It is an impressive spot and there is no impossibility about its being the place."

From Nazareth, Phillips Brooks traveled to Jerusalem, and was perhaps reminded of the Holy Trinity before entering the city, symbolically noting in his journal that at this time he saw three eagles soar over him, and his path was crossed by three gazelles. He spent three days here, leaving on Christmas Eve for a two-hour horseback trip to Bethlehem. Along the way,

just before dark, he found the area where the shepherds first saw the guiding star. He paused to ponder its sacred significance, noticing "the shepherds still keeping watch over the flocks and leading them home."

According to Brook's biographer, Raymond W. Albright, it is now "almost certain that Phillips wrote 'O Little Town Of Bethlehem' that night in or near those fields, just as on other occasions when deeply moved he wrote his best poetry." A second biographer, A.V.G. Allen, corroborated this fact. There is further evidence he gave birth to the song during this time based on an 1886 letter he sent to an author wanting to know more about the hymn's history.

He missed the children of his parish, most likely creating the poem in remembrance of them. Later, when he traveled on to Rome, he wrote to tell them about the five-hour Christmas service he attended near the place of Jesus' birth: "I cannot tell you how many Sunday mornings since I left you I

*Where children pure and happy
Pray to the blessed Child;
Where misery cries out to thee,
Son of the mother mild*

have seemed to stand in the midst of our crowded schoolroom again, and look about and know every face just as I used to. I remember especially on Christmas Eve, when I was standing in the old church at Bethlehem, close to the spot where Jesus was born, when the whole church was ringing hour after hour, how again and again it seemed as if I could hear voices I knew well, telling each other of the 'Wonderful Night' of the Savior's birth, as I had heard them a year before. I assure you I was glad to shut my ears for a while and listen to the more familiar strains that came wandering to me halfway round the world."

In September 1866, Brooks returned from his trip with heightened physical and mental power, yet for reasons unknown it would be two years before Lewis Redner wrote the music for their yuletide masterpiece. Though there is a question as to exactly when the minister gave his organist the lyrics, and requested him to write the children's hymn, it is known that words and music were joined on Christmas Day 1868.

Apparently Redner had plenty of time to write the music, but by Christmas Eve, due to a lack of inspiration, he had yet to pen a note. Heavenly intervention must have been at play, for

Where Charity stands watching
And Faith holds wide the door,

after a divine muse visited him in the middle of the night, he sprung out of bed, quickly wrote down the melody, and slipped into slumber for a few more hours. Upon awakening, he composed the song's harmony, which was sung for the first time by thirty-six children and six Sunday School teachers at Philadelphia's Holy Trinity Church, on December 27, 1868.

Above artwork is taken from Phillips Brooks' 19th century book, "Heartsease."

The dark night wakes,
the glory breaks,
And Christmas comes
once more.
O holy Child of
Bethlehem,

Descend to us,
we pray;
Cast out our sin
and enter in,
Be born in us
to-day.

Phillips Brooks.

Above artwork is taken from Phillips Brooks' 19th century book, "Heartsease."

ity when it was published in the Episcopal Hymnal of 1892, a year before Phillips Brooks' death. It is a powerful testament of some of the most poetic thoughts he ever imagined during his Middle East transformation:

"As concerns Jesus," he wrote in his diary, "I know nothing which can more adjust our views of him than a visit to the Holy Land. While by fastening the New Testament story in its place by geographical positions it rescues it from vagueness and obscurity and makes the humanity a clear and palpable fact. It is like the relation between an immortal word and the mortal lips that uttered it. The lips die and you go and look at them when they are dead and see at once how they were made to utter the word, their whole mechanism built for it and yet how, while they uttered it even they were dying in giving expression to what in its very nature was Eternal."

For Phillips Brooks, who died of diphtheria on January 23, 1893, and is buried just outside Boston at Mount Auburn

Though the holy duo would create a second seasonal song together, "Everywhere, Everywhere Christmas Tonight," only "O Little Town Of Bethlehem" would go on to achieve worldwide popular-

Cemetery, eternity became his song of hope, a metaphor of the love that can be found on a journey to Bethlehem where light transcends darkness.

Phillips Brooks' tombstone, located in Mount Auburn Cemetery, Cambridge, Massachusetts

O LITTLE TOWN OF BETHLEHEM

LITTLE town of Bethlehem,
How still we see thee lie!
Above thy deep and dreamless sleep
The silent hours go by.
Yet in thy dark street shineth
The everlasting Light;
The hopes and fears of all the years
Are met in thee to-night.

Pages from the 1904 book, "Christmas Songs And Easter Carols," by Phillips Brooks. Upper right page is a list of Christmas songs Brooks wrote during his lifetime.

[II]

MORE ON "O LITTLE TOWN OF BETHLEHEM"

Record Guild Of America single with vocal by the Boy Choristers, St. Patrick's Cathedral, New York City (c. 1950)

- Phillips Brooks became friends with famous poet Alfred Tennyson. In 1892 the Brooks family sent a copy of "O Little Town" as a gift to Tennyson's grandson Lionel.

- His hymn was first published in 1874 in *The Church Porch*, but did not attain wide popularity until it was included in the *Episcopal Hymnal of 1892*.

- The fifth stanza was usually omitted in hymnals.

- Lewis Redner re-discovered an abandoned verse years later when looking back at Holy Trinity's 1868 Christmas program. He said it wasn't initially published in any of the hymn books.

- People in England have been singing a different melody for the song since 1903, when a man named Vaughan Williams wrote a new arrangement for it based on the existing ballad, "The Ploughboy's Dream." This new setting was known as "Forest Green."

- Lewis Redner's melody still remains most popular in The United States. Henry Walford Davies, once an organist for The Temple Church in London, created another version of the song, published in 1978. It starts out with a recitative from St. Luke's gospel, followed by a soloist singing the first two verses with piano. The last verse is sung by a choir.

- Brooks originally named the carol "St. Louis" after its co-creator, Lewis Redner.

"O Little Town Of Bethlehem" was quite popular in the 1950's. Elvis Presley and Mario Lanza (upper left and right) both included it back then on their respective Christmas sets, as did Mitch Miller, who released it as part of an EP in 1958 (lower left). Burl Ives sang Brooks' evergreen on his 1957 "Christmas Eve" collection. The tune is also contained on his posthumous 1999 release, "The Very Best Of Burl Ives Christmas" (lower right).

PHILLIPS BROOKS:

Phillips Brooks photo (c. 1880)

- A towering presence, who grew to be 6 feet 4 inches, eventually weighing in at nearly 300 pounds

- Two-term Harvard Overseer, university preacher and student counselor

- A steadfast champion of emancipation, who fought to give former slaves the right to vote. In 1862, he created a campaign to desegregate the streetcars of Philadelphia, and often preached to African-American Civil War soldiers.

Phillips Brooks was a powerful inspiration whose memory lives on more than 100 years after his death, in song, and in the following monuments:

Saint Gaudens' statue of Phillips Brooks

- The Phillips Brooks House, located in the northwest corner of Harvard Yard

- The wooden pulpit inscribed with his name at Harvard's Memorial Church

- The stained glass window bearing his image in Harvard's Memorial Hall

- Trinity Church, Boston, Massachusetts, which he helped design. The famous sculptor, Augustus Saint Gaudens, created a dramatic model of Brooks, the church's first rector, that still stands at the holy building's northeast corner.

- Holy Trinity Church, Philadelphia, located in Rittenhouse Square

- His tombstone at Mount Auburn Cemetery, Cambridge, Massachusetts

A Christmas letter written by Phillips Brooks in 1868:

1

Philada
Dec 30 1868

Dear Wm

I wish you a merry Christmas & a happy New Year — Isn't it queer how quick they come — I wish I could be at home this one, but I will send on the Boy Arthur who shall speak & eat for both of us & who will tell you how it fares with us here — He & I have been doing the Musical pretty largely lately — We went to

2

hear Miss Kellogg Friday night & Ole Bull yesterday afternoon & had a very pretty time on both occasions —

You seem to have been very fine at the big wedding. Take care. This adulation of society is apt to turn young couples' heads & make them frivolous & worldly & fricassee & grecian bendy & all that — To pause on your headlong career of reckless fashion, you & Mary

3

& look out for yourselves —

I passed a pleasant week in Virginia — saw Freedmen's schools which look first-rate — & all the beautiful faces of the sulky beasts who crowd that delectable land — They didn't look nicer. A fellow from these parts has to wait awhile before he can go down there for the pleasure of social life —

Jim was on this week — He really says that girl of his is stunning — He was

4

quite spoony & of course so annoying. The Allmouth girl who was here the other day says He (Jim) "has made a ten-strike" which is the free & festive Grace Church way of putting a solemn matrimonial engagement —

Schuyler Colfax is here Arthur went to another concert last night with a girl

I am
Yours affecty
P.B.

AN INTERVIEW WITH JOHN WOOLVERTON, AUTHOR OF
THE EDUCATION OF PHILLIPS BROOKS

How did Phillips Brooks become famous?

In 1865, he became famous overnight when he preached a sermon for the death of Lincoln — it was immediately reprinted all over the country. His legacy lived on up until World War II, but he's largely forgotten today, except for his song. Brooks said that poetry, like that found in "O Little Town," is the highest expression that the human mind can achieve, and that you begin to use the unused machinery of the mind when you create it.

What were some of the driving forces behind Brooks becoming a poet/minister?

First of all, he had a literary education in Latin and Greek at The Boston Latin School. He excelled there and was very hard-working. At home, there was a lot of reading out loud, particularly English literature. And he and his brothers all had to memorize a hymn every week.

Was "O Little Town Of Bethlehem" an anomaly in his life?

He wrote a lot of poetry. In fact, he expressed his inner most deeply held emotions in poetry. Not all of the poetry was great, but he was very adept at writing verse because of his education.

Other than his Christmas song, did he write another hymn that has lasted?

He wrote another one that survives to this day — "The Groton School Hymn." He was a moving figure behind the founding of this famous school in Massachusetts, whose most prominent student was Franklin Delano Roosevelt.

Did he have the traits of a charismatic leader early on?

No one expected him to be a great preacher. He painted very well and had artistic talent.

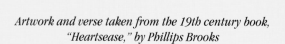

*Artwork and verse taken from the 19th century book,
"Heartsease," by Phillips Brooks*

I must have
some notion in gen-
eral of what I am alive
for, or I cannot live rightly
from hour to hour this evening
and to-morrow morning.

Give our lives room to grow to truth, and they
will grow to symmetry; give them leave to ripen,
and they will richen too.

Did he have some kind of spiritual calling as a young man?

I don't think so — he didn't have any kind of conversion experience. He was simply brought up in the church, and it became second nature to him. He thought in Christian terms and simply built on that, but he built hesitantly. He was slow in deciding what to do with his life, slow to make a commitment until he had worked it out intellectually in theological school with great concentration. Then he took a stand, and aesthetically put the person of Jesus Christ at the center, without separating the heart from the head.

What happened when he failed as a school teacher?

He was only nineteen when he started teaching and was not a disciplinarian. It was an unmitigated disaster and a cause of shame for him. But writing poetry helped pull him out of the depression of failing, and through the eyes of the poet, he was able to stand outside himself and reach a degree of sanity and stability by using the language of the day.

What does "O Little Town Of Bethlehem" say about the human spirit?

If you look closely at the symbols in this song, you'll find that the metaphor of light shining in darkness dominates. It's an ancient Christian metaphor, which goes all the way back to the prologue of John's gospel. Jesus Christ is the light that shines in the darkness, and this darkness cannot comprehend or overcome it.

Phillips Brooks' portrait and signature, taken from the 1894 book, "A Sketch Of The Late Rt. Rev. Phillips Brooks, D.D.," by his private secretary, the Rev. William Henry Brooks, D.D.

WE THREE KINGS OF ORIENT ARE —

c. 1857

WRITER: JOHN HENRY HOPKINS, JR.

John Henry Hopkins, Jr.

The son of the second Episcopal bishop of Vermont, John Henry Hopkins, Jr., was born on October 28, 1820. In addition to living his life as a poet, musicologist, composer and designer of stained glass windows, he was ordained a minister in 1839, and became rector of Christ's Church in Williamsport, Pennsylvania. While serving there, he wrote "We Three Kings Of Orient Are" around 1857 for a Christmas pageant, loosely basing it on the gospel of Matthew 2:1-12. Hopkins wrote other hymns, yet this was the only one to achieve lasting popularity after it was published in his 1865 collection, *Carols, Hymns And Songs*. Upon its first printing, Hopkins, who died in Troy, New York, on August 13, 1891, was criticized for calling the Wise Men "Kings," since the Bible refers to them only as "men from the East."

Record Guild Of America single release

Leroy Anderson, who wrote the music to "Sleigh Ride," released a complete album of carols in 1955 that included Hopkins' "Kings" (upper left). Dennis Day and the Mitchell Boychoir covered it in 1950 (upper right), and it's also on "Bing Crosby Sings Christmas Songs" (1986, lower left) and "Rudolph The Red Nosed Reindeer" (1977, Kid Stuff Records, lower right).

IT CAME UPON THE MIDNIGHT CLEAR — 1849

Edmund Hamilton Sears

WRITERS:
EDMUND HAMILTON SEARS
RICHARD S. WILLIS

ivil unrest ominously lurked, and on a wintry day in 1849, Edmund Hamilton Sears (1810 — 1876), a Unitarian minister, wrote a poem for his times titled, "It Came Upon The Midnight Clear." Like Longfellow's seasonal elegy, "The Christmas Bells," Sears' soothing balm was a vision of universal peace, and the gifted preacher penned it during his ministry at First Church in Wayland, Massachusetts. In 1850, it was published in a Boston-based magazine called, *The Christian Register.* Sears graduated from Union College in Schenectady, New York, briefly studied law, and went on to higher learning at Harvard's Divinity School. He was ordained in 1839, and spent the rest of his life ministering at churches in Massachusetts, as well as writing books and hymns. The music for his most famous hymn, "It Came Upon The Midnight Clear," was written in New York City by a Boston-born composer named Richard S. Willis (1819 — 1900), who once studied with Felix Mendelssohn. His onetime collaboration with Sears went on to attain lasting success when it was included in England's 1870 edition of the *Hymnal Companion To The Book Of Common Prayer.*

Record Guild of America single with vocal by the Boy Choristers, Saint Patrick's Cathedral, New York City (c. 1950)

Bing Crosby sang "It Came Upon The Midnight Clear" in the 1960 movie, "High Time." Rosemary Clooney's version of it appears on the 1998 Crosby/Clooney "Silver Bells Of Christmas" compilation (upper left). The Sears/Willis classic is also included on the Disneyland record, "Christmas Songs For Children" (1968, upper right), Guy Lombardo's "Sing The Songs Of Christmas" (1960, lower right), and the 1957 Robert Shaw Chorale LP, "Christmas Hymns And Carols, Vol. 1" (lower left).

GO TELL IT ON THE MOUNTAIN

ARTIST:
THE JUBILEE
SINGERS OF
FISK UNIVERSITY

The Jubilee Singers

Founded in 1866, Fisk University, located in Nashville, Tennessee, was first established as a place of formal learning for recently freed African-American slaves. Four months after opening, the liberal arts institution, originally known as The Fisk Free Colored School, had enrolled up to 900 students. Among them was a small group of performers known as The Jubilee Singers. They specialized in performing slave songs, also known as Negro spirituals, which included one that went on to become a Christmas favorite — "Go Tell It On The Mountain." By 1871, Fisk was on the brink of financial collapse, and as a way of saving their university, The Jubilee Singers embarked upon a stateside, and subsequent European, tour. Unwittingly, they introduced a body of work to people who had never heard their tales of oppression and sacred transcendence. Some of their early fans included influential people of the day, like Mark Twain, Ulysses S. Grant and Queen Victoria. As they traveled along the old Underground Railroad, they made stops along the way singing their songs to people in local churches and private homes. Around 1889, John Wesley Work, Jr. (1872 — 1925), son of a freed slave, who later became a professor at Fisk, began leading The Jubilee Singers. He is believed to be the first African-American collector of Negro spirituals, and the first to write down the words and music to "Go Tell It On The Mountain."

Sheet music featuring The Jubilee Singers (1881)

Known as one of the finest gospel singers ever, Mahalia Jackson released "Go Tell It On The Mountain" in the early 1950's as a single paired with "Silent Night." Her interpretation of this popular African-American spiritual appears on many albums including "Silent Night" (1967, upper left). The song has been covered by many performers such as Bing Crosby (upper right), The Robert Shaw Chorale (lower right) and Mom & Pop Winans (lower left).

AWAY IN A MANGER

1949 Voco Records release

For quite some time, it was believed that "Away In A Manger," was a European carol written by Martin Luther (1483 — 1546), leader of Germany's Protestant Reformation. The song was at times printed in the United States with a picture of Luther and his family at Christmas, but it is now widely held that the hymn has ties to the American Lutheran Church. Although the author and date of it remain unknown, some attest that it originated from a colony of German Lutherans living in Pennsylvania. Most agree that the creation of it took place sometime in the nineteenth century.

Martin Luther

In 1885, with the approval of the Evangelical Lutheran Church of North America, the first two verses of it were published in the *Little Children's Book For Schools And Families* (Philadelphia). Its third verse appeared in a Lutheran songbook seven years later. Over the years, "Away In A Manger" has been sung to over forty different melodies, but the arrangement we sing today is ascribed to James R. Murray. It first appeared in his 1887 book *Dainty Songs For Little Lads And Lasses*. Confusion over the carol's origin can also be attributed to him, as he, like others, mistakenly believed it was written by Martin Luther. He printed the song with the title, "Luther's Cradle Hymn (Composed By Martin Luther For His Children, And Still Sung By German Mothers To Their Little Ones)." Upon investigation, musical scholars discovered that the song was virtually unknown in Germany.

Popular versions of "Away In A Manger" have been sung by Julie Andrews, Joan Baez, The Mormon Tabernacle Choir and The Judds. Nat King Cole covered it for his 1963 holiday LP, and it's also a part of his 1992 "Christmas Favorites" compilation (upper left). Others who have recorded it include Andy Williams (upper right), Judy Collins (lower right) and Take 6 (lower left).

The European Classics

IV

ANGELS WE HAVE HEARD ON HIGH

Like a brilliant melodic triptych, this exalted telling of what the angels sang on the night of the nativity is one of the oldest surviving Christian Christmas songs, and is actually three different tunes taken from three different times merged into one. The words of its Latin chorus, "Gloria In Excelsis Deo (Glory To God In The Highest)," started appearing in second-century Christian hymns, and some credit Pope Telesphorus with introducing them into the mass. The English verses of "Angels We Have Heard On High" are a loose translation of a French carol titled "Les Anges Dans Nos Campagne" (Angels In Our Countryside), and were most likely written in the 1700's. The angelic music we hear today is also taken from a French carol that may have been penned around the same time, yet is thought to be older. No one knows for sure who cleverly united these sources, but in 1855 the three parts were woven into one for publication, and the song became quite popular at England's Westminster Abbey, where some say it was first sung.

O COME, O COME EMMANUEL

Originally a Latin hymn sung in the Roman Church, this song may be as old as the 12th century, and was translated into English by John Mason Neale (1818 — 1866) in 1851. An Anglican minister, Neale was born in England, and spent most of his life translating Latin and Greek hymns. The word, "Emmanuel," isn't Latin, but is Hebrew, and means "God Is With Us."

John Mason Neale

The Anita Kerr Singers released a single version of "Angels We Have Heard On High" in 1970, and the cherished carol has been cut by acts like Ralph Carmichael, The Harry Simeone Chorale, Kitaro and the Trans-Siberian Orchestra. It's also featured on the above sets (clockwise): Mannheim Steamroller's "The Christmas Angel" (1998), The St. Nicholas Boys Choir's "Christmas Carols" (1956), Ella Fitzgerald's "Christmas With..." (1973) and Bing Crosby's "That Christmas Feeling" (1958).

DECK THE HALLS

The date and author of this traditional Welsh folk carol are a mystery, but this lively tune is thought to be quite ancient, and was popular enough by the year 1700 for Mozart to use it in a piano and violin composition. Once known as "Nos Galan" (New Year's Eve), the song's initial Welsh lyrics had nothing to do with Christmas. Instead it was a ditty sung by merry makers dancing around a harpist, which celebrated the New Year and the joyful customs associated with the pagan winter festival known as Yule. Some of those festivities described in "Deck The Halls" illustrate the custom of cutting down a tree in the forest and dragging it back to a party hall decorated with holly, evergreen and mistletoe. Known as the yule log, the tree was then set on fire. A raucous party subsequently ensued, with sumptuous drinking and feasting lasting for as long as it burned. Although the song's ancient melody has been kept intact, the lyrics we sing today are not the original Welsh words, but were written by an American around 1880, whose "fa la la la la" was typical of the playful nonsense syllables that became a feature of folk songs from old Wales.

THE HOLLY AND THE IVY

Like "Deck The Halls," "The Holly And The Ivy" is a very long-standing European song of unknown authorship. Although its lyrics use holly and ivy as Christian images that portray Jesus' birth and resurrection, the festive foliage was first an ancient pagan symbol that represented masculine and feminine energy. In many old European Yuletide carols, holly was associated with men, ivy with women. The one brought into the home first during the Christmas season determined who would dominate the house that year.

In 1950, Coral Records issued legendary producer Owen Bradley's take on "Deck The Halls," with "Ring Out The Bells" as its flip side. Two other Nashville cats, Boots Randolph (lower left) and Chet Atkins (lower right) included it on albums released in the 1990's. Also shown above are The Record Guild Of America single release of it (upper left), and "Punk Rock Xmas," which contains Metal Mike's odd interpretation (upper right).

GOD REST YE MERRY, GENTLEMEN

Published in 1827 yet thought to go much further back, this minor-key English carol of obscure authorship was once considered to be that country's most popular Christmas song, and it was the custom for poor shivering street "waits," wishing for a coin or two, to sing it to warm, merry gentlemen sitting inside by the fire. "God Rest Ye Merry, Gentlemen" is the song's original title, but over the years the comma between "merry" and "gentlemen" has either been misplaced or entirely omitted. Since the meaning of "rest" is "keep," the carol really means "may God keep you merry." By the mid-1800's this musical blessing had become so familiar that a starving "wait" sang it to Scrooge in Charles Dickens' 1843 *A Christmas Carol.* While the miserly curmudgeon was busy counting his money in his counting house on Christmas Eve, "at the first sound of 'God rest you merry, gentlemen, let nothing you dismay,' Scrooge seized the ruler with such energy of action that the singer fled in terror."

THE WASSAIL SONG (HERE WE COME A-CAROLING)/ WE WISH YOU A MERRY CHRISTMAS

Two other "wait" carols of ambiguous origin, these are believed to be from England circa the 19th century. At that time, English "waits" wandered the streets during the holidays, hoping to get money, food or drink, as they sang and played carols for those more fortunate than themselves. When singing "The Wassail Song" they were most likely asking for a drink, as well as bestowing a blessing. "Wassail" was what we would today call eggnog, and it was made up of ale, egg, nuts and spices. The word, wassail, is old English for "be healthy." The waits' request as they sing "We Wish You A Merry Christmas," is for figgy pudding, and they are adamant in their pursuit as "they won't go until they get some."

Lionel Barrymore portrayed Scrooge on this 1955 album of Dickens' "A Christmas Carol" (upper left). On that set, The Canterbury Choir sings "God Rest Ye Merry, Gentlemen." The "wait" carol is also a part of (clockwise): 98 Degrees' "This Christmas" (1999, upper right), Randy Travis' "An Old Time Christmas" (1989, lower right) and "A Motown Christmas," with vocals by Smokey Robinson & The Miracles (1973, lower left).

HARK! THE HERALD ANGELS SING

Record Guild Of America single release

The original words of "Hark! The Herald Angels Sing," as well as the music it was later matched with, had nothing to do with angels and were never intended for holiday purpose. Its writer, Charles Wesley, first published it in 1739 as a work dealing with the incarnation of Christ, but at first didn't regard it as a Christmas hymn. Initially, he opened his song with the lines "Hark how all the welkin rings, Glory to the king of kings," and churchgoers sang it throughout the year.

Shortly after that first version was released, a friend convinced him to add the herald angels and get rid of the ringing welkin, an old English word meaning "vault of heaven." Those opening words, which we still sing today, first appeared in a 1743 revision he simply named "The Christmas Hymn."

Come, Desire of Nations, come,
*   Fix in us thy humble home;*
Rise, the woman's conquering seed,
*   Bruise in us the serpent's head;*

Now display thy saving power,
*   Ruined nature now restore;*
Now in mystic union join
*   Thine to ours, and ours to thine.*

(Shown above are the last two verses of Wesley's original "Hark! The Herald Angels Sing")

Charles Wesley

An ordained English minister, and the brother of fellow tunesmith John Wesley (founder of The Methodist Church), Charles Wesley was born in 1707, and wrote over six thousand hymns in his lifetime, making him one of history's most prolific composer's of religious music. He died in 1788 and for over a hundred years, the music and lyrics he penned for "Hark!" went through a series of revisions.

The most dramatic change occurred in 1855 when Dr. William Cummings, an organist at

Waltham Abbey England, not only altered its lyrical structure, but coupled Wesley's words with *Festgesang #7,* an 1840 classical cantata specifically written for a German Guttenberg Festival, commemorating what was believed to be the 400th anniversary of the printing press.

The author of this piece was Jewish-born Felix Mendelssohn (1809 — 1847), a much sought after festival organizer, conductor and com-

Felix Mendelssohn

poser. He grew up in Germany, and was a leading figure of 19th-century European romanticism in classical music, who also wrote the still widely popular *Wedding March*, along with many other seminal pieces. Surprisingly, he felt his "Festgesang" wasn't suitable for sacred text, and didn't approve of its use as a Christmas song. Since then, more lyrical changes have occurred with "Hark!" but Mendelssohn's music has survived the test of time.

Before Bing Crosby's "White Christmas" came along, recorded versions of old carols by choruses were quite common. The above right choral set from the early 1940's contains Wesley's masterpiece, and is an example of this. Shown above left, is a 1952 children's Little John Records vinyl version of it. The tune also appears on "Christmas With Frank Sinatra & Nat King Cole" (lower right), and Natalie Cole's 1999 set, "The Magic Of Christmas," in which she, through the magic of technology, duets with her father, Nat, on "The Christmas Song" (lower left).

JOY TO THE WORLD

Joyeux Noël

Joy To The World" is adapted from five verses English hymnist Isaac Watts (1674 — 1748) took from the Old Testament's *Psalm 98*. Once re ferred to as "the father of English hymnody," Watts wrote over 450 religious songs, and his vivacious poetic style helped revolutionize church singing in the 1700's.

As a teenager, Watts' puritanical Deacon father angrily challenged him to write better songs when his young son expressed dissatisfaction with the lack of quality he felt existed in the hymns he was hearing in church. By the next Sunday, at the age of eighteen, he penned his first work, and went on to become an Anglican preacher until illness forced him to move into a friend's estate and abandon his ministry. Although Isaac Watts would never recover, he spent the rest of his life creating music for the church, and wrote "Joy To The World" while convalescing.

The original tune is not the song we sing today, and while most of Watts' lyrics have survived, the current melody was created sometime in the early 1800's. Lowell Mason, once the leading Presbyterian hymn composer in America, is credited with uniting this new strain with Watts' old lyrics. He published a new version of "Joy" in 1836. For over a hundred years, it was believed that Mason adapted this music from part of classical composer George F. Handel's *The Messiah*. It is now commonly held that the new notes were most likely crafted by an English choir conductor named William Holford.

Isaac Watts

WHILE SHEPHERDS WATCHED THEIR FLOCKS BY NIGHT

Like Watts, who relied on the Bible for his "Joy," English poet laureate Nahum Tate (1652 — 1715) paraphrased Luke 2:8-14 when he wrote the lyrics for "While Shepherds Watched Their Flocks By Night," which were first published in 1700. In England, the song was radical for its time, since before it, Christmas hymns weren't sung in church. Because Tate's tune was so closely associated with scripture, it became the only one officially accepted by the Church of England, and was the first Christmas song people could freely sing during divine services. The melody most closely associated with it in America is an adaptation of an aria taken from "Siroe, Re di Persia," a 1728 George F. Handel opera. In that aria, a princess disguised as a man, finds herself obligated to make love to a woman.

*George F. Handel
(1685 —1759)*

Whitney Houston warbles "Joy To The World" on her 1996 soundtrack, "The Preacher's Wife" (upper left). Published in 1719, Watts' hymn was also released in the 1950's by The Record Guild Of America (upper right). Carl Cotner's arrangement of it is on "Christmastime With Gene Autry" (1974, lower right), and it's also a part of the 1983 holiday LP, "Merry Christmas — Judy Garland And The Mantovani Orchestra" (lower left).

O CHRISTMAS TREE (O TANNENBAUM)

Joyeux Noël.   Ida

The Christmas tree originated over two thousand years ago and was considered to be a symbol of renewed life force during the pagan winter solstice celebration. At Roman festivals known as Saturnalia, it was a common tradition to adorn trees with gifts and decorations, but it took Christianity quite a long time to adopt this spiritual practice — it didn't become a symbol of Jesus' birth until the sixteenth century. Some credit Martin Luther with introducing Christmas trees into the home during this same period. By 1824, they had become so popular in Germany that a Leipzig schoolmaster named Ernst Anschutz sat down and wrote a song about them to teach his students the importance of dressing up evergreens. Anschutz actually borrowed an old German folk melody that may have started out in medieval times as a Catholic hymn, and had been used in the past for a Latin school song. He set these old strains to new words he wrote in German, and titled the composition, "O Tannenbaum," which simply means, 'O Fir Tree.' Over the years the melody of what we now call "O Christmas Tree" has been used in non-holiday ways. It was once the setting for "Lauriger Horatius," a popular college song, and the official state tunes of Maryland, Delaware and Missouri.

THE TWELVE DAYS OF CHRISTMAS

Known as a cumulative carol, the twelve days in "The Twelve Days Of Christmas" are thought to be the dozen which stretch from the day after December 25, to the Epiphany on January 6. This carol may have started out as a traditional children's pastime known as a "forfeit" game. The origin of its lyrics and music are obscure, but various versions of its words began appearing in the early 1700's. The carol we sing today was first published in 1864, however, what we now know as four calling birds started out as four "cally-birds," which are blackbirds. In addition, the five golden rings may actually have been five "goldspinks" (Scottish for goldfinches).

1976 Disneyland record

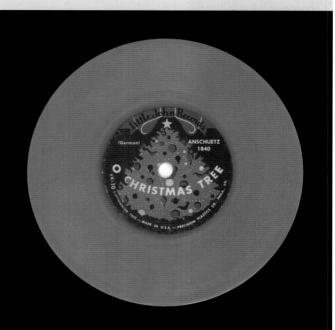

In 1956, Decca Records launched "O Tannenbaum, Christmas On The Rhine," a full album of carols sung in German by a mixed chorus (upper left). A Little John children's record of "O Christmas Tree," was released in 1952 (upper right), and the secular carol has also been interpreted by They Might Be Giants (1993, lower left), as well as the Jingle Dogs and Jingle Cats (1995 & 1998, lower right).

O COME ALL YE FAITHFUL (ADESTE FIDELES)

Record Guild Of America single release

Adeste Fideles" is the original name of this hymn, once a favorite of Theodore Roosevelt, which for a long time many mistakenly believed was either written by a Portuguese monk, or an English composer named John Reading. Five manuscripts of the song were discovered in 1946, however, and they were all signed by John Francis Wade (1711 — 1746), leading many to conclude that he wrote or copied it down for the first time in the 1740's. By then the hymn was popular enough that a similar melody was used in a vulgar French comic opera. Born in Britain, Wade eventually moved to Douay, a renowned Catholic center in France, where he spent most of his life teaching and transcribing music for the church.

Wade was also a teacher of Latin, and the manuscripts he left behind were all written in this ancient language of the early Roman Catholic Church. In 1841, Francis Oakeley, once an English Catholic Bishop, translated the Latin into the English words most of us sing today. Although Wade's name is now associated with what had become the fourth most commonly played song on church organs in 18th and 19th century England, some say he could have copied an already existing old French carol that was used by religious orders as a Christmas Eve processional hymn.

Adeste Fideles, laeti triumphantes,
 Venite, Venite in Bethlehem:
Natum videte
 Regem angezorum,
Venite adorate, Venite Adorate,
 Venite Adorate
Dominum.
(a sample of "O Come All Ye Faithful's" original Latin lyrics)

"Adeste Fideles" was one of the first Christmas songs to be recorded by popular singers. Bing Crosby cut it in 1935, while Frank Sinatra's take debuted in 1946 (upper left). The hymn also appears on "Great Songs Of Christmas" (1966, upper right), Fred Waring and his Pennsylvanians' "'Twas The Night Before Christmas" (1949, lower right), and Vic Dana's "Little Altar Boy" (1965, lower left). Dana, who was born in Buffalo, New York, popularized the album's title song in 1961.

O HOLY NIGHT

"O Holy Night" sheet music (1951)

"Cantique de Noel" is the real title of this 19th century French carol. At one time it was such a Christmas favorite in Paris that people flocked there to hear it sung in churches, despite the fact that religious authorities disapproved of its "lack of taste and spirituality." Based on a poem written by M. Cappeau de Roquemaure, Parisian composer Adolphe Charles Adam (1803 — 1856) subsequently crafted a melody for the tune that was translated into English by John S. Dwight (1813 — 1893), a Boston music teacher and co-founder of The Harvard Music Society. As a young man, Adam was forced to study music in secret because his father wanted him to become a lawyer. Defiantly, he went on to write *Giselle,* eventually becoming France's most famous composer of comic operas. Unfortunately, the eruption of revolution caused him to close the opera theater he founded in 1847, and although bankruptcy followed, his famous song would go on to spiritually unite people for years to come. One dramatic example of the carol's power occurred on Christmas Eve, 1870, during the Franco-Prussian War, a time when Germany was attacking France. As French and German soldiers faced each other in trenches before the city of Paris, and prepared for bloody slaughter, one French man unexpectedly jumped out and began singing "Cantique de Noel" in a voice so divine that it shocked the Germans into ceasing fire. When the young man finished, a tall German fighter came out of hiding to reciprocate in his own language by singing Martin Luther's then-famous Christmas hymn "From Heaven Above To Earth I Come."

THE FIRST NOEL

There is disagreement as to whether this carol is French or English, but most authorities agree that its roots go all the way back to the 17th century, and that it could be even older. William Sandys, an English lawyer, was the first to publish this re-telling of the New Testament's Luke 2:10 in his 1833 book, "Christmas Carols, Ancient And Modern," and he titled it "The First Nowell." Some scholars believe the word, "Nowell," is Old English for "now all is well."

Johnny Mathis' interpretation of this French carol debuted in 1958 on "Merry Christmas," his first holiday LP (upper left). Recorded by many others over the years, it's also sung by The Lettermen ("Christmas America," 1974, upper right), Perry Como ("Home For The Holidays," 1968, lower right) and Hanson ("Snowed In," 1997, lower left).

SILENT NIGHT

Near Salzburg on Christmas Eve 1818, in the obscure alpine Austrian town of Oberndorf, Catholic priest Josef Mohr (1792 — 1848), and his organist Franz Gruber (1787 — 1863), wrote "Silent Night" for the parishioners of their St. Nicholas Church. Although some believe it's a myth, one story claims the church organ broke down the day before Christmas, and that the holy duo quickly wrote the song in a state of emergency as a way of dealing with the impending silence of a holiday mass without music. Mohr penned the lyrics, and Gruber specifically crafted the simple melody for two voices backed by one lone guitar. Both are thought to have sung it that night, possibly accompanied by a small girls' choir. While some accounts blame mice for disabling the instrument, and others state a winter blizzard kept a repairman from getting to the church to fix the problem in time, whatever the case may have been, Mohr and Gruber are credited with writing one

I SAW THREE SHIPS

Based on a European folk legend about what happened to the Three Wise Men's bodies after they died, this carol, also known as "Christmas Day In The Morning," can be traced back to the 17th century, and may go further back than this. Legend has it that in the 4th century, Helena, mother of Constantine the Great, carried the Magi's corpses to Byzantium. Later in time, they were moved to Milan, Italy, and in 1162, three mysterious ships transferred their skulls to Cologne, Germany. Over time, the legend changed, with the three skulls becoming Christ and his mother Mary, who in the song, "I Saw Three Ships," sailed to Bethlehem on Christmas morning. The skulls are believed to still exist today, and lie in jeweled coffins at Cologne Cathedral.

Franz Gruber, depicted above
Joseph Mohr

of the world's greatest Christmas songs in 1818, a tune they penned in their native German and titled "Stille Nacht."

Over the next twenty years, wandering groups of folk singers popularized the song in Austria and Germany. It is believed that when one famous professional group in particular, The Strasser Sisters, added the song to their repertoire, it quickly spread throughout the rest of Europe. First published in 1832, the remainder of the world, including America, wasn't introduced to "Silent Night" until 1849, when it was added to a Methodist hymn book. Not everyone loved it though — England considered it vulgar and removed it from most of their carol publications. In 1935, over one hundred years after Mohr and Gruber composed it, the song would help revolutionize the Christmas music industry when it became the first holiday tune Bing Crosby recorded as a solo artist. (See *WHITE CHRISTMAS*)

A children's version of "Silent Night" was released in the 1950's by The Record Guild Of America (upper left). Voco Records also issued one in 1949 (upper right). In 1917, the Neapolitan Trio recorded it for Victor Records (lower right), and Destiny's Child brought it into the new millennium when they included it on their "8 Days Of Christmas" CD (lower left).

WHAT CHILD IS THIS?

What song is this?" could be a relevant question when one looks at the myriad uses of this English carol's lovely folk melody, and the chameleon-like nature of its ever-changing lyrics over the past five hundred years. Though the writer remains anonymous, its music can be traced all the way back to the 16th century, yet some think it may be much older than this. The first known words to accompany what was during the Elizabethan period a popular fast-paced dance tune, had nothing to do with religion, but were in fact a bit bawdy for the time. In the 1500's it was known to some as "My Lady Greensleeves," and during Queen Elizabeth's reign she herself is said to have danced to it. Apparently, she wasn't the only famous person to have fallen in love with its contagious strains, for it shows up on two occasions in Shakespeare's play *The Merry Wives of Windsor.*

Over the next one hundred years, the tune transformed itself into a song whose lyrics wistfully celebrated the arrival of the New Year, and in 1642 it was published with the title, "The Old Year

GOOD KING WENCESLAS

Like "I Saw Three Ships," "Good King Wenceslas" is based upon an old legend. John Mason Neale, responsible for translating "O Come, O Come Emmanuel," wrote its words to honor both St. Stephen's Day and King Wenceslas, who presided over 10th century Bohemia (later known as Czechoslovakia). St. Stephen's Day is December 26, and was known as a day of giving to the poor. According to legend, King Wenceslas was greatly loved for his generosity toward the needy, and he became a martyr after he was murdered by his jealous brother.

Neale's lyrics are an imaginary dialogue between Wenceslas and his page, and they tell of good deeds the ruler performs for the poor. The melody of the tale is an old Latin springtime carol called "Tempest Adest Floridum," ("Spring Has Now Unwrapped The Flowers"). Neale discovered it in a 16th century hymn collection compiled by Martin Luther. First published in 1853, John Stainer added harmony to "Good King's" melody, and printed a new arrangement of it in 1871.

William Dix

Now Away Has Fled." Throughout the ages, the melody, among other things, has also been used as a lullaby, a children's Christmas song, and the theme for a midnight radio program broadcast by WNBC in the 1930's. Two Englishmen, John Stainer (1840 — 1901), and insurance man/poet William Dix (1837 — 1898), are credited with finding the true beauty of the song by slowing the tempo down and thus turning it into the elegiac religious hymn we sing today as "What Child Is This?" Best known for a cantata he wrote called *The Crucifixion*, and his 1871 book, *Christmas Carols New And Old*, Stainer was an organist and a prolific composer of church music. He took part of an 1865 poem Dix wrote while ill on the day of the Epiphany, and merged it with the melody that is now also referred to as "Greensleeves."

Alas, my love, you do me wrong
To cast me off discourteously,
For I have loved you so long
Delighting in your company.

Greensleeves was all my joy,
Greensleeves was my delight,
Greensleeves was my heart of gold,
And all for my Lady Greensleeves.

(Original lyrics sung during Queen Elizabeth's reign)

Three years following Bing Crosby's death, Reader's Digest issued "Christmas With Bing," which includes "What Child Is This?" paired with "The Holly And The Ivy" as part of a medley (1980, upper left). Mannheim Steamroller breathed new life into the ancient carol on their "A Fresh Aire Christmas" project (1988, upper right), and it's also on "Christmas In New York" (1967, lower right) and Vince Gill's "Let There Be Peace On Earth" (1993, lower left).

Charted Christmas Songs

V

THE *Chipmunk Song*

(CHRISTMAS DON'T BE LATE!)

Words and Music by Ross Bagdasarian

Recorded by DAVID SEVILLE on Liberty Records

SIMON

ALVIN

THEODORE

Copyright © 1958 by Monarch Music Company, Inc.

MONARCH MUSIC COMPANY, INC.

Sole Selling Agents: KEYS-HANSEN, INC. • 119 West 57th Street • New York 19, N. Y.

CHARTED CHRISTMAS SONGS
(1900 — 2000)

SONG	ARTIST	INITIAL YEAR
ADESTE FIDELES (O COME ALL YE FAITHFUL)	Peerless Quartet	1905
	John McCormack	1915
	Associated Glee Clubs Of America	1925
	Bing Crosby	1960
ALL I WANT FOR CHRISTMAS IS MY TWO FRONT TEETH	Spike Jones	1949
AULD LANG SYNE	Frank Stanley	1907
	Peerless Quartet	1921
AVE MARIA	Frances Alda & John McCormack *(Bach & Gounod)*	1910
	Enrico Caruso *(Kahn)*	1913
	John McCormack *(Mascagni & Weatherly)*	1914
	Perry Como *(Schubert)*	1949
BLUE CHRISTMAS	Russ Morgan	1949
	Hugo Winterhalter	1949
	Ernest Tubb	1950
	The Browns	1960
	Elvis Presley	1964
THE CHIPMUNK SONG	The Chipmunks	1958
THE CHRISTMAS SONG	Nat King Cole	1946
	Les Brown	1947
	James Brown	1966
	Herb Alpert	1968
DO THEY KNOW IT'S CHRISTMAS?	Band Aid	1984
DO YOU HEAR WHAT I HEAR?	Bing Crosby	1963
	Andy Williams	1965
FROSTY THE SNOWMAN	Gene Autry	1951
	Nat King Cole	1951
	Guy Lombardo	1951

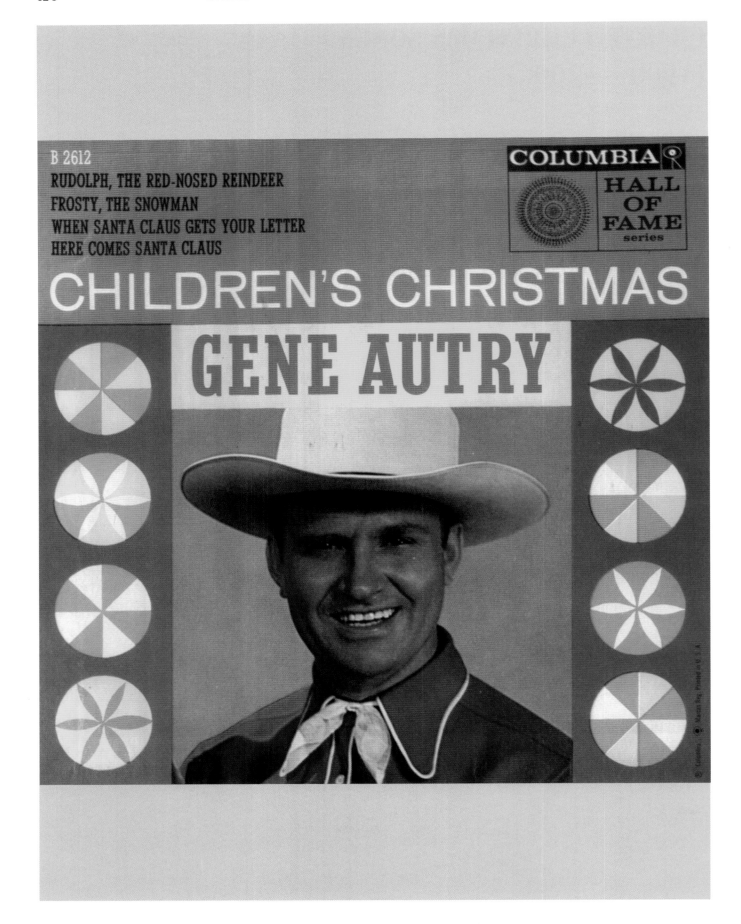

SONG	ARTIST	INITIAL YEAR
GRANDMA GOT RUN OVER BY A REINDEER	Elmo & Patsy	1983
GREENSLEEVES (WHAT CHILD IS THIS?)	Mantovani	1952
HAPPY XMAS (WAR IS OVER)	John & Yoko/Plastic Ono Band	1971
HARK! THE HERALD ANGELS SING	Trinity Choir	1912
	Columbia Mixed Quartet	1916
HAVE YOURSELF A MERRY LITTLE CHRISTMAS	Judy Garland	1944
HERE COMES SANTA CLAUS	Gene Autry	1947
A HOLLY JOLLY CHRISTMAS	Burl Ives	1964
HOME FOR THE HOLIDAYS	Perry Como	1954
HOW LOVELY IS CHRISTMAS	Bing Crosby	1957
I SAW MOMMY KISSING SANTA CLAUS	Jimmy Boyd	1952
	Spike Jones	1953
	Molly Bee	1953
	The 4 Seasons	1964
I'LL BE HOME FOR CHRISTMAS	Bing Crosby	1943
	The Brothers Four	1966
IF EVERYDAY WAS LIKE CHRISTMAS	Elvis Presley	1966
IT'S BEGINNING TO LOOK LIKE CHRISTMAS	Perry Como	1952
JINGLE BELL ROCK	Bobby Helms	1957
	Bobby Rydell/Chubby Checker	1961
	Brenda Lee	1964
JINGLE BELLS	Benny Goodman	1935
	Glenn Miller	1941
	Bing Crosby & the Andrews Sisters	1943
	Primo Scala	1949
	Les Paul	1952
	Perry Como	1957

"The Little Drummer Boy" LP (1965) was arranged and conducted by Anita Kerr, and includes songs sung by Living Voices.

SONG	ARTIST	INITIAL YEAR
JINGLE BELLS (continued)	Booker T. & The M.G.'s	1966
	The Ramsey Lewis Trio	1965
	The Singing Dogs	1971
JOY TO THE WORLD	Trinity Choir	1911
LET IT SNOW! LET IT SNOW! LET IT SNOW!	Vaughn Monroe	1946
	Woody Herman	1946
	Connee Boswell	1946
	Bob Crosby	1946
LET'S START THE NEW YEAR RIGHT	Bing Crosby	1943
LITTLE ALTAR BOY	Vic Dana	1961
THE LITTLE DRUMMER BOY	The Harry Simeone Chorale	1958
	Johnny Cash	1959
	The Jack Halloran Singers	1961
	Johnny Mathis	1963
	Joan Baez	1966
	Lou Rawls	1967
	Kenny Burrell	1967
	Moonlion	1975
LITTLE SAINT NICK	The Beach Boys	1963
MARSHMALLOW WORLD	Bing Crosby	1951
MARY'S BOY CHILD	Harry Belafonte	1956
	Boney M	1978
MERRY CHRISTMAS BABY	Chuck Berry	1958
	Charles Brown	1964
	Otis Redding	1968
MERRY CHRISTMAS DARLING	Carpenters	1970
NIGHT BEFORE CHRISTMAS SONG	Gene Autry & Rosemary Clooney	1952
NUTTIN' FOR CHRISTMAS	The Fontane Sisters	1955
	Stan Freberg	1955
	Barry Gordon	1955
	Joe Ward	1955
	Ricky Zahnd	1955

1945

SONG	ARTIST	INITIAL YEAR
PLEASE COME HOME FOR CHRISTMAS	Charles Brown	1961
	The Uniques	1967
	Eagles	1978
PRETTY PAPER	Roy Orbison	1963
ROCKIN' AROUND THE CHRISTMAS TREE	Brenda Lee	1960
RUDOLPH THE RED-NOSED REINDEER	Gene Autry	1949
	Spike Jones	1950
	Bing Crosby	1950
	The Chipmunks	1960
	The Melodeers	1960
	The Temptations	1968
SAME OLD LANG SYNE	Dan Fogelberg	1980
SANTA BABY	Eartha Kitt	1953
SANTA CLAUS IS COMIN' TO TOWN	George Hall	1934
	Bing Crosby & the Andrews Sisters	1947
	The 4 Seasons	1962
	The Jackson 5	1970
	Bruce Springsteen	1985
SILENT NIGHT	Haydn Quartet	1905
	Ernestine Schumann-Heink	1908
	Elsie Baker	1912
	Neapolitan Trio	1917
	Paul Whiteman	1928
	Bing Crosby	1936
	Mahalia Jackson	1962
	Barbra Streisand	1966
	The Temptations	1969
SILVER BELLS	Bing Crosby & Carol Richards	1953
	Al Martino	1964
	Earl Grant	1966
SNOOPY'S CHRISTMAS	The Royal Guardsmen	1967
STEP INTO CHRISTMAS	Elton John	1973

What Are You Doing New Year's Eve
by FRANK LOESSER

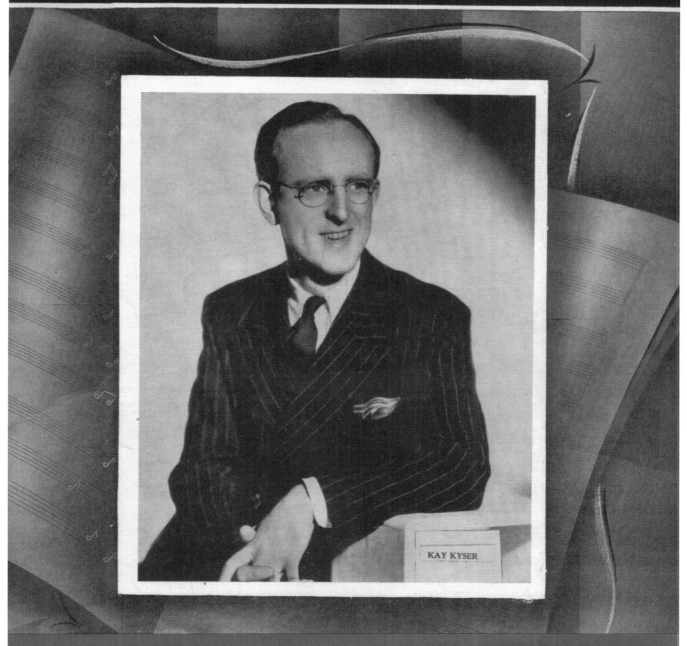

Frank Loesser, composer of Broadway hits like *Where's Charley?* (1948) and *Guys And Dolls* (1950), wrote "What Are You Doing New Year's Eve" in 1947. It was introduced that year by popular singer Margaret Whiting, as well as dance-band leader Kay Kyser (shown above). In 1965, jazz chanteuse Nancy Wilson reintroduced what has become a sentimental year-end evergreen.

FAMOUS MUSIC CORP., • 1619 BROADWAY, New York City, N. Y.

SONG	ARTIST	INITIAL YEAR
THIS ONE'S FOR THE CHILDREN	New Kids On The Block	1989
TOYLAND	Corrine Morgan & Haydn Quartet	1904
WHAT ARE YOU DOING NEW YEAR'S EVE	Nancy Wilson	1965
WHAT CAN YOU GET A WOOKIEE FOR CHRISTMAS?	The Star Wars Intergalactic Droid Choir & Chorale	1980
WHITE CHRISTMAS	Bing Crosby	1942
	Charlie Spivak	1942
	Gordon Jenkins	1942
	Freddy Martin	1942
	Frank Sinatra	1944
	Freddy Martin	1945
	Jo Stafford	1946
	Eddy Howard	1947
	Perry Como	1947
	Mantovani	1952
	The Drifters	1955
	Andy Williams	1963
	Otis Redding	1968
WINTER WONDERLAND	Guy Lombardo	1934
	Ted Weems	1935
	Perry Como	1946
	Andrews Sisters	1946
	Johnny Mercer	1947
	The Rasey Lewis Trio	1966
	Dolly Parton	1984
WONDERFUL CHRISTMASTIME	Paul McCartney	1984
YOU'RE ALL I WANT FOR CHRISTMAS	Frank Gallagher	1948
	Frankie Laine	1949
	Eddie Fisher	1953
	Brook Benton	1963

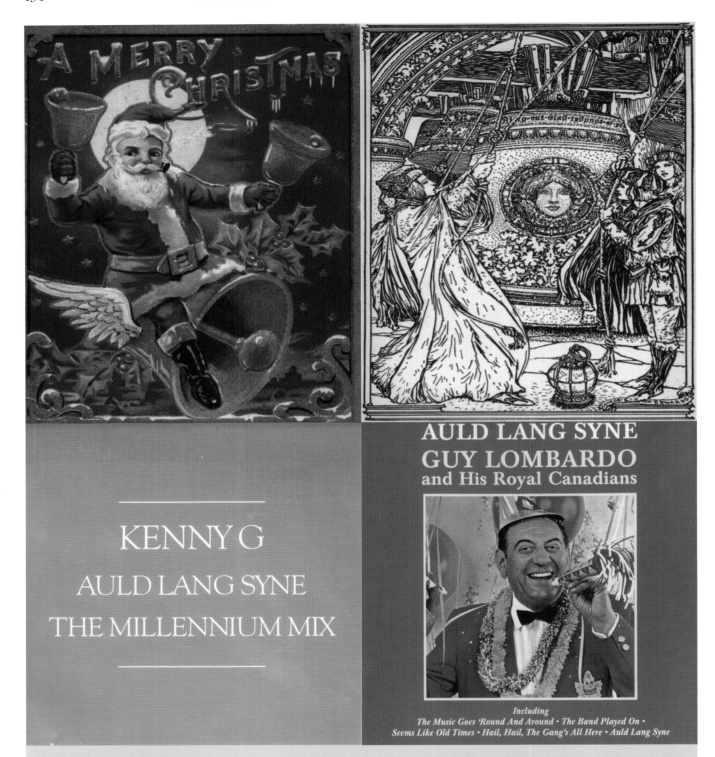

KENNY G
AULD LANG SYNE
THE MILLENNIUM MIX

AULD LANG SYNE
GUY LOMBARDO
and His Royal Canadians

Including
The Music Goes 'Round And Around · The Band Played On ·
Seems Like Old Times · Hail, Hail, The Gang's All Here · Auld Lang Syne

The origin of "Auld Lang Syne's" music is unknown, and although Scottish poet Robert Burns (1759 — 1796) wrote the words to it in 1788, scholars believe the first verse may have been written by someone else. Popular versions of the song were recorded by Frank Stanley (1907) and The Peerless Quartet (1921), and on December 31, 1929, Guy Lombardo and His Royal Canadians performed a live radio broadcast of it. Since then, "Auld Lang Syne," which is Scottish for "Old Long Ago," has been associated with him and with New Year's Eve. Lower left is Kenny G's 1999 "Millennium Mix," which married the music to myriad sound bites representing moving moments in history. Guy Lombardo's version of it appears on the 1998 set appropriately titled *Auld Lang Syne* (lower right).

Bells are ringing, hearts are
    singing!

Ding Dong Ding!

Bells are ringing, angels singing!

Ding Dong Ding!

Oh, Christmas is inside us

Every moment of the day

It's December twenty-second

And the twenty-fifth of May

It's the love we give ourselves

When we give up all the fear

Yes Christmas is inside us

every moment of the year

Bells are ringing, angels singing

Ding Dong Ding!

We were looking for the message

In a mall and credit card

Now we see that it's so simple

What the world has made so hard

Oh the snow melts all our silence

Silver crystals swirl delight

Shining colors light the meaning

of that shimmering star night

Bells are ringing hearts are
    singing

Ding Dong Ding!

Can somebody open Christmas?

Will somebody ever see?

What was once wrapped up inside
    a box

Is now inside of me

Let angels voice our silence

Ding Dong Ding!

Dreamy crystals swirl delight

Ding Dong Ding!

Shining colors light the meaning

Of that clear and sacred night

We can give our love all seasons

What was sold is now for free

And the Christmas once outside
    myself

Is Christmas inside me!

Bells are ringing hearts are
    singing!

Let the whole world see

Bells are ringing angels singing!

Christmas is in me!

End Notes

SANTA CLAUS IS COMIN' TO TOWN

1. "seeing whiskey bottles all over the house." William E. First with Pasco E. First, *Drifting and Dreaming — The Story of Songwriter Haven Gillespie.* St. Petersburg, FL: Seaside Publishing, 1998, p. 8.

2. "It was through printing:" Ibid., p. 11.

3. "many of his masterpieces:" Ibid., p. 21.

4. "It got beyond anything:" Eddie Cantor with Jane Kesner, *Take My Life.* Garden City, NY: Doubleday, 1957, p. 215.

5. "Say you played in a Ziegfeld show:" Ibid., p. 214.

6. "historically interesting depression-era shows:" John Dunning, *On The Air: The Encyclopedia of Old-Time Radio.* New York: Oxford University Press, 1998, p. 225.

Haven Gillespie's quotes on " Santa Claus Is Comin' To Town" are taken from his letters (see pages 30 – 31).

Interviews with the following were conducted for this chapter:
- Audrey Gillespie — March 25, 1999
- Patricia Coots Chester — March 26, 1999
- Thomas H. Carlisle — March 28, 1999
- William First — March 31, 1999
- Herbert Goldman — April 1, 1999

WHITE CHRISTMAS

1. "I used to sing:" unidentified news clipping, The Irving Berlin Scrapbooks at The Library of Congress.

2. "I suppose it was singing:" Michael Freedland, *Irving Berlin.* New York: Stein and Day, 1974, p. 19.

3. "I was a little Russian-born kid:" *Saturday Evening Post,* January 14, 1944.

4. "In 1893, the year Irving Berlin:" Philip Furia, *Irving Berlin: A Life In Song.* New York: Schirmer Books, 1998, p. 15.

5. "He had just come from his mission:" *Good Housekeeping,* December 1955.

6. "The plan was to take the royalties:" Bing Crosby, *Call Me Lucky.* New York: Simon & Schuster, 1953, p. 142.

7. "Like "God Bless America:" Laurence Bergreen, *As Thousands Cheer: The Life of Irving Berlin.* New York: Penguin Books, 1990, p. 385.

8. "In September 1941, my father went:" Mary Ellin Barrett, *Irving Berlin: A Daughter's Memoir.* New York: Simon & Schuster, 1994, p. 194.

9. "We working composers all too often:" *Saturday Evening Post,* January 14, 1944.

10. "It was morning when he finished the song:" Laurence Bergreen, *As Thousands Cheer: The Life of Irving Berlin.* New York: Penguin Books, 1990, p. 386.

11. "Impressed by the amount of energy:" Ibid., p. 388.

12. "Of course, he's not the one to throw his arms about:" Ibid.

13. "although 'White Christmas became the best-selling song:" Philip Furia, *Irving Berlin:* A Life In Song. New York: Schirmer Books, 1998, pp. 205-206.

14. "didn't think 'White Christmas' would make it:" Laurence Bergreen, *As Thousands Cheer: The Life of Irving Berlin. New York: Penguin Books, 1990,* p. 407.

15. "It became a peace song:" Michael Freedland, *Irving Berlin.* New York: Stein & Day, 1974, p. 148.

16. "Often in the midst of rainy muggy weather:" *Good Housekeeping,* December 1955.

17. "When the first pressing of 'White Christmas:'" Laurence Zwisohn, *Bing Crosby: A Lifetime Of Music:* Los Angeles: Palm Tree Library, 1978, p. 48.

18. "He looked quite worried:" Chris Thompson, *Bing:* New York: David McKay Co., 1975, p. 176.

19. "Many years later, when Christmas:" Mary Ellin Barrett, *Irving Berlin: A Daughter's Memoir:* New York: Simon & Schuster, 1994, pp. 127-128.

Interviews with the following were conducted for this chapter:
- Philip Furia — November 30, 1998
- Ken Barnes — December 6, 1998

HAVE YOURSELF A MERRY LITTLE CHRISTMAS

Interviews with the following were conducted for this chapter:
- Hugh Martin — September 14, 1998
- George Blane — September 23 & October 6, 1998
- John Fricke — October 9 & 22, 1998

HERE COMES SANTA CLAUS

1. "After the war:" Gene Autry with Mickey Herskowitz, *Back In The Saddle Again.* Garden City, NY: Doubleday & Co., 1978, p. 27.

2. "This was an event:" Ibid.

3. "The parade route jangled:" Ibid.

4. "Gene turned a sketch he had:" Douglas B. Green, *Sing, Cowboy, Sing! The Gene Autry Collection.* New York: Rhino Records, 1996.

5. "I tried to stick with my policy:" Gene Autry with Mickey Herskowitz, *Back In The Saddle Again.* Garden City, NY: Doubleday & Co., 1978, p. 100.

6. "People like him:" *Life,* June 28, 1948.

7. "You hear all the time about performers:" Gene Autry with Mickey Herskowitz, *Back In The Saddle Again.* Garden City, NY: Doubleday & Co., 1978, p. 22.

Interviews with the following were conducted for this chapter:
- Gene Autry — October 1997
- Virginia Long (Oakley Haldeman's daughter) — November 6, 1997
- Alex Gordon — January 16, 1998

RUDOLPH THE RED-NOSED REINDEER

1. "It seemed I'd always been a loser:" *Guideposts*, January 1975.

2. "In January 1939:" *Today's Health,* December 1959.

3. "First I decided that nuts:" *Newsweek,* December 7, 1964.

4. "Why isn't my mommy:" *Coronet,* December 1948

5. "Separate analyses of Santa's needs:" Robert L. May, *Rudolph The Red-Nosed Reindeer.* Chicago: Follett, 1954.

6. "I'll never forget that day:" *Today's Health,* December 1959.

7. "In 1949, I was in the market:" Gene Autry with Mickey Herskowitz, *Back In The Saddle Again.* Garden City, New York: Doubleday, 1978, p. 28.

8. "We finished the first three numbers:" Ibid., p. 29.

9. "The electric success of it:" *Billboard,* November 23, 1959.

10. "In December 1949 Rudolph moved:" *Today's Health,* December 1959.

11. "For me, the story has appeal:" *The Highland Park News,* December 20, 1990.

12. "My dad liked the story:" *The Chicago Tribune,* December 13, 1990.

Interviews with the following were conducted for this chapter:
- Gene Autry — October 1997
- Alex Gordon (Vice President of Autry's movie company) — January 16, 1998
- Thomas H. Carlisle — March 22, 1998

On February 17, 1998, Dartmouth University granted permission to examine documents Robert L. May bequeathed to his alma mater, located in Hanover, New Hampshire.

CAROLING, CAROLING

1. "I was there that eventful day:" *Christmas*, December 1984.

2. "I shall never forget:" *Choral Journal,* December 1992.

3. "In 1953 our whole life would change:" *Christmas,* December 1984.

4. "For the demo tape:" Ibid.

The following interview was conducted for this chapter:
- Anne Burt — May 19, 1998 & May 29, 1998.

JINGLE BELL ROCK

Interviews with the following were conducted for this chapter:
- Owen Bradley — June 6, 1997 & September 19, 1997
- Anita Kerr — October 23, 1997
- Robert Helms — November 5, 1997
- Maud Jennings — November 24, 1997

ROCKIN' AROUND THE CHRISTMAS TREE

Interviews with the following were conducted for this chapter:
- Brenda Lee — June 11, 1997
- Owen Bradley — June 6 & September 19, 1997
- Anita Kerr — October 23, 1997
- Michael Marks — May 16, 1997

A HOLLY JOLLY CHRISTMAS

1. "When I tour the country:" Rick Goldschmidt, *The Enchanted World of Rankin/Bass.* Issaquah, Washington: Tiger Mountain Press, 1997, p. viii.

2. "The mind controls the heart:" *The Burl Ives Official Website: www.burlives.com*

3. "Our hearts are the eternal part of us:" Ibid.

A HOLLY JOLLY CHRISTMAS (cont.)

Interviews with the following were conducted for this chapter:
- Owen Bradley — June 6, 1997 & September 19, 1997
- Anita Kerr — October 23, 1997
- Dorothy Ives — December 5, 1997
- Rick Goldschmidt — January 22, 1998

MERRY CHRISTMAS DARLING

1. "I gave him an on the spot vocal audition." Ray Coleman, *The Carpenters — The Untold Story.* New York, NY: Harper Collins, 1994, p. 55.

2. "*Christmas Portrait* assumed its own momentum." Ibid., p. 236.

The following interview was conducted for this chapter:
- Frank Pooler — May 11, 2000

HAPPY XMAS (WAR IS OVER)

1. "The least Yoko and I can do:" Carole Lynn Corbin, *John Lennon.* New York, NY: Franklin Watts, 1982, p. 84.

2. "We got just thank-you's:" Ibid., p. 86.

3. "I always wanted to write a Christmas record:" Paul Du Noyer, *We All Shine On.* New York, NY: Harper Perennial, 1997, p. 58.

4. "As long as people imagine:" Ibid., p. 59.

O LITTLE TOWN OF BETHLEHEM

The following interview was conducted for this chapter:
- John Woolverton — May 15, 1997

In June, 1997, Harvard University's Houghton Library granted permission to examine Phillips Brooks' letters and journals. Excerpts from those documents are included in the chapter.

N.B. Dates listed for some songs and sheet music are the dates of the original copyright, and not necessarily the dates they were written or commercially released.

Photo Credits

Additional Credits

Bibliography

Albright, Raymond W. *A Life of Phillips Brooks: Focus on Infinity.* New York: The Macmillan Co., 1961.

Allen, Alexander V.G. *Life and Letters of Phillips Brooks.* E.P. Dutton and Company, 1900.

Barnes, Ken. *The Crosby Years.* New York: St. Martin's Press, 1980.

Country Music Foundation. *Country: The Music And The Musicians.* Abbeville Press, 1994.

The Editors of Country Music Magazine. *The Illustrated History of Country Music.* Random House/Times Books, 1995.

Emurian, Ernest K. *Stories of Christmas Carols.* W.A. Wilde Co., 1958.

Fricke, John. *Judy Garland World's Greatest Entertainer.* New York: MJF Books, 1992.

Hotten, John. *A Garland of Christmas Carols.* London: John Camden Hotten, Piccadilly, 1861.

Jacobs, Dick & Jacobs, Harriet. *Who Wrote That Song?* Cincinnati, Ohio: Writer's Digest Books, 1994.

Jones, Margaret. *Patsy: The Life and Times of Patsy Cline.* New York: Harper Collins, 1994.

Kvamme, Torstein O. *The Christmas Caroler's Book In Song And Story.* Hall & McCreary Co., 1935.

Malone, Bill C. *Country Music U.S.A.* University of Texas Press, 1985.

Mottinger, Alvina H. *Christmas Carols, Their Authors and Composers.* New York: G. Schirmer, Inc., 1948.

Nassour, Ellis. *Honky Tonk Angel: The Intimate Story of Patsy Cline.* St. Martin's Press, 1993.

Neely, Tim. *Goldmine Christmas Record Price Guide.* Iola, Wisconsin: Krause Publications, 1997.

Robertson, William. *k.d. Lang: Carrying The Torch.* Toronto: ECW Press, 1992

Shipman, David. *Judy Garland: The Secret Life Of An American Legend.* New York: Hyperion, 1992.

Simon, William L. *The Reader's Digest Merry Christmas Songbook.* Pleasantville, NY: The Reader's Digest Assoc., 1981.

Starr, Victoria. *k.d. Lang: All You Get Is Me.* St. Martin's Press, 1994

Wernecke, Herbert H. *Christmas Songs and Their Stories.* Philadelphia: The Westminster Press, 1957.

Whitburn, Joel. *Joel Whitburn's Pop Memories 1890 - 1954.* Menomonee Falls, Wisconsin: Record Research Inc., 1986.

Woolverton, John F. *The Education of Phillips Brooks.* University of Illinois Press, 1995.

For additional bibliographical information, please see End Notes.

Index

I SAW MOMMY KISSING SANTA CLAUS

Words And Music By
TOMMIE CONNOR

Price 40c

Published for

SONG
SIMPLIFIED SONG (CHILDREN'S EDITION)
ACCORDION (CHILDREN'S EDITION)
ORGAN (EASY ARRANGEMENT FOR WURLITZER & HAMMOND)
DANCE ORCHESTRA
BAND
CHORAL ARRANGEMENTS
    SA
    SAB
    SSA
    SATB
    TTBB

HARMAN MUSIC, INC.
Music Publishers
1619 BROADWAY · NEW YORK 19, N.Y.

About the Author

James Richliano grew up in Western New York, majored in English, and graduated with honors from The State University of New York at Buffalo. After moving to New York City, over 200 of his articles were published internationally in *Billboard* magazine, where he was employed for four years as a writer and Chart Production Manager. Some of his responsibilities there included editing, proofreading and producing all of *Billboard's* charts. Subsequently, for several years he wrote music reviews for *The Boston Globe* and also worked as associate producer for a nationally syndicated modern rock/pop radio show called *Cross Currents*. In addition, he has written for various other newspapers and has worked as a researcher/ interviewer on several books including *The Billboard Book of Number One Hits, The Billboard Book of Number One R&B Hits* and *Billboard's Hottest Hot 100*. He currently resides in the Hudson Valley of New York State. *Angels We Have Heard: The Christmas Song Stories* is James' first book.

(The Toys Gave A Party For)
POPPA SANTA CLAUS
WORDS BY JOHNNY BURKE · MUSIC BY JAMES VAN HEUSEN
THE SNOWMAN
(The Toys Gave A Party For)
POPPA SANTA CLAUS
I'D LIKE TO HITCH A RIDE WITH SANTA CLAUS
THAT CHRISTMAS FEELING
PHILLIP
GARY
BING
DENNIS
LINDSAY
Bing Crosby with Gary, Phillip, Dennis and Lindsay Crosby as recorded by Decca Records and as featured on Chesterfield's radio program.
BURKE-VAN HEUSEN & ASSOCIATES MUSIC CORP.
Sole Selling Agent
FAMOUS MUSIC CORPORATION
1619 BROADWAY, NEW YORK 19, N. Y.